SPD

37
THE BEST OF
2001

[THE SOCIETY OF PUBLICATION DESIGNERS]
[37TH PUBLICATION DESIGN ANNUAL]

acknowledgments

The Sponsors

The Society thanks its corporate sponsors
for their continuing support:

AOL/Time Warner, Inc.
Adobe Systems Incorporated
Apple Computers, Inc.
Condé Nast Publications, Inc.
Donnelly Printing
Herlin Press
Meredith Corporation
The New York Times Company Foundation
Spectragraphics, Inc.
Westvaco Corporation

The Society of Publication Designers wishes to
thank the New York Times Company
Foundation for its ongoing generosity to The
New York Public Library which enables us to
hold our annual Awards Gala in this very
special place.

Pub37 Competition

The Co-Chairs, John Korpics and Rockwell
Harwood, would would like to extend
special thanks to the judges of the 37th
Annual Competition, Linda Root and her
corps of volunteers and the group of
dedicated professionals who work tirelessly
for the Society.

The Gala

PROGRAM DESIGN: Mimi Park
PAPER: Westvaco Corporation
PRINTING: Spectragraphics Inc.
AWARD PRESENTATION GRAPHICS: Mimi Park
AUDIO VISUAL PROGRAM: David Solin
Audio Visual Services
AWARDS: Nick Fasciano Design, Inc.

CALL FOR ENTRIES DESIGN: Rockwell Harwood
and John Korpics
POSTER PHOTOGRAPH: Mark Hooper
COLOR WORK: Quad Graphics
PRINTING: Herlin Press
PAPER: Westvaco Corporation

INVITATION DESIGN: Francesca Messina
PRINTING: Lightning Printing/Greg Sachs

Spots Competition

Chairperson Christine Curry would like to
extend a special thanks to Bob Newman and,
of course, Bride Whelan for keeping us in line
and helping us tally up the ratings for the
hundreds and hundreds of entries.

CALL FOR ENTRIES DESIGN: Christine Curry
ILLUSTRATION: Philippe Petit-Roulet
SEPARATIONS & PRINTING:
Condé Nast Publications, Inc.
Special Thanks to Gary Van Dis
PAPER: Westvaco Corporation

The Society of Publication Designers, Inc.

60 East 42nd Street, Suite 721
New York, NY 10165
Telephone: (212) 983-8585
Fax: (212) 983-6043
Email: SPDNYC@aol.com
Web site: http://www.SPD.org

Executive Board

PRESIDENT
Fred Woodward
Design Director, GQ

VICE PRESIDENTS
Diana LaGuardia
Art Director, GOURMET

David Matt
Partner, DANILO/BLACK, INC.

SECRETARY
Christine Curry
Illustration Editor, THE NEW YORKER

EXECUTIVE DIRECTOR
Bride Whelan
SOCIETY OF PUBLICATION DESIGNERS

Board of Directors

Gail Anderson
Art Director

Florian Bachleda
Art Director, VIBE

Janet Froelich
Art Director, THE NEW YORK TIMES MAGAZINE

David Harris
Art Director, VANITY FAIR

Mimi Park
Principal, DESIGN PARK INC.

Ina Saltz
Principal, Saltz Design, Associate Professor of
Electronic Design and Multimedia, CCNY

Veronique Vienne
Principal, YOUNG VIENNE, INC.

Ex Officio

Robert Newman
Design Director, REAL SIMPLE

The SPD 37th Publication Design Annual

Book produced and designed by Mimi Park,
Design Park, Inc., Stillwater, New Jersey
and Francesca Messina,
Francesca Messina Design, New York

JACKET PHOTOGRAPH: Mark Hooper
IMAGING ASSISTANCE: Joe Calviello
INDEXING; SCANNING; DESIGN AND MORAL SUPPORT:
Michael Aron

First published
in the United States of America by:
Rockport Publishers, Inc.
33 Commercial Street
Gloucester, Massachusetts 01930
Telephone: (978) 282-9590
Fax: (978) 283-2742

ISBN 1-56496-885-5 55500

Printed in China

contents

Established in 1965, the Society of Publication Designers was formed to acknowledge the role of the art director and designer in the visual understanding of the printed word. The art director as a journalist brings a unique skill to the editorial mission of the publication and clarifies the editorial message. The specialized skills of the designer confront the challenges of technology within a constantly expanding

Bride Whelan, Executive Director

industry. ■ The Society provides for its members Speaker Luncheons and Evenings, the monthly newsletter GRIDS, the publication design annual, the Design Exhibition and the annual SPOTS Competition and Exhibition for illustrators, and the SPD Auction and Awards Gala. It has developed a working network of opportunities for job seekers and student interns. It actively participates in related activities that bring together members of the numerous design communities in the New York area.

SPD 37 competition

The judging of Pub37 was one of the most spirited and varied in memory. Forty-nine design, photography, and illustration professionals spent two days viewing 7,952 submissions from around the world. The 669 merit, 40 silver, 17 gold and the Magazine of the Year awards are the result of their efforts and are recorded in this annual. ■ This judging represented many viewpoints and is a subjective process affected by style and contemporary taste. We hope that certain universal values prevail and that over time this body of work will continue to represent high journalistic standards, innovative problem solving and the pure pleasure of design.

COMPETITION CO-CHAIRS

Rockwell Harwood, Details
John Korpics, Esquire

JUDGES

YELLOW GROUP
Kelly Doe, Kelly Doe Design
Francesca Messina, CAPTAIN,
Francesca Messina Design
Ellen Lupton, Maryland Institute
College of Art
James Dunlinson, Martha Stewart Living
Amy Rosenfeld, Smart Money
Stephen Fay, The Wall Street Journal Weekend
Arthur Hochstein (not pictured), Time

GREEN GROUP
John Walker, Entertainment Weekly
Diana Laguardia, CAPTAIN, Gourmet
Lynn Staley, Newsweek
Yvette Francis, PSP Sports
Pamela Berry, Travel & Leisure
David Armario, David Armario Design

ORANGE GROUP
Jill Armus, Teen People
Anthony Jazzar, House & Garden
Jane Palacek, Mother Jones
Kati Korpijaakko, CAPTAIN, Self
Jeanette Hodge Abbink, Dwell
Rip Georges, InStyle

PHOTOGRAPHY BY **SVEND LINDBAEK**

RED GROUP
Eletherios Kardamakis, Lucky
Rina Migliaccio, Talk
Florian Bachleda, Vibe
Janet Froelich, CAPTAIN,
The New York Times Magazine
Greg Klee, The Boston Globe
Carla Frank, O, The Oprah Magazine

BLUE GROUP
Kit Hinrichs, Pentagram, San Francisco
Debra Bishop, Martha Stewart
Kids/Baby
D J Stout, CAPTAIN, Pentagram, Austin
Carmen Dunjko, Shift
Chee Pearlman, Chee Pearlman, Inc.
Jay Porter, The Washingtonian

BLACK GROUP
Fo Wilson, W Design and Consulting
Lloyd Ziff, CAPTAIN, Lloyd Ziff Photography
Darrin Perry, Wired
David Whitmore, National Geographic
Joele Cuyler, The New York Times Magazine
Mimi Dutta, Business 2.0

ONLINE & INTERACTIVE
John Grimwade, Conde Nast Traveler
Melanie McLaughlin, CAPTAIN,
The Feedroom.com
David Matt, Danilo Black Inc.
Mimi Park, Design Park Inc.
Nancy Eising, Art Director
Paul Schreynemakers, iVillage

September 11, 2001: A Day in TIME

Journalism, we've been told, is the first draft of history. And the history now simply known as 9/11 was an unforgettable date in all our lives. But to those of us in the media, or, like me, who work at a newsweekly, it had an extra dimension. For a magazine such as Time an event like this was a rare opportunity—an obligation, even—to try to make some sense for readers who need information, emotional context and, to some degree, reassurance.

Like issues of magazines that were kept by families when John Kennedy was assassinated, this issue of Time, produced in the first hours after the event, was one for history's time capsule.

How to proceed? First, we had to decide whether we would close on our regular schedule (late Friday night and through the day on Saturday) or publish a quick-closing special edition. Almost immediately, our collective instincts told us the magnitude of the event called for a special issue, as fast as we could publish one. Here was the plan: 48 pages plus front and back covers, with no advertising. Open with strong photography and then do a mix of stories that captured the drama and detail of the day. To be on the newsstand Thursday, we had to close by 6 p.m. Wednesday.

Uncharacteristically, we started with the cover. On the suggestion of Managing Editor Jim Kelly, we replaced our traditional red border with black. We had a spellbinding picture, shot by a photographer who was working downtown. There was no time for deliberation; it was a great shot, it was a high-quality chrome, and it was ours exclusively. One image, one layout, and that was the cover. Time to move on.

The scenario was daunting—only three art directors could even get into our Rockefeller Center office, and we'd have to make do. More daunting was the task of gathering, editing and presenting the thousands of photos that were flooding in through the efforts of our picture department. (Picture Editor MaryAnne Golon actually abandoned her car in the South Bronx and hitched a ride into Manhattan by bribing an EMS driver, making deals along the way with agencies and contacting people like legendary war photographer James Nachtwey, who lives in New York and was already on the scene.) Pictures were digital, transparencies, prints—almost any format possible, making editing and presentation process more difficult.

We edited through the night. Around midnight, Jim suggested we all sleep for a few hours in our offices or nearby hotels and re-convene at 6 a.m.

As the designer of the photo act, I decided that things would proceed more efficiently if I stayed up and put our picture selects into layouts. Between 2 a.m. and 6 a.m. I designed 64 pages of double-truck spreads so the editors could see the pictures in context. Taking a break, I encountered photographer Nachtwey, who had brought in his last batch of film. He sat dazed and eerily placid. He smelled of smoke and was dust-covered from head to toe, the only un-ashen part of his body his reddened and tearing eyes. This was, for me, what it is all about. To be able to help produce this issue—to be confident and focused about how to design it—was the distillation of years of training and experience.

We gathered at 6 A.M., a loose collection of editors, designers, writers and picture editors. With everyone weighing in, we selected our favorites and prepared to move on to other tasks. It seemed fine, but not great. This feeling was certified when MaryAnne came to my office, in tears, saying that we weren't running our very best photography. I suggested she call Jim Kelly, who was

The morning of 9/11, from my rooftop

under immense deadline pressure, and ask for another session. "All right," he said. "You, Arthur and me, in the viewing room in five minutes. No one else."

The next time around we got it right. The picture story grew to 26 pages. It had drama, epic scale, pacing, flow. The text narrative that followed told its own story, providing emotional context that balanced against the visual statement that had preceded it. We wrapped up the layouts and went home. I went to bed early because the next day—Thursday—we had to get to work on a double issue, closing in two more days.

In the morning I decided to stop at my neighborhood newsstand on 14th St., hoping but not expecting to see the issue. When I walked in, there it was, which was mindblowing. Forty-eight hours after the event, we designed, wrote, edited, picture edited, engraved, color corrected, transmitted, printed and distributed an issue that would become part of the permanent historical record. A magazine!

A big newsstand seller for us these days is 300,000. (Most copies go to our 4 million subscribers.) A mega-seller like Princess Diana or JFK Jr. sells a million or a million-two. This issue sold over 3.5 million on the newsstand alone, meaning that we sold almost 7.5 million copies of Time. I added to that total by buying a few myself. Souvenirs.

—*Arthur Hochstein, Art Director, Time Magazine*

special section

The New York Times Magazine
SEPTEMBER 23, 2001 / SECTION 6

Remains of the Day By Richard Ford Colson Whitehead Richard Powers Robert Stone James Traub Stephen King Jennifer Egan Roger Lowenstein Judith Shulevitz Randy Cohen William Safire Andrew Sullivan Jonathan Lethem Michael Lewis Margaret Talbot Charles McGrath Walter Kirn Deborah Sontag Allan Gurganus Michael Ignatieff Kurt Andersen Jim Dwyer Michael Tolkin Matthew Klam Sandeep Jauhar Lauren Slater Richard Rhodes Caleb Carr Fred R. Conrad Joju Yasuhide Angel Franco Joel Sternfeld Katie Murray Steve McCurry Carolina Salguero Lisa Kereszi Jeff Mermelstein William Wendt Andres Serrano Richard Burbridge Paul Myoda Julian LaVerdiere Taryn Simon Kristine Larsen

■ 1
Publication The New York Times Magazine
Art Director Janet Froelich
Designer Joele Cuyler
Photo Editor Kathy Ryan
Photographers Julian LaVerdiere, Paul Myoda, Fred R. Conrad
Publisher The New York Times
Issue September 23, 2001

DAY OF INFAMY

MAXIMUM IMPACT More than 40,000 people—the population of a small city—worked in the Twin Towers, and tens of | thousands more visited every day

SPENCER PLATT—GETTY IMAGES

HOLY WAR As large swaths of lower Manhattan were turning to dust, farther uptown, at First Presbyterian on Fifth Avenue, the | faithful gathered to hear the Rev. Jon Walton's "service of mourning and lament"

EVACUATION Rescue workers rushed the dead and injured away from the choking soot. One construction crew donated plywood to fashion emergency gurneys.

ASH TUESDAY Everything and everybody was coated with a layer of soot. "You know those refugees you see in stories about war?" asked one woman. "That was me"

■ 2
Publication Time
Art Director Arthur Hochstein
Designer Arthur Hochstein
Photo Editor MaryAnne Golon
Photographers Spencer Platt, Suzanne Plunkett,
David Surowiecki, James Nachtwey, Gulnara Samiolava,
Angel Franco, Justin Kane, Harry Zernike, Ruth Fremson,
Timothy Fadek
Publisher AOL Time Inc.
Issue September 11, 2001
Category Photography: Reportage: Story

A SPECIAL ISSUE — THE REALITIES OF GROUND ZERO . . .
HEROES OF NEW YORK . . . ELEGIES FOR AMERICA . . . MUSICIANS
UNITED . . . INSIDE THE HOLY WAR . . . MEMO TO THE PRESIDENT

RollingStone

rollingstone.com
ISSUE 880 — OCTOBER 25, 2001 / $3.95

9.11.01

I ♥ NY

MIRKO ILIĆ *transformed Milton Glaser's famous 1975 logo into a tribute to the ultimate devotion shown to New York by so many. "It's one of Milton's best pieces," says Ilić, a Bosnian native. "I just wanted to make it appropriate for this moment in time."*

VOICES OF AMERICA

STOP MAKING SENSE

JONATHAN LETHEM's *crime-fiction and crime-novel writer who returned to his native Brooklyn after living in the San Francisco Bay area for a decade. His latest novel is "Motherless Brooklyn."*

ROLLING STONE 52 OCTOBER 25, 2001   ROLLING STONE 53 OCTOBER 25, 2001

AT GROUND ZERO

THE WORD ON THE STREET IS RUN

Since the Fifties,
Pulitzer Prize winner
JIMMY BRESLIN has
virtually defined the big-city
newspaper column. He was
on Liberty Street, just two
blocks from the WTC, when
Tower One collapsed.

* * * * *

I WAS DIGGING, and then they told me to come here," the firefighter said. He was dressed in a white short-sleeve shirt and a green plaid kilt, and if you think this sounds unusual then you should have been in Queens County, which is part of New York City, in the middle of September. The men in kilts are Fire Department bagpipers. This one was sent to a Catholic church in a neighborhood called Middle Village.

He was waiting around until it was time to pipe Mike Weinberg out of the church. It was a good assignment. It gave the guy a couple of hours away from digging through wreckage.

"Yesterday I found a tie that was knotted," he said.

He took a gulp from a bottle of soda.

"You know how you get a tie that's knotted and there's nothing else with it, don't you?" he said.

"I can imagine," I said.

"I took it to the cop in charge. I say, 'Look at this.' What does he say? We're not interested in that,' I told him, 'I just found it, don't you want to at least look at it?' He didn't. Dumb cop. What's he going to say if I bring him the head?"

Tuesday, September 11th, 2001: The remains of the World Trade Center

Photograph by JAMES NACHTWEY

The New York Times Magazine
SEPTEMBER 23, 2001

After the Fall

This issue of The New York Times Magazine is made up of words written and images captured in the immediate aftermath
of the terrorist attack, sent forward to Sept.
23, 2001, like a message in a bottle. In these
pages, the magazine's contributors have
tried to explain what it is like where we live,
at this particular moment in history: the
first few days after four planes made sudden, unexpected turns and delivered us into
a world we do not yet fully understand. ■

6:30 p.m., Sept. 11, 2 World Financial Center
Photograph by Steve McCurry

'I do not have a
conscious memory of taking
most of these pictures.
I was on total autopilot
the day of the attack. I don't
really remember finding
that statue covered in debris.
And I can barely
recall those firefighters who
are struggling to clean out
their eyes — though, looking
at it now, I can remember
exactly how much
my own eyes burned
from the smoke.'

This Is What A Day Means
By Andrew Sullivan

'America was a symbol that the world need not always
be the imperturbably dark place it has often been. It was a sign that
complacency, somewhere, was always secure.'

*Around 12 a.m., Sept. 11, walkway to the back of the
World Financial Center*
Photograph by Carolina Salguero

Andrew Sullivan is a contributing writer for the magazine.

3
Publication Rolling Stone
Art Director Fred Woodward
Designers Fred Woodward, Gail Anderson,
Siung Tjia, Ken DeLago, Leslie Long
Photo Editor Fiona McDonagh
Photographer Davies + Starr
Publisher Wenner Media
Issue October 25, 2001
Category Design: Entire Issue

4
Publication The New York Times Magazine
Art Director Janet Froelich
Designers Joele Cuyler, Claude Martel, Nancy Harris,
Chris Dixon, Andrea Fella, Lisa Naftolin
Photo Editors Kathy Ryan, Jody Quon, Kira Pollack,
Evan Kriss, Cavan Farrell
Photographers Fred R. Conrad, Steve McCurry,
Carolina Salguero, Jeff Mermelstein
Publisher The New York Times
Issue September 23, 2001
Category Design: Entire Issue
A MERIT: Photography: Reportage: Story

The Guardian
A declaration of war

50p
Wednesday
September 12 2001
Published in London
and Manchester
guardian.co.uk

2 | **G2**   12.09.01 | 3

Yesterday's apocalyptic scenes far outstripped anything Hollywood has ever imagined. Amid the confusion, only one thing seemed certain, says Ian McEwan – the world would never be the same again

Beyond belief

A person jumps to their death as flames engulf the World Trade Centre

Mid-morning Manhattan, the aftermath of terror

■ 6

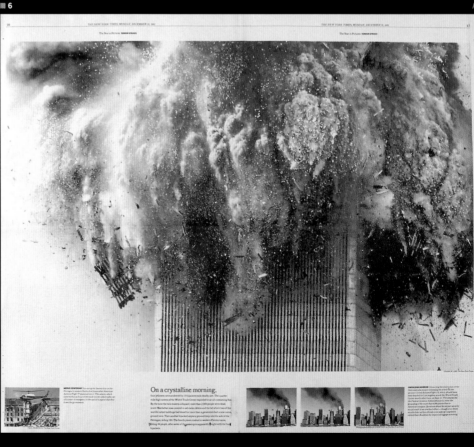

On a crystalline morning,

■ 5
Publication The Guardian G2
Creative Director Mark Porter
Photo Editor Roger Tooth
Publisher Guardian Newspapers LTD.
Issue September 12, 2001
Category Design: Entire Issue

■ 6
Publication The New York Times
Art Director Michael Valenti
Photo Editor Margaret O'Connor
Photographers Chang W. Lee, Kelly Guenther,
Paul Hosefros
Publisher The New York Times
Issue December 31, 2001
Category Design: Entire Issue
     A **MERIT:** Features: Spread

GHOSTLY REMAINS **Buried in the rubble of 1 World Trade Center were relics of the work taking place there only hours earlier,** including expense reports, memos and computer discs

JAMES NACHTWEY VII FOR TIME

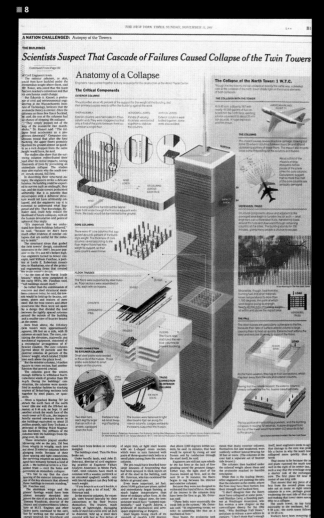

7
Publication Time
Art Director Arthur Hochstein
Designer Arthur Hochstein
Photo Editor MaryAnne Golon
Photographer James Nachtwey
Publisher AOL Time Inc.
Issue September 11, 2001
Category Photography: Reportage:
Spread/Single Page

8
Publication The New York Times
Designers Steve Duenes, Mika Gröndahl
Publisher The New York Times
Issue November 11, 2001
Category Information Graphics:
Story/Spread/Single Page

special section

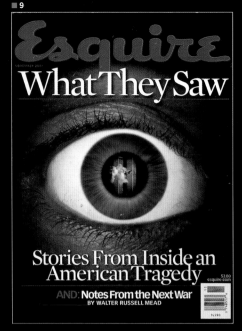

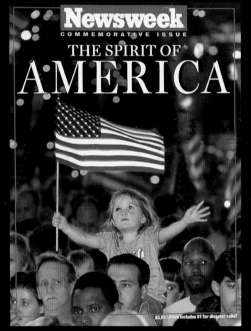

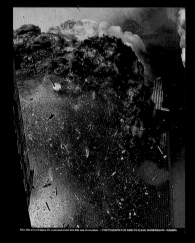

■ 9
Publication Esquire
Design Director John Korpics
Photographer Matt Mahurin
Publisher The Hearst Corporation-Magazines Division
Issue November 2001
Category Design: Cover

■ 10
Publication Guardian Weekend Magazine
Creative Director Mark Porter
Publisher Guardian Newspapers LTD
Issue December 29, 2001
Category Design: Cover

■ 11
Publication Newsweek
Design Director Lynn Staley
Art Director Bruce Ramsay
Photo Editor Simon Barnett
Photographer Ethan Miller
Publisher The Washington Post Co.
Issue December 3, 2001
Category Design: Cover

■ 12
Publication Newsweek
Design Director Lynn Staley
Art Director Bruce Ramsay
Illustrator Joe Zeff
Photo Editor Simon Barnett
Photographer Spencer Platt
Publisher The Washington Post Co.
Issue January 7, 2002
Category Design: Cover

■ 13
Publication Time
Art Director Arthur Hochstein
Designer Arthur Hochstein
Photo Editor MaryAnne Golon
Photographers James Nachtwey, Allan Tannenbaum, Thomas Hart Shelby,
Andrew Lichtenstein, Frank Fournier, Alex Webb, Sean Hemmerle, Timothy
Fadek, Rachel Cobb, Marilyn Bridges
Publisher AOL Time Inc.
Issue December 31, 2001
Category Photography: Reportage: Story

jetzt:
Süddeutsche Zeitung
#39

The Washington Post Magazine

08.45

09.03

'I dreamed in a dream I saw a
city invincible to the attacks of
the whole rest of the earth.'
—WALT WHITMAN

After the Fall

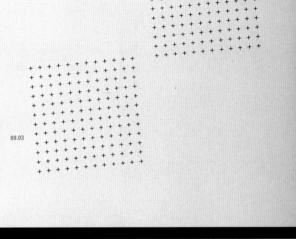

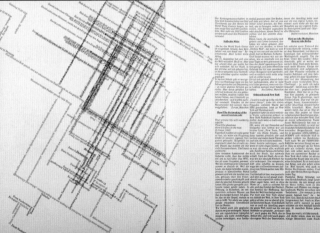

■ 14

Publication Jetzt
Art Director Mirko Borsche
Illustrator Mirko Borsche
Photo Editor Bettina Beust
Publisher Süddeutsche Zeitung
Issue September 24, 2001
Category Design: Entire Issue

■ 15

Publication The Washington Post Magazine
Art Director Brian Noyes
Designers Brian Noyes, Lisa Schreiber
Photo Editors Keith Jenkins, Jennifer Beeson, Molly Roberts, Emilie Sommer, Meaghan Wolff
Photographer Yoni Brook
Publisher The Washington Post Co.
Issue October 7, 2001
Category Entire Issue

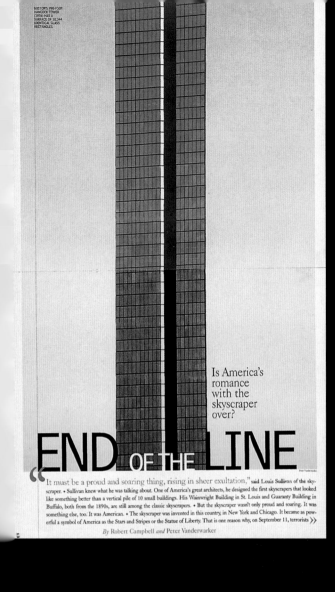

BOSTON'S 790-FOOT
HANCOCK TOWER
(1976) HAS A
SURFACE OF 10,344
IDENTICAL GLASS
RECTANGLES.

Is America's
romance
with the
skyscraper
over?

"END OF THE LINE

"It must be a proud and soaring thing, rising in sheer exultation," said Louis Sullivan of the sky-scraper. • Sullivan knew what he was talking about. One of America's great architects, he designed the first skyscrapers that looked like something better than a vertical pile of 10 small buildings. His Wainwright Building in St. Louis and Guaranty Building in Buffalo, both from the 1890s, are still among the classic skyscrapers. • But the skyscraper wasn't only proud and soaring. It was something else, too. It was American. • The skyscraper was invented in this country, in New York and Chicago. It became as powerful a symbol of America as the Stars and Stripes or the Statue of Liberty. That is one reason why, on September 11, terrorists ≫

By Robert Campbell *and* Peter Vanderwarker

Süddeutsche Zeitung
MAGAZIN

62 AUGENBLICKE

■ 18

WAR ON TERROR

Phase Two: The Hard Part

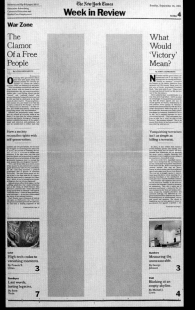

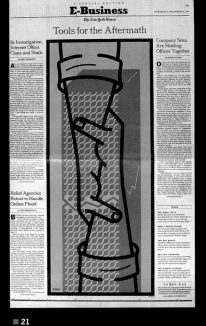

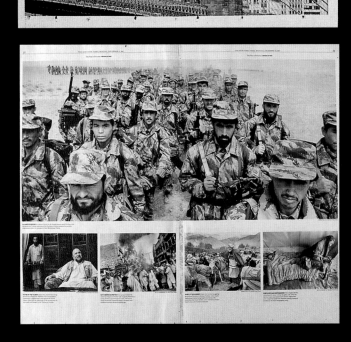

■ 19
Publication The New York Times
Art Director Corinne Myller
Illustrator John Hersey
Publisher The New York Times
Issue September 26, 2001
Category Design: Features: Single Page

■ 21
Publication The New York Times Magazine
Art Director Janet Froelich
Designer Joele Cuyler
Photo Editor Kathy Ryan
Photographer Jeff Mermelstein
Publisher The New York Times
Issue September 23, 2001
Category Photography: Reportage: Story

■ 20
Publication The New York Times
Art Director Greg Ryan
Designer Greg Ryan
Publisher The New York Times
Issue September 16, 2001
Category Design: Features: Single Page

■ 22
Publication The New York Times
Art Director Michael Valenti
Photo Editor Margaret O'Connor
Publisher The New York Times
Issue December 31, 2001
Category Design: Entire Issue
▲ **MERIT:** Design: Features: Single Page

The New York Times

VOL. CL...No. 51,874   Copyright © 2001 The New York Times   NEW YORK, WEDNESDAY, SEPTEMBER 12, 2001   *Beyond the greater New York metropolitan area.*   75 CENTS

Late Edition

New York: Today, sunny, a few afternoon clouds. High 77. Tonight, slightly more humid. Low 63. Tomorrow, sun then clouds. High 81. Yesterday, high 81, low 63. Weather map, Page C19.

U.S. ATTACKED

HIJACKED JETS DESTROY TWIN TOWERS AND HIT PENTAGON IN DAY OF TERROR

A CREEPING HORROR

Buildings Burn and Fall as Onlookers Search for Elusive Safety

By N. R. KLEINFIELD

President Vows to Exact Punishment for 'Evil'

By SERGE SCHMEMANN

A Somber Bush Says Terrorism Cannot Prevail

By ELISABETH BUMILLER with DAVID E. SANGER

AMERICAN TARGETS A ball of fire erupted outward after the second of two jetliners slammed into the World Trade Center.

Awaiting the Aftershocks

Washington and Nation Plunge Into Fight With Enemy Hard to Identify and Punish

By R. W. APPLE Jr.

MORE ON THE ATTACKS

RESCUERS BECOME VICTIMS Firefighters who rushed to the trade center were killed. PAGE A7

SEARCH FOR SURVIVORS Some people trapped in the rubble for hours were rescued. PAGE A14

OFFICIALS SUSPECT BIN LADEN Eavesdropping intercepts after the attacks were cited. PAGE A4

TERRORISTS EXPLOIT WEAKNESS Investigators had criticized precautions against hijacking. PAGE A17

CASUALTIES IN WASHINGTON An unknown number of people were killed at the Pentagon. PAGE A6

A DAY OF TERROR

Rescue Workers Rush In, And Many Do Not Return

Survivors Are Found In the Rubble

Towers Believed to Be Safe Proved Vulnerable to an Intense Jet Fuel Fire, Experts Say

Two Crashes, Then Two Collapses

Columbia's Seismographs Log Quake-Level Impacts

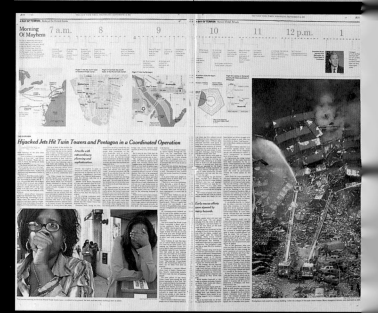

Morning Of Mayhem   7 a.m.   8   9   10   11   12 p.m.   1

Hijacked Jets Hit Twin Towers and Pentagon in a Coordinated Operation

---

23
Publication The New York Times
Art Director various
Photographer various
Publisher The New York Times
Issue September 12, 2001
Category Design: Entire Issue
A **MERIT**: Design: Features: Spread

24
Publication TIME
Creative Director Arthur Hochstein
Illustrator Ed Gabel
Graphics Director Jackson Dykman
Publisher AOL Time Inc.
Issue September 11, 2001
Category Illustration: Information Graphics: Single Page

25
Publication The New York Times
Art Director John Macleod
Designer Kareen Freeman
Illustrator Don Foley
Publisher The New York Times
Issue September 18, 2001
Category Illustration: Information Graphics: Single Page

■ 24

TWIN TERRORS

When two hijacked airliners ripped through the World Trade Center towers, the real horror was only beginning

PLANES SLAM TOWERS ...   ... AND WEAKENED BUILDINGS COLLAPSE

8:45 a.m. American Airlines Flight 11, a Boeing 767 hijacked en route from Boston to Los Angeles with 92 passengers aboard, slams into the north tower

9:06 United Airlines Flight 175, a Boeing 767 hijacked en route from Boston to Los Angeles with 65 passengers aboard, slams through the south tower

10:00 the south tower collapses

10:29 the north tower collapses

5:25 p.m. 7 World Trade Center building falls

FIRST IMPACT

SECOND IMPACT

WHY DID THEY COLLAPSE?

■ 25

Science Times

The New York Times

Emptying a Hazardous 'Bathtub'

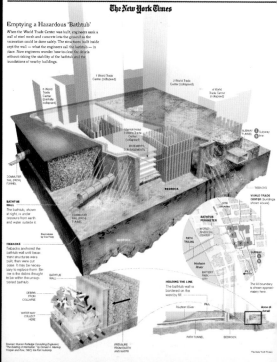

THE LONG FALL "You saw their ties flying up in the air," recalls David Burrell, a broker, who watched several people fall or jump to their death. A man and a woman held hands on the way down

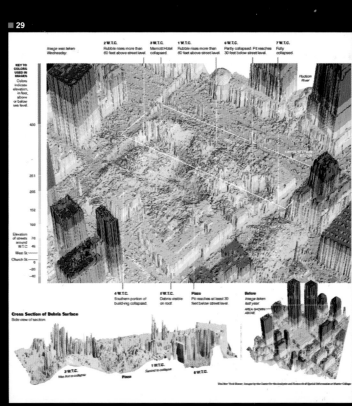

■ 26
Publication Time
Art Director Arthur Hochstein
Designer Arthur Hochstein
Photo Editor MaryAnne Golon
Photographer David Surowiecki
Publisher AOL Time Inc.
Issue September 11, 2001
Category Photography:
Reportage: Spread

■ 27
Publication Time
Art Director Arthur Hochstein
Designer Arthur Hochstein
Photo Editor MaryAnne Golon
Photographer James Nachtwey
Publisher AOL Time Inc.
Issue September 11, 2001
Category Photography:
Reportage: Spread

■ 28
Publication Time
Art Director Arthur Hochstein
Designer Arthur Hochstein
Photo Editor MaryAnne Golon
Photographer Angel Franco
Publisher AOL Time Inc.
Issue September 11, 2001
Category Photography:
Reportage: Spread

■ 29
Publication The New York Times
Designer Archie Tse
Publisher The New York Times
Issue September 23, 2001
Category Illustration:
Information Graphics: Single Page

DETAILS

HERE'S JOHNNY
TO HELL AND BACK

KILLER SEX
The Dark Truth
About Young
Men and Viagra

GOOD CATCH
Why Fishing Is
the New Golf

PERP WALK
The Bizarre Prison
Break That's
Embarrassing L.A.

**PASSING
THE BUCK**
Does Money
Still Matter?

PLUS: The New King of the NFL,
8 Steps to Building a Better Man,
and the Surprising Cure for Baldness

OCTOBER/US $3.00 CAN $3.95

10>

0 754904 7

08435

THE

XXX

MEN

Boogie Nights, Serge Ferrari and David James have dared to be Vivid Entertainment, the country's top porn producers. And now, with an IPO looming and Wall Street beckoning, the industry, can they legitimize porn on the Internet and become the next Beta, Disney, Vivendi.

BY ALLEN SALKIN

DETAILS

SPECIAL MUSIC EDITION

BONO

+ No Doubt, Michael Jackson, Moby, Gene Simmons, Oscar De La Hoya, the Ultimate Home Stereo, and Why Beautiful Women Love Ugly Rockers

SNOW JOB
A Complete Guide to Skiing, Boarding, and the World's Most Extreme Escapes

JUST SAY NO
Virginity: Why Everyone's Doing It

CLASS WARFARE
Inside America's Controversial Blue-blood Reform School

PLUS: Rose McGowan, Michael Jordan's New Teen Idol, and How to Get Your Own Lamborghini

DETAILS

WHO'S
PUFFY
FIRES BACK

49
PAGES OF MUST-HAVE CLOTHES FOR FALL

FAST AND FURIOUS
Test-driving the latest hot rides

BROKER GONE BAD
The Wall Street hustler who stole Hef's centerfold

HIGH INFIDELITY
Portrait of the new American adulterer

BRITS AND ASS
Inside Oxford's invitation-only orgy

PLUS: Julia Stiles, Conan O'Brien, Macy Gray, and the next Babe Ruth

B

■ 30

Publication Details
Creative Director Dennis Freedman
Design Director Edward Leida
Art Director Rockwell Harwood
Photo Editors Alice Rose George, Amy Steigbigel, Jeannine Foeller
Photographers Michael Thompson, Steven Klein, Tom Munro, Larry Sultan
Publisher The Condé Nast Publications Inc.
Issues September 2001, November 2001, December 2001
Category Magazine of the Year
A **MERIT:** Design: Entire Issue
B **MERIT:** Design: Features: Story

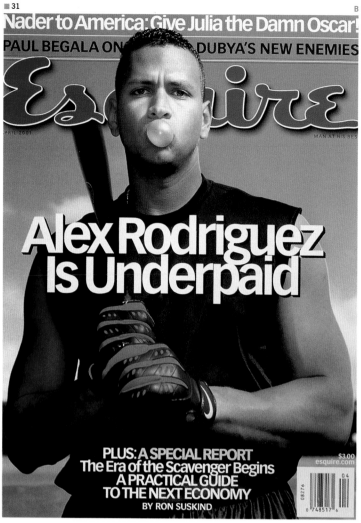

A

TheEnlightenedMan

One of the best athletes in the NFL has never scored a touchdown or recorded a sack. KOREY STRINGER is six feet four inches, 340 pounds of supersized, liver-and-onions-eating, deep-thinking, dreadlocked delight. By JEANNE MARIE LASKAS

First we have the bull. Yeah, that was his first piece. He's stretching his V-neck down to provide a view of that bull depicted on his splendid left breast. Yeah, he knows. It's the size of a pasta bowl, that breast. Yeah, it's a dark-brown hunk of human worthy of fear and awe and God's glory. It's a rock-solid, bulbous slab of man-flesh commanding adoration. Yeah. But what about the bull? Now, ain't that a good bull? ¶ Tattoo-wise, the bull was an obvious first choice for a man whose body has always been the main event. A more or less 338-pound, six-foot-four body with a forty-six-inch waist and a size-14 foot, a body that could easily bring to mind thoughts of steak and hide and cowboys getting thrown off it. The kind of body that was always different, always extreme; you know, his mom would get so sick of having to take his birth certificate to T-ball games back home in Warren, Ohio, to prove that, in fact, her son really was only eight years old, even though he looked more or less like a sycamore tree. ¶ He shrugs. This movement makes him sweat. Yeah, he almost always sweats, beads of liquid pooling and spilling, pooling and spilling down a deep brown brow. A thoughtful, earnest brow that seems to bear the weight of centuries but actually is topped by dreadlocks sprouting happily, joyfully, as if dancing maybe to the theme song from *Wally Gator*.

PHOTOGRAPHS BY CHRIS BUCK

SEPTEMBER 2001 ESQUIRE 15

B

Penninger

The Digital Man 2003

Body Tech

B

THE CRUSADER

■ 31

Publication Esquire
Design Director John Korpics
Designers Hannah McCaughey, Todd Albertson, Erin Whelan, Kim Forsberg
Illustrator John Craig
Photo Editors Nancy Jo Iacoi, Catriona NiAolain
Photographers Martin Schoeller, Chris Buck, Nigel Dickson, Julian Broad, Jeffrey Braverman, Norman Jean Roy
Publisher The Hearst Corporation-Magazines Division
Issues April 2001, July 2001, September 2001
Category Magazine of the Year
    A **SILVER:** Design: Entire Issue
    B **MERIT:** Design: Entire Issue

FEBRUARY/MARCH 2001 | THE MAGAZINE FOR GLOBAL EXECUTIVES | VOL. 4, NO. 1

GLoBAL

Mideast Diary

The Unbuttoning of the Workplace

The Power of Alliances

The Humorist as Business Strategist

linking up:
five e-trends in supply chain management

A

GLoBAL

JULY/AUGUST 2001 THE MAGAZINE FOR GLOBAL EXECUTIVES | VOL. 4, NO. 2

Dot-Com Diary

Philanthropy's Uncharitable Instincts

Korea: The Road to Reform

predicting the next
global currency crisis:
a question of where, not if

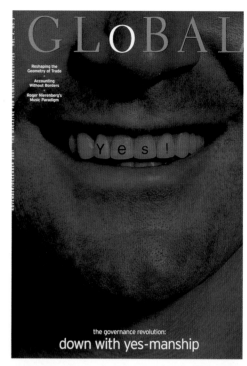

GLoBAL

Reshaping the Geometry of Trade

Accounting Without Borders

Roger Nierenberg's Music Paradigm

the governance revolution:
down with yes-manship

Q

A
Question
of
Degree

It's time
to turn down
the heat
on the global
warming
debate,
says Richard
Lindzen.

Interview by Beth Browde

photo-illustration by Mark Hooper • portraits by Kyoko Harada

FIX ING KOREA

The Seoul government has made tangible progress toward economic reforms. Now comes the hard part.

Surviving the Loss of Your

.com

The sting of death may be sharpest for the clients left behind.

BY JOSH MARTIN

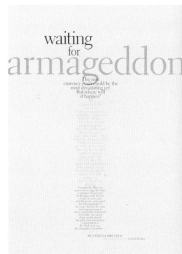

waiting for armageddon

The next currency crisis could be the most devastating yet. But where will it happen?

Wired for **Growth**

>> Spain's Telefonica reinvents itself as a global telecommunications leader.

BY JOSH MARTIN

■ 32
Publication Global
Art Director David Armario
Designers David Armario, Candela D, Ethan Fowler
Illustrators Tavis Coburn, Jason Holley, Alain Pilon
Photographers Fredrik Brodén, Mark Hooper, Gary Tannhauser, Dan Winters
Studio David Armario Design
Publisher Deloitte & Touche, LLP
Issues January 2001, July/August 2001, November/December 2001
Category Magazine of the Year
    A **MERIT:** Design: Cover

MARTHA STEWART

baby

SPECIAL ISSUE

BIRTHDAY CAKES

MAKING COSTUMES

ALPHABET NURSERY

ALL ABOUT TEETH

MUSIC AND DANCE

DISPLAY UNTIL 11/5/01

13>

$4.75 USA (CAN. $5.75)

www.marthastewart.com

Gentle botanical details fill a bright, simple nursery. The glass in an armoire's doors is replaced with screening that's been spray-painted white with silhouettes of ferns and butterflies. These mesh panels (opposite) let sound float through, making the armoire the perfect hiding place for a radio to play softly at nap time (see page 108 for how-tos).

spring nursery

why milk?

milk

breast milk.

Crochet

decorating with letters

■ 33
Publication Martha Stewart Baby
Creative Director Gael Towey
Art Director Deb Bishop
Designers Deb Bishop, Jennifer Wagner, Sara Hicks, Jennifer Dahl
Photo Editor Jodi Nakatsuka
Photographers Gentl + Hyers, Lisa Hubbard, Anna Williams, William Abranowicz, Christopher Baker, Maria Robledo, Formula z/s, Frank Heckers, Sang An, Maura McEvoy
Stylists Jodi Levine, Ayesha Patel, Amy Gropp Forbes, Melanio Gomez, Cyndi DiPrima, Katie Hatch, Lynn Butler
Publisher Martha Stewart Living Omnimedia
Issues Spring 2001, Fall 2001
Category Magazine of the Year
  A **MERIT:** Design:Features: Story

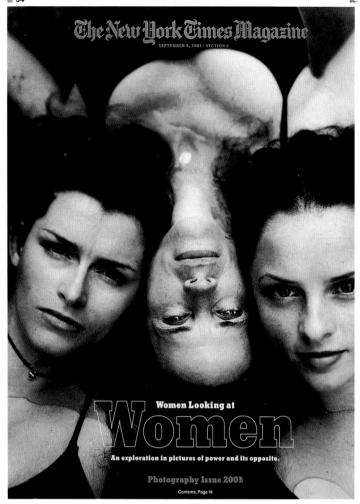

The New York Times Magazine

SEPTEMBER 9, 2001 / SECTION 6

Women Looking at

Women

An exploration in pictures of power and its opposite.

Photography Issue 2001

Contents, Page 16

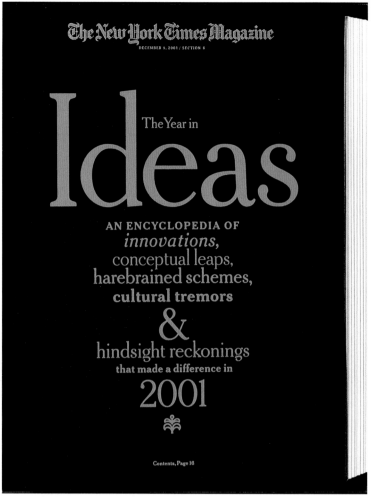

The New York Times Magazine

DECEMBER 9, 2001 / SECTION 6

The Year in

Ideas

AN ENCYCLOPEDIA OF
innovations,
conceptual leaps,
harebrained schemes,
cultural tremors

&

hindsight reckonings

that made a difference in

2001

❦

Contents, Page 16

Strength

Big Women on Campus

Delts, quads, pecs, mascara, lipstick.

Photographs and interview by
Lauren Greenfield

Misty Hyman, Olympic gold medalist, Stanford University, Class of '01:
"I've been a swimmer all of my life. It's a big part of who I am, and the physical attributes that go along with the swimming are definitely something I'm proud of. I've gone through periods when I've felt like, gosh, I'm so big and bulky. There are occasions where I just forget that I am so strong. I definitely get a lot of stares. But you can make it negative attention or you can make it positive attention. You can say, look, this is who I am. This is beautiful.

"I like to get my nails done and I like to dress up and I like to be taken out on

Some of Stanford's star swimmers
(from left) Jessie Carr, 20, a junior who swims distance freestyle; Jessica Foschi, 21, a senior and champion distance freestyler; Misty Hyman, 22, who won an Olympic gold medal for the 200-meter butterfly; Katy Blakemore, 19, a sophomore who swims distance freestyle; Tara Kirk, 19, a sophomore and a champion in the breaststroke.

148

THE NEW YORK TIMES MAGAZINE / SEPTEMBER 9, 2001 149

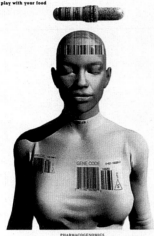

play with your food

Play With Your Food The idea that food might also furnish a creative diversion is as old as alphabet soup. But playing with floating bits of pasta is fairly staid when you can make like Jackson Pollock with fluorescent hues of ketchup.

It was Heinz that had the bold idea to add blue and yellow dye to their traditional formula to create "Blastin' Green" ketchup. The company quickly sold 10 million plastic squirt containers filled with the stuff. Just this summer, Heinz added a "Funky Purple" variety. Joining the party, ConAgra Foods has begun to offer its Parkay margarine in bright blue and pink.

Manufacturers have long known that an element of playfulness enhances the appeal of food products to children, whose aggressive lobbying (or nagging) is frequently responsible for their parents' purchasing decisions. But never before have foods been so overtly marketed as toys. Flavored varieties of Mott's applesauce now come in turquoise, red and acid green. You can buy Nabisco fruit snacks cut into X's and O's for playing tick-tack-toe. Milk Changer Oreo cookies, with orange creme filling, are designed to create colorful swirly patterns when dunked in a glass of milk. And Quaker Instant Oatmeal Treasure Hunt contains miniature treasure chests that melt as you mix in hot water, revealing edible jewels and coins contained within.

Anyone old enough to have been imprinted with the notion that ketchup is "supposed" to be red and margarine yellow may find neon-colored condiments unappetizing. But for children coming fresh to the table, it's all equal, a matter of choice — and for them, yellow margarine and red ketchup will most likely be an important part of the action-food-painting palette. It may be some time before children get into sirloin sculpture or broccoli-and-green-pea bonsai gardens, but clearly playtime is no longer over when mealtime begins. JAIME WOLF

Populist Editing Despite the popular conception of the Internet as our most interactive medium, on the great majority of Web pages the interaction all goes in one direction. But an intriguing new subgenre of sites, called WikiWikiWebs, really are interactive: users can both read and write. If you don't like the perspective of the article you are perusing, you can go in and rephrase the concluding paragraph. If you stumble across a spelling mistake, you can fix it with a few quick keystrokes. Wikis are like communal gardens of data: some participants do a lot of heavy planting, while others prefer to pull a weed here and there.

The most ambitious Wiki project to date applies this governing principle to the encyclopedia, that Enlightenment-era icon of human intelligence. The result is the Wikipedia, created in early 2001 by a philosophy Ph.D. named Larry Sanger and billed as "a collaborative project to produce a complete encyclopedia from scratch." Wikipedia has attracted more than 1,000 new entries a month on everything from astronomy to the visual arts. With a total of 16,000 articles in the database, the Wikipedia is already large enough to be a source of generally reliable information, though stronger in some areas ("Star Trek" spinoffs) than others (the novels of Charles Dickens).

Wikipedia differs from conventional encyclopedias in that each article is a work in progress: a visitor will draft a new entry, sometimes merely jotting down a few random data points, with a handful of links to other related entries; a few weeks later, another visitor might add a paragraph or two or a few more hyperlinks. Each entry has a revision history, like those featured in modern word processors, that lets you see at a glance any changes that have been made to the document.

What prevents a crank or a saboteur from deliberately undermining

positive asymmetry

PLAY WITH MARGARINE
Photograph by Davies + Starr

the quality of entries? Only the steady force of constant revisions, doled out by thousands of contributors. A few jokers in the mix will invariably get washed out by the overwhelming number of contributors who are genuinely interested in the site's meeting its objectives. There is a saying in the open-source software community (from which the Wiki movement borrows more than a few moves): given enough eyeballs, all bugs are shallow. The slogan works for programmers collectively writing an operating system like Linux, so why shouldn't it work for hobbyists and armchair enthusiasts stringing together an encyclopedia? STEVEN JOHNSON

Positive Asymmetry The United States defense establishment has awakened to an unsettling paradox. America's military power vastly outstrips that of most potential adversaries, but unrivaled military superiority does not make the U.S. invulnerable to attack. Instead, Pentagon planners now realize, conventional military dominance only encourages potential adversaries to look for "asymmetrical" ways to neutralize our strengths by exploiting our vulnerabilities.

The events of Sept. 11 — in which a handful of hijackers armed with box cutters transformed several civilian airliners into precision guided missiles — provided a horrific testament to the destructive power of asymmetric threats. In response, some national-security experts now argue that the U.S. should take advantage of all the resources — military and civilian — that can be brought to bear as part of a broader national-security policy designed to halt the spread of terrorism. The challenge, in other words, is to fight an asymmetrical foe asymmetrically by using those U.S. assets that can best undermine the social, cultural and economic factors that foment extremism.

In a paper published earlier this year, Steven Metz, chairman of

PHARMACOGENOMICS
A map of genetic variations can guide drug therapy.

promises to make this process a lot more precise. As it turns out, 25 percent of breast-cancer patients exhibit a unique genetic variation called Her2 overexpression. When Her2 overexpression is present in a patient, doctors can now prescribe a drug that is specifically designed to block the proteins created by this genetic variation. Doing so improves patient survival rates by 25 percent.

Genaissance Pharmaceuticals, a biotech company based in New Haven, Conn., has made pharmacogenomics the centerpiece of the company's business by mapping patterns of genetic variation that influence responsiveness to specific medications. For example, Genaissance is studying high cholesterol with an eye toward seeing how certain genetic variations affect the efficacy and safety of drugs like Lipitor and Zocor. One goal is to come up with a screening test that will allow patients to figure out which anticholesterol drug is best suited for them.

It's not clear yet how fully pharmaceutical companies will embrace the pharmacogenomics idea. Will drug companies bother to produce specifically tailored drugs in small quantities? Or will they pass in order to focus on drugs that enjoy more widespread utility?

From a patient's perspective, however, pharmacogenomics promises to radically change the way doctors treat disease — for the better. As Dr. Susan Hellmann, the chief medical officer at the pioneering biotech firm Genentech puts it, "It's as if our old weapon was an ax, and now we have a scalpel." TODD LAPPIN

THE NEW YORK TIMES MAGAZINE / DECEMBER 9, 2001 91

90

B

acquired situational narcissism

A to Z.

Acquired Situational Narcissism

ACQUIRED SITUATIONAL NARCISSISM
Photograph by Rodney Smith

Faith

Keeper
of the
Flame

The paradox of the rabbi's wife.

Photographs by
Mary Ellen Mark
Text by
Samantha M. Shapiro

■ 34

Publication The New York Times Magazine
Art Director Janet Froelich
Project Designer Joele Cuyler
Designers Claude Martel, Nancy Harris, Andrea Fella, Chris Dixon
Photo Editors Kathy Ryan, Jody Quon, Evan Kriss, Kira Pollack, Cavan Farrell
Photographers Mary Ellen Mark, Lauren Greenfield, Jeff Mermelstein, Lisa Kereszi, Rodney Smith, Davies + Starr, Julian LaVerdiere, Paul Myoda, Fred R. Conrad, Justine Kurland, Sally Mann
Publisher The New York Times
Issues September 9, 2001, September 23, 2001, December 9, 2001
Category Magazine of the Year
    A **MERIT:** Design: Entire Issue
    B **GOLD:** Design: Entire Issue

MARTHA STEWART

baby
SPECIAL ISSUE

SPRING NURSERY

ALL ABOUT MILK

CHANGING TABLE

COOKING WITH CARROTS

SWADDLING

EMBROIDERY

DISPLAY UNTIL 5/14/01

11>

0 92567 10152 8

$4.75 USA (CAN. $5.75)

www.marthastewart.com

easter

the hide-and-seek workbook

Children love to pretend, so help your baby become a bunny for the day. Slip a pair of handmade felt rabbit ears gently over her head. The slippers you can make using our instructions, too; she will love watching these furry friends come to life when she wiggles her toes. Then send her off on a hopping hunt for a basket full of goodies (see following pages).

PHOTOGRAPHS BY CHRISTOPHER BAKER · TEXT BY BRENNAN TRAVIS KEARNEY

pillowcase dress

cow's milk

MILK

■ 35

Publication Martha Stewart Baby
Creative Director Gael Towey
Art Director Deb Bishop
Designers Deb Bishop, Jennifer Wagner, Sara Hicks, Jennifer Dahl
Illustrator Raymond Booth
Photo Editor Jodi Nakatsuka
Photographers Frank Heckers, Lisa Hubbard, Anna Williams, William Abranowicz, Christopher Baker, Maria Robledo, Sang An, Formula z/s, John Dolan
Stylists Jodi Levine, Ayesha Patel, Amy Gropp Forbes, Lynn Butler, Melanio Gomez, Cindi DiPrima, Katie Hatch
Publisher Martha Stewart Living Omnimedia
Issue Spring 2001
Category Entire Issue
   A MERIT: Design: Cover

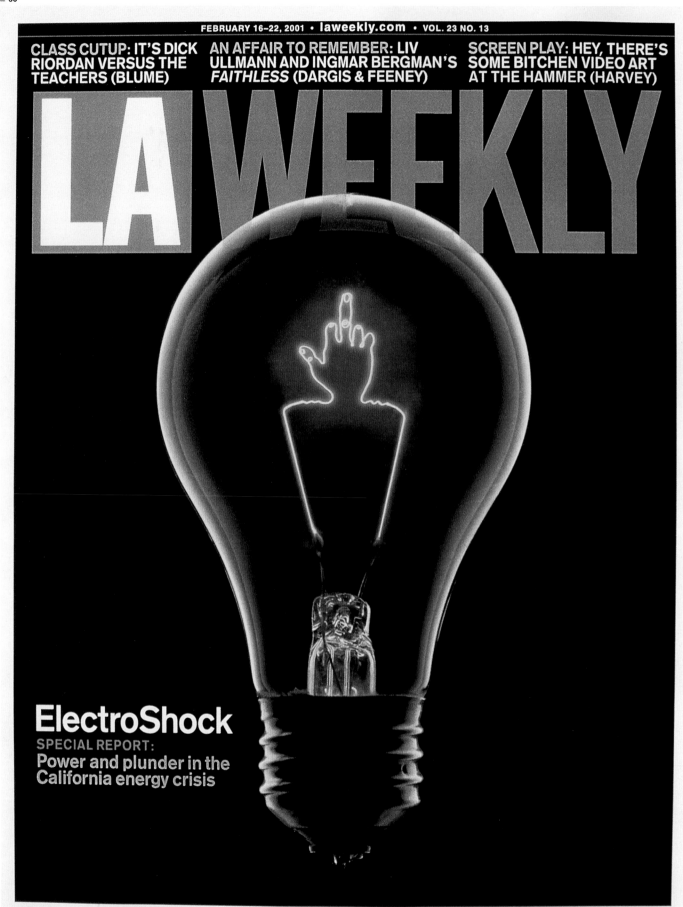

■ 36
Publication LA Weekly
Art Director Bill Smith
Illustrator Bill Smith
Publisher Village Voice Media
Issue February 16, 2001
Category Cover

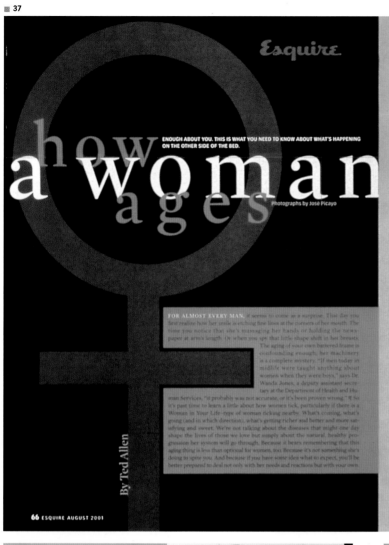

how a woman ages

ENOUGH ABOUT YOU. THIS IS WHAT YOU NEED TO KNOW ABOUT WHAT'S HAPPENING ON THE OTHER SIDE OF THE BED.

Esquire

Photographs by José Picayo

By Ted Allen

FOR ALMOST EVERY MAN, it seems to come as a surprise. That day you first realize how her smile is etching fine lines at the corners of her mouth. The time you notice that she's massaging her hands or holding the newspaper at arm's length. Or when you spy that little shape shift in her breasts. The aging of your own battered frame is confounding enough; her machinery is a complete mystery. "If men today in midlife were taught anything about women when they were boys," says Dr. Wanda Jones, a deputy assistant secretary at the Department of Health and Human Services, "it probably was not accurate, or it's been proven wrong." If So it's past time to learn a little about how women tick, particularly if there is a Woman in Your Life–type of woman ticking nearby. What's coming, what's going (and in which direction), what's getting richer and better and more satisfying and sweet. We're not talking about the diseases that might one day shape the lives of those we love but simply about the natural, healthy progression her system will go through. Because it bears remembering that this aging thing is less than optional for women, too. Because it's not something she's doing to spite you. And because if you have some idea what to expect, you'll be better prepared to deal not only with her needs and reactions but with your own.

66 ESQUIRE AUGUST 2001

IN HER TWENTIES. Building muscle, packing on the bone mass, and pumping estrogen.

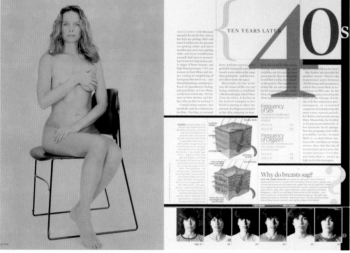

TEN YEARS LATER

40s

Frequency of Sex

Frequency of Orgasm

Why do breasts sag?

THE WOMAN TO COME

60s

X vs.Y

Why do women live longer?

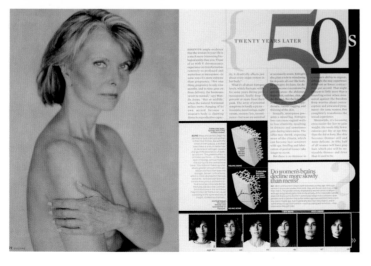

TWENTY YEARS LATER

50s

Do women's brains decline more slowly than men's?

■ 37

Publication Esquire
Design Director John Korpics
Designer Hannah McCaughey
Photo Editor Nancy Jo Iacoi
Photographer José Picayo
Publisher The Hearst Corporation-Magazines Division
Issue August 2001
Category Features: Story

33

normal story length

(Esquire Fiction)

[a] [b] [c]

3

short
short
stories

[a] *Russell Banks*
[b] *T. R. Pearson*
[c] *Arthur Bradford*

Photographs by James Fee

JUNE 2001 ESQUIRE **149**

■ 38
Publication Esquire
Design Director John Korpics
Photo Editor Nancy Jo Iacoi
Photographer James Fee
Publisher The Hearst Corporation-Magazines Division
Issue June 2001
Category Features: Spread/Single Page

■ 39
Publication Magazine El Mundo
Design Director Carmelo Caderot
Art Director Rodrigo Sánchez
Designers Rodrigo Sánchez, María González
Photo Editor Rodrigo Sánchez
Photographer Gerard Rancinan
Publisher Unidad Editorial S.A.
Issue April 22, 2001
Category Entire Issue

DOMINGO 22 DE ABRIL DE 2001　EL ⊕ MUNDO　Nº 52 SEGUNDA ÉPOCA

MAGAZINE

ÉL ES EL NUEVO PICASSO

SE LLAMA PAUL McCARTHY Y EN SUS OBRAS UTILIZA EL "KETCHUP" PARA DENUNCIAR LA VIOLENCIA Y EL CONSUMO. LA FRANCESA ORLAN SE HACE IMPLANTES DE SILICONA FRENTE A LA ESTÉTICA IMPUESTA, Y DAMIEN HIRST DISECA ANIMALES PARA MOSTRAR LA PASIÓN POR LA VIDA. ¿SON LOS GENIOS DEL ARTE CONTEMPORÁNEO O UNA PANDILLA DE LOCOS? SUS COTIZACIONES MILLONARIAS LES DAN LA RAZÓN

LA SEMANA
PAUL McCARTHY

LA SEMANA
DAMIEN HIRST

22 IV 01
LA SEMANA
ORLAN

Es la primera artista que ha utilizado la cirugía estética para hacer de sí misma una obra de arte. Su cuerpo está totalmente modificado por intervenciones quirúrgicas que la francesa convierte en impactantes *performances*. Para las operaciones Orlan se aplica sólo anestesia local, lo cual le permite dirigir el evento, que graba en vídeo o retransmite vía satélite por televisión, e incluso participar activamente en la acción mediante la lectura de textos psicoanalíticos o filosóficos. También diseña los trajes de los cirujanos a los que encarga a modistos de la talla de Paco Rabanne y decora el quirófano, convertido en escenario de un sorprendente acto creativo. Aquí, el vehículo de la labor artística es el artista mismo. La primera reacción ante este tipo de proyectos es de terror pero, en realidad, se trata de un trabajo profundamente humanista que se cuestiona los cimientos sociales y morales y la tradición estética de nuestra época. Orlan utiliza la medicina y el progreso tecnológico para deformar su cuerpo con el propósito de penetrar en los misterios del organismo y de imaginar cómo serán los cuerpos en el futuro. Su objetivo es superar los tabúes, ofrecer al mundo la posibilidad de escapar de la prisión de lo físico proponiendo la creación de tantos cánones de belleza como personas, en un mundo ideal que favorece la diferencia. A sus 54 años, se atreve a pensar en el momento de su muerte, cuando su cuerpo descanse, más que en un cementerio, en las instalaciones de algún museo. El cuerpo agredido y mutilado se encuentra en el corazón del mundo artístico contemporáneo. En su opinión, ¿se debe a una reacción contra los problemas de nuestra época? Los artistas no trabajan tanto con la violencia como con la agresión a terceros, aquellos que contemplan su obra. Además, el artista es un cronista de nuestro tiempo y, más aún, de lo que traerá el mañana. Todos estamos adscritos a nuestro tiempo pero el artista, a diferencia de otros muchos, lo cuestiona. En contraposición con otros movimientos artísticos, usted no se expone al dolor. En el contexto de mi trabajo, yo me he sometido a operaciones de cirugía cosmética. El primer acuerdo al que llegué con mi cirujano fue que nada de dolor, ni antes, ni durante, ni después. Sobre este tema, precisamente, escribo mi propio papel en la próxima película de David Cronenberg. El guión está basado en un futuro donde no existe el dolor y las relaciones sexuales se viven de manera distinta. Al igual que Cronenberg, intento pensar en el futuro y abolir la frontera entre lo virtual y lo real. No estamos acostumbrados a ver el interior del cuerpo. La mutilación del mismo constituye una mutilación de la política y de la cultura que nos moldea. Las imágenes de una operación a cuerpo abierto están siempre asociadas con la guerra, la tortura y el sufrimiento. Aún no hemos asimilado la idea de que podemos vivir sin sufrimiento. La performance que realizaré para la película no consistirá en una intervención de cirugía estética, sino en una operación de apertura y cierre del cuerpo. Una operación poética en el sentido de que no tendrá ningún otro fin salvo el demostrar que un cuerpo puede abrirse y que después se puede reír, hablar, leer y jugar. Ésa es la gran contribución de nuestra era, la supresión del dolor. ¿De qué manera resumiría el tema central de sus "performances", incluidas estas operaciones? El tema central ha sido siempre el mismo: denunciar las presiones sociales sobre el cuerpo. Estas operaciones no son un fin en sí mismas. Demuestran que la belleza puede asumir una apariencia que no es implícitamente bella. Demuestran que nuestros cuerpos han sido alienados por la religión, por el trabajo, por el deporte e incluso por la sexualidad, y que se han sido formateados en función de unos modelos estandarizados. Y ya sea mediante operaciones quirúrgicas o imágenes virtuales, siempre obtengo seres híbridos, cuerpos mutantes, posibles apariencias de civilizaciones que no poseen las mismas ideas preconcebidas que nosotros. Por tan-

EL QUIRÓFANO SE HA CONVERTIDO EN EL ESTUDIO DE TRABAJO DE ESTA ARTISTA FRANCESA QUE OPERA SU CUERPO PARA DENUNCIAR LA IMPOSICIÓN DE UN MODELO DE BELLEZA ÚNICO. BAJO LOS EFECTOS DE LA ANESTESIA LOCAL, DIRIGE LAS INTERVENCIONES EN LAS QUE AÑADE PRÓTESIS A UN FÍSICO EN CONSTANTE EVOLUCIÓN, UN PROCESO RECOGIDO EN FOTOGRAFÍAS QUE HAN VISITADO VARIOS MUSEOS. COTIZACIÓN: DESDE SIETE MILLONES DE PESETAS.

La cabeza de la artista, con una prótesis de silicona en la frente, descansa gracias al montaje fotográfico sobre un enorme compact disc.
FOTOGRAFÍA DE GERARD RANCINAN

MAGAZINE PÁG. 9

US $ 15 CANADA $ 20   www.bigmagazine.com   39   U T O P I A

■ 40
Publication Big
Creative Director Marcelo Jünemann
Art Directors Rafic Farah, Eduardo Hirama
Publisher Big Magazine, Inc.
Issue November 2001
Category Entire Issue

■ 41
Publication The New York Times Magazine
Art Director Janet Froelich
Designer Joele Cuyler
Illustrators Moonrunner Design LTD, Natasha Tibbott
Photo Editors Kathy Ryan, Kira Pollack
Photographers Rodney Smith, Davies + Starr,
Eika Aoshima
Publisher The New York Times
Issue December 9, 2001
Category Entire Issue
     A MERIT: Design: Cover

The New York Times Magazine
DECEMBER 9, 2001 / SECTION 6

The Year in
Ideas

AN ENCYCLOPEDIA OF
innovations,
conceptual leaps,
harebrained schemes,
cultural tremors
&
hindsight reckonings
that made a difference in
2001

Contents, Page 16

---

selling fast. Still, Jordan insists his motivation is "love of the game."

For many, that's hard to believe, coming from a man whose will to win is notorious. In his first half-dozen seasons, Jordan royally derided his championship-deficient Chicago Bulls teammates as "my supporting cast." He once bought a Pac-Man machine and brought it home to practice — so he could beat all comers during idle time in airports. His onetime Bulls teammate Luc Longley, asked to describe Jordan in a word, replied, "Predator." When the Bulls won their first title in 1991, Jordan famously wept in vindication and relief. As he has said, "Winning is everything."

MICHAEL JORDAN

Now an older and largely earthbound Jordan, playing for a team that won only 19 games last year, speaks enigmatically of "a different criteria for winning." He says he'll savor (nonwinning) moments: "smiling with the crowd, joking with the referees, challenging the other players, jawing with them." While his old Zen master Phil Jackson returned from retirement with a new colossus — monstrous Shaq and telegenic Kobe — Jordan and a bunch of kids will struggle to go .500. But maybe this will be one of Jordan's most endearing contributions — popularizing the beauty of imperfection and élan in defeat. ANDREW HSIAO

The 'X-Files' Conspiracy Trope Is Dead

According to "The X-Files," the C.I.A. and the F.B.I. are involved in a vast and exquisitely executed scheme to hide the presence of extraterrestrials on earth. According to Don DeLillo's novel "Libra," they plotted the assassination of John F. Kennedy. And in James Ellroy's "American Tabloid" and "Cold Six Thousand," they engineered every political killing and scandal of the past 40 years. According to the newspapers, however, America's elite intelligence and law-enforcement agencies are a bunch of bumblers. They have botched investigations, lost files, harbored double agents in their ranks and, despite the clamorous wake-up call of the 1993 bombing of the World Trade Center, failed to both anticipate and prevent the worst terrorist attack in American history.

"THE X-FILES"

Conspiracy theory, like garden-variety paranoia, has always contained a kernel of yearning; you only wish you were important enough for people to plot against you. After Sept. 11, however, it's acquired the sepia glow of nostalgia. If America's intelligence community were ever capable of pulling off the elaborate, masterful intrigues detailed by such paranoid classics as the alternative radio program "Hard Rain" — which featured reports suggesting that the C.I.A. intentionally started the AIDS epidemic — it certainly doesn't seem to be now. After-the-fact pleas for Arabic speakers to enlist in the C.I.A. and for suggestions from the public on how to pursue the hunt for whoever slipped anthrax-filled envelopes into the postal system don't inspire much confidence that either agency can even attend to its appointed rounds, let alone play puppet master. Could it be that setting Fidel Castro's beard on fire is the best idea they ever had? LAURA MILLER

Your Very Own Breakfast Cereal

Advances in niche marketing have made it possible for Americans to buy a wide array of individually tailored products. At a Levi's store, you can be fitted for a pair of individual, custom-tailored jeans; online, you can order your own personally selected compilation CD. Now the power of niche marketing is being brought to your breakfast table. Next spring, General Mills is expected to introduce www.mycereal.com, a Web site that allows users to mix and match more than 100 different ingredients to create and name their own breakfast cereals, delivered to their homes in single-serving portions.

You want Cheerios to come with the marshmallows from Lucky Charms? Done. Mix Cinnamon Toast Crunch with French Toast Crunch? Sure. Wheaties with blueberries, almonds and grains? No problem. Add a tropical touch to your Cocoa Puffs? Have them throw in some coconut shreds and dried mango. Databases connected to the Web site are set up to provide suggestions on health and nutritional criteria, including cholesterol, blood pressure and sugar content.

For a price of approximately $1 per serving, General Mills will deliver a one- or two-week supply of your personalized cereal mix to your home. There may always be a mass market for the popular varieties available on grocery-store shelves, but the high-tech interactive fantasy of www.mycereal.com is a creative solution to the problem of serving people with particularized, nonmainstream tastes or specific health needs. You will not be able to — at least at first — design your own cereal box, but you will be able to name your concoction. During a test run of the site last year, a customer at risk for osteoporosis designed a calcium-rich blend of chocolate- and peanut-butter-flavored cereals, studded with macadamia nuts and marshmallows. She called it Chocolatey-Calci-Yumm. JAIME WOLF

CUSTOM CEREAL

Zeroing In on a Killer

Geoprofiling — the science of predicting where criminals live based on where they commit crimes — was transformed this year from an academic novelty into a mainstream crime-fighting technique. It is now used by Scotland Yard, the F.B.I., the Royal Canadian Mounted Police, the A.T.F. and others to solve apparent serial crimes. Kim Rossmo, the former police detective from Vancouver, who invented it, flew more than 100,000 miles in 2001 to consult on various high-profile investigations. He has advised on everything from serial murders in New York to serial rapes in Louisiana.

The theory of geoprofiling was first articulated in Rossmo's Ph.D. thesis — but it didn't take long to be put into practice. On the very day in 1995 that Rossmo defended his thesis, two young girls were attacked by an unknown man in the town of Abbotsford, not far from Vancouver. Both girls were sexually assaulted. One was killed. A series of 911 calls followed in which the killer taunted police from five different phone booths. Within days the police had gathered more leads in more locales than they could ever check out, and so Rossmo was charged with winnowing those leads down and closing in on the killer by using the equation at the heart of his research.

It had come to him, the math of it, in a classic eureka moment five years before. "I was riding the train and staring out the window," he says, "and suddenly it hits me, this idea hits me, and I can kind of see the algorithm that expresses it, and then I'm grabbing for a napkin to scribble it all down." Of course it helped, vis-à-vis his ability to receive such an idea, that he'd first earned a degree in sociology and then logged a few years in grad school while walking a beat, reading widely — a book about the hunting patterns of African lions proved most helpful — and puzzling over the geographic logic hidden beneath most criminal acts. Rossmo's equation (now converted into a commercial software program called Rigel) leans heavily on what psychologists call the least-effort principle. In

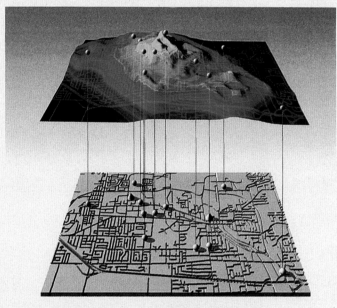

GEOPROFILING
Dots represent crime scenes; peaks, in yellow, indicate most likely locations of criminal's home.
Illustration by Moonrunner Design Ltd.

the realm of crime fighting, that principle holds that most offenders will do their dirty work relatively close to home, in a comfort zone defined by where they live, work, play and commute. They will not, however, do it too close to home; they tend to travel at least several blocks to avoid detection. When five or six related crime scenes can be identified, the model can reduce an investigator's prime search area by more than 90 percent.

In the case of the Abbotsford murders, Rossmo's model narrowed a 10-square-mile crime scene into a half-square-mile in which the killer was most likely to reside. When the culprit was found within Rossmo's square, geoprofiling was suddenly more than a hypothesis.

CHOCOLATE LAB
These Café Crunch treats, slathered with coffee-flavored chocolate, were hatched via a process known as "supercritical fluid extrusion." Have no fear: They're distantly related to Cheetos and Rice Krispies.

junkies

Meet the Ivy league iron chefs who think the world would be a better place with caffeinated breakfast cereals, orange milk, and chicken-flavored potato chips. Test-tube food is the answer for those who've lost that oven feeling.

BY ALEC FOEGE   PHOTOGRAPHS BY MATTHEW MONTEITH

Net COMPANY

WHERE DOES THE NET STAND?

The Internet economy is in disarray, but the Internet itself remains a powerful force or transformation: of strategy, of leadership, of day-to-day operations. This special report offers lessons from Cisco, Intel, and Microsoft—along with insights from top CEOs—about the next phase of the Internet revolution.

Illustration by ALISON SEIFFER

Fast Company 143

■ 42

Publication Details
Creative Director Dennis Freedman
Design Director Edward Leida
Art Director Rockwell Harwood
Photo Editors Alice Rose George, Amy Steigbigel, Jeannine Foeller
Photographer Mathew Monteith
Publisher The Condé Nast Publications Inc.
Issue August 2001
Category Features: Story

■ 43

Publication Fast Company
Design Director Patrick Mitchell
Designer Kristin Fitzpatrick
Illustrator Alison Seiffer
Publisher Gruner & Jahr USA Publishing
Issue July 2001
Category Department

(you are here)

PHOTOGRAPHS BY MICHAEL THOMPSON

Can't tell our models from the celebutante DJs, publicists, and party photographers on these pages? That's the point. Make it past the velvet rope by following the insiders' dress code: understated suits, graphic T-shirts, beat-up jeans.

158 DETAILS OCTOBER 2001

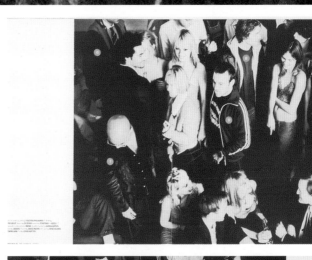

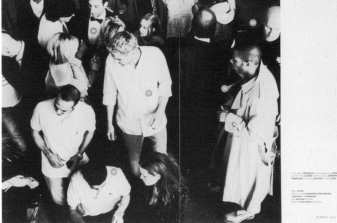

44
Publication Details
Creative Director Dennis Freedman
Design Director Edward Leida
Art Director Rockwell Harwood
Photo Editors Alice Rose George, Amy Steigbigel, Jeannine Foeller
Photographer Michael Thompson
Publisher The Condé Nast Publications Inc.
Issue October 2001
Category Features: Story

FLARE

unforgettable

Part showman, part soul man, he's been saving the world for a quarter of a century. As U2's Elevation Tour returns to America, the last rock star may have finally found what he's looking for. The ongoing beatification of Bono.

BY ANDREW ESSEX | PHOTOGRAPHS BY STEVEN KLEIN

all over white middle-class college kids with guitars."

CANCER

are compounds that occur naturally in the body, and in cancerous tissues, there is a higher concentration. In the past, scientists have developed agents to stimulate the production of phorphyns to selectively kill cancer cells. This state-of-the-art chemical research is not exactly a lifelong project of Bornhop's. It is, however, the blend of two careers.

Before coming to Texas Tech in 1994, Bornhop worked in the medical device industry for three years. He was familiar with visualization technology that allowed physicians to examine almost any part of a patient's body – knees, the heart, arms, ankles, the colon – through in-cavity microsurgery.

In his first semester as a faculty member at Texas Tech, he sat in on a lecture given by Garry Kiefer from the Dow Chemical Company. The lecture, Bornhop said, was about the chemical synthesis. At the end of the lecture, Kiefer showed a picture of a piece of bone that was glowing in a blue-green

color. Bornhop said a "light" went on for him. The "light" for him was sight-directed chemistry.

"I saw the correlation of early detection and making a chemical associate with or attach to a specific target site," said Bornhop.

In this case, the target site was cancer cells.

After the lecture, he talked to Kiefer and showed him Texas Tech's micro-endoscopy technology. The next day, Bornhop flew to Houston to present his research on fluorescence endoscopy at the Dow Chemical Company.

"Fluorescence is the most recently developed detection application," said Kiefer, who is the research leader in pharmaceutical development at Dow Chemical. "It's our hope to be able to detect cancer lesions before they become visible to the naked eye."

Soon after, Bornhop secured grants from the Whitaker Foundation, the

Inc

The Inc 500
AMERICA'S FASTEST-GROWING PRIVATE COMPANIES

October 30, 2001
$4.95 US $6.95 Canada

■ 46
Publication Vistas: Texas Tech Research
Creative Director Artie Limmer
Art Directors Alyson Keeling, T.J. Tucker
Designer Alyson Keeling
Photo Editor Artie Limmer
Photographer Artie Limmer
Studio Texas Tech University Creative Services
Publisher Texas Tech University
Client Texas Tech University
Issue Winter 2001
Category Features: Spread/Single Page

■ 47
Publication Inc.
Design Director Patrick Mitchell
Designer Patrick Mitchell
Photo Editor Alicia Jylkka
Photographer Christopher Harting
Publisher Gruner & Jahr USA Publishing
Issue October 2001
Category Cover

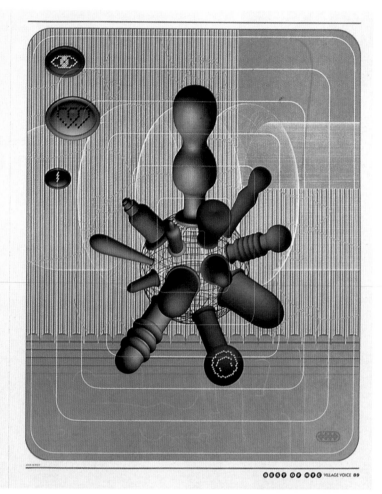

BEST CONDOM SELECTION

With such a large variety of rubbers, you may feel overwhelmed at CONDOMANIA, but remember to take your time when deciding whether the Kimono Micro Thin or the Bareback will allow for superior cock sensitivity. Looking for more head room? Condomania recommends Maxx for you lucky, well-endowed fellows. (If you actually want to downsize, the Trojan Ultra-Fit is code for small.) For studs and ridges designed to make her squeal and squirm, go straight for the Trojan Pleasure Mesh—unless you know she's daring enough to climb aboard Rough Rider. Not sure whether to test-run cola- or grape-flavored for that special safer-sex fellatio occasion? Just ask the prophylactic know-it-all behind the counter. 351 Bleecker Street, 691-9442, www.condomania.com

sex continues page 93

48
Publication The Village Voice
Design Director Ted Keller
Art Director Minh Uong
Designer Kimberly Hall
Illustrator John Hersey
Publisher Village Voice Media
Issue October 22, 2001
Category Features: Story

49
Publication Esquire
Design Director John Korpics
Designers Hannah McCaughey, Todd Albertson, Erin Whelan, Kim Forsberg
Illustrators David Plunkert, Mark Matcho, Eddie Guy, David Hughes, Tim Bower, Robert Parada
Photo Editors Nancy Jo Iacoi, Catriona NiAolain
Photographers Nigel Dickson, Julian Broad, Martin Schoeller, Jeffrey Braverman, Matt Jones, Norman Jean Roy, Dana Gallagher, Fabrizio Ferri, Stephen Danelian, Larry Sultan, Bruce Davidson, Frank W. Ockenfels 3, Chris McPherson
Publisher The Hearst Corporation-Magazines Division
Issue July 2001
Category Entire Issue

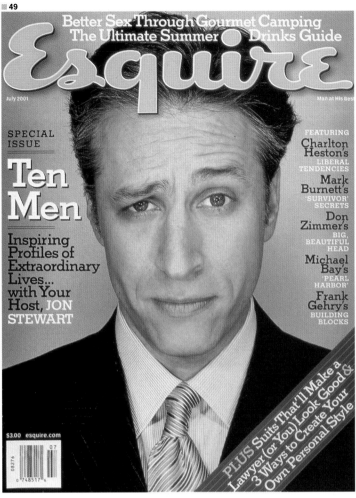

Esquire

Better Sex Through Gourmet Camping
The Ultimate Summer Drinks Guide

July 2001

Man at His Best

SPECIAL ISSUE

Ten Men

Inspiring Profiles of Extraordinary Lives... with Your Host, JON STEWART

FEATURING

Charlton Heston's LIBERAL TENDENCIES

Mark Burnett's 'SURVIVOR' SECRETS

Don Zimmer's BIG, BEAUTIFUL HEAD

Michael Bay's 'PEARL HARBOR'

Frank Gehry's BUILDING BLOCKS

PLUS Suits That'll Make a Lawyer (or You) Look Good & 3 Ways to Create Your Own Personal Style

$3.00 esquire.com

07

tenMEN

[Photograph by NIGEL DICKSON]

JOSEF PENNINGER He's thirty-six. He's the son of Austrian farmers. He's saved the world once. He's on the verge of saving it again. And his greatest discovery is just around the corner. He's going to save you. **BY MARY ROGAN**

Penninger

THE GREATEST SCIENTIST OF OUR TIME worries about you every day. He worries about the diseases lurking in your genes, the ache in your bones, the viruses sneaking up on your heart. And he worries about your soul, too. He worries whether you have one, and he worries about what you're going to do with it. But he's working while he's worrying. He's finding the genes that will make your bones feel good again, he's flipping the switch for your immune system, and he's hunting down the virus that is going to murder your heart. And he's getting closer, every day, to discovering the gene that will rock your world.

Josef Penninger may well save your life someday, but he'll still wish he could have touched your soul. When he wins the Nobel prize for discovering God, he'll feel his own troubled soul pounding away inside him, nestled between his heart and his thymus, protected by an army of T cells. But that's a long bicycle ride from here. Right now, he's just getting started.

CD45 IS THE GENE that controls the on/off switch for your immune system. When CD45 is switched on, T cells are released to fight infection. After the T cells have done their job, CD45 is switched off and your T cells go home to wait for the next battle. It's a great system when it works. When it doesn't, the results are disastrous. Until recently, scientists weren't sure which gene told your T cells when it was time to come in swinging and when it was time to call it quits.

CD45 is huge. It could be the heart of autoimmune diseases. Think of it this way: There's trouble in your neighborhood; some guy is knocking over trash cans and keeping your daughter out late. So you call in the big guy who keeps order in the neighborhood—CD45—to reach out and set things straight. CD45 unleashes his heavy hitters—T cells—which is a good thing, unless these heavy hitters get hooked on the juice of being heavy and won't stop. Pretty soon, they're killing everyone in the neighborhood, including your daughter and your wife, and after a few beers and crazy talk, they'll be coming for you. That's what hap-

tenMEN

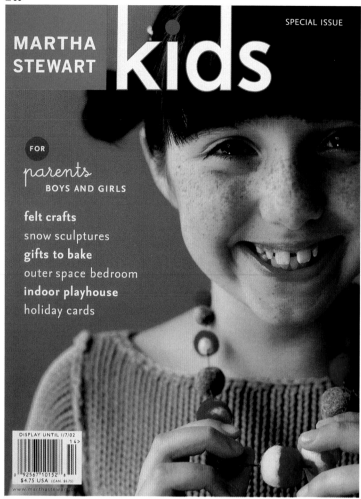

■ 50
Publication Martha Stewart Kids
Creative Director Gael Towey
Art Director Deb Bishop
Designers Jennifer Wagner, Sara Hicks, Jennifer Dahl, Deb Bishop
Photo Editors Jodi Nakatsuka, Jamie Bass
Photographers Ulla Nyman, Anna Williams,
Philip Newton, William Abranowicz, Gentl + Hyers
Stylists Jodi Levine, Ayesha Patel, Amy Gropp Forbes,
Melanio Gomez, Cyndi DiPrima, Laura Romandin
Publisher Martha Stewart Living Omnimedia
Issue Holiday 2001
Category Entire Issue

cooking with **Carrots**

HOW TO HELP YOUR BABY ENJOY EATING HIS VEGETABLES
FROM INFANCY THROUGH TODDLERHOOD

Sweet and colorful,
carrots are immediately appealing to
horses, bunnies, and children of all ages.
Carrots' color comes from carotenoids,
orange pigments, some of which are converted
in the body to vitamin A, essential for eyesight,
tooth and bone development, and immune
function. In the Middle Ages, carrot juice was
sometimes used to tint batches of butter
a golden yellow. Carrots contain more natural
sugars than any other vegetable except
beets. Carrots are related to parsley and dill
(note their similarly lacy greens) and
also to Queen Anne's lace, which appeared
in this country when carrots, brought here
by the colonists, escaped their gardens
and reverted to a wild state.
Nature designed the carrot, a root,
to be a fuel tank for these
greens, so if you buy fresh
carrots with their greens
still attached, twist them off.
They will continue to
draw moisture and
nutrients from
the carrot after
harvest.

PHOTOGRAPHS BY MARIA ROBLEDO   TEXT BY STEPHANA BOTTOM

114

■ 52

$6

ARCADE   the journal for architecture and design in the northwest
autumn 2001 volume 20 number 1

2001

the idea
of regionalism
guest editor john cava

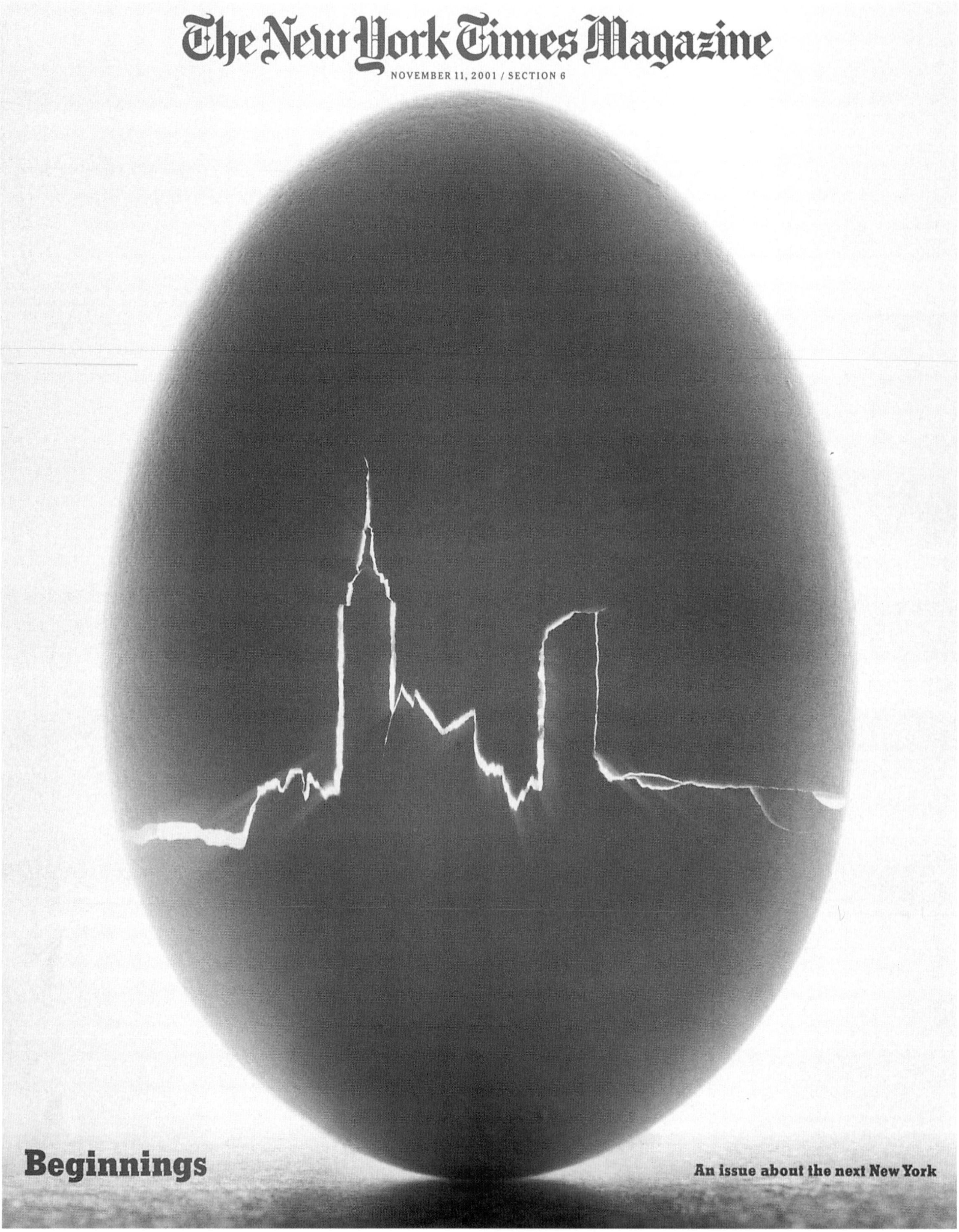

The New York Times Magazine

NOVEMBER 11, 2001 / SECTION 6

Beginnings

An issue about the next New York

НОВЫЕ ТЕНДЕНЦИИ

PLUS

→ **ПРАЗДНИКИ!** Примите гостей?

Конкорд снова в полете

Дизайн дома и в гостях

Geländewagen и тридцать Жигулей

Одеваемся на вечеринку стр. 56

Модный взгляд на вещи стр. 53-111

ISSN 1681-6269

ГОРЯЧИЕ ТРЕНДЫ С ХОЛОДНЫХ УЛИЦ | КАК ЗДОРОВО ВЫГЛЯДЕТЬ?

Стрижём круглосуточно

Рабочая Одежда

Что носить +

Звонят: откройте дверь!

53
Publication The New York Times Magazine
Art Director Janet Froelich
Designer Nancy Harris
Photo Editors Kathy Ryan, Jody Quon
Photographer Raymond Meier
Publisher The New York Times
Issue November 11, 2001
Category Cover

54
Publication New Trends Plus
Creative Directors Anton Ioukhnovets, Oleg Diachenko
Designer Anton Ioukhnovets
Illustrator Vasco Colombo
Photo Editors Anton Ioukhnovets, Oleg Diachenko
Photographers Michael Korolev, Sergei Gavrilov, Victoria Rich,
Jorge Colombo, Andrei Bihov, Andrei Bronikov,
Vladimir Mishukov, Angela West, Tim Davis, Robert Veimer
Publisher Plus Publications LLC
Issue December 2001
Category Entire Issue

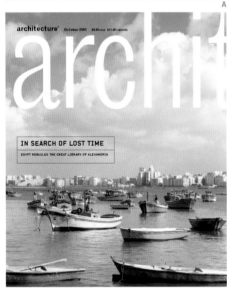

■ 55
Publication Architecture
Art Directors Martin Perrin, Lisa Naftolin
Designers Adam Michaels,
Claudia Brandenburg, Lynn Yeo
Photo Editor Alexandra Brez
Publisher VNU, Inc.
Issues January 2001, June 2001, October 2001
Category Magazine of the Year
    A **MERIT:** Design: Cover

■ 56
Publication Entertainment Weekly
Design Director Geraldine Hessler
Art Directors John Walker, Jennifer Procopio,
Tamaye Perry, Robert Festino, Jennie Chang
Designers Sara Osten, Lee Berresford, Amy Won
Photo Editors Sarah Rozen, Denise Sfraga,
Michael Kochman, Michele Romero, Luciana
Chang, Richard B. Maltz, Suzanne Reagan,
Fredya C. Tavin, Nola Tully, Marian Isel Barragn
Photographers Matthew Rolston,
Andrew Macpherson
Publisher Time Inc.
Issues June 29, 2001, September 7, 2001,
December 21, 2001
Category Magazine of the Year

■ 57
Publication Fast Company
Design Director Patrick Mitchell
Designers Melanie deForest, Emily Crawford,
Julia Moburg, Kristin Fitzpatrick
Illustrators Peter Hoey, Scogin Mayo,
Michael McLaughlin, Michael Lewis, Catherine Ledner
Photo Editors Alicia Jylkka, Lauren Bollettino
Publisher Gruner & Jahr USA Publishing
Issues February 2001, June 2001, September 2001
Category Magazine of the Year

BIG 34 : THIS ENGLAND

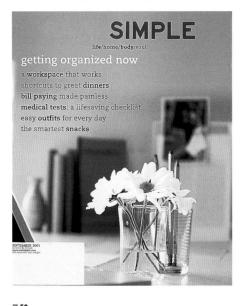

■ 58
Publication Big
Creative Director Marcelo Jünemann
Design Director Daren Ellis
Art Directors Daren Ellis, Starr Foundation NY,
Christophe Brunnquell
Photo Editors Lisa Ano, Sarah Colette
Studio Big
Publisher Big Magazine, Inc.
Issues April 01, 2001, September 2001,
October 2001
Category Magazine of the Year
    A MERIT: Design: Cover

■ 59
Publication Real Simple
Creative Directors Roland Bello, Michael Grossman
Design Director Jill Armus
Art Directors Chalkley Calderwood-Pratt, Eva Spring
Designers Jill Armus, Roland Bello,
Chalkley Calderwood-Pratt, Millie Rossman Kidd,
Eva Spring, Chad Tomlinson
Photo Editors Jean Herr, Naomi Nista
Photographers Jim Franco, Thayer Allyson Gowdy,
William Waldron
Publisher Time Inc.
Issues June/July 2001, August 2001, September 2001
Category Magazine of the Year
    A MERIT: Design: Cover   **49**

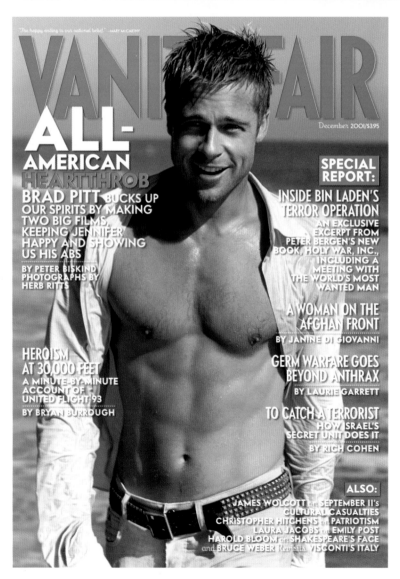

■ 60
Publication Vanity Fair
Design Director David Harris
Art Directors Julie Weiss, Gregory Mastrianni
Designers Adam Bookbinder, Lee Ruelle, Lisa Meipala
Kennedy, Christopher Israel, Chris Mueller, Glenn Bo
Photo Editor Susan White
Photographers Annie Leibovitz, Herb Ritts
Publisher The Condé Nast Publications Inc.
Issues April 2001, November 2001, December 2001
Category Magazine of the Year

MERIT / MAGAZINE OF THE YEAR design

■ 61

■ 63

■ 65

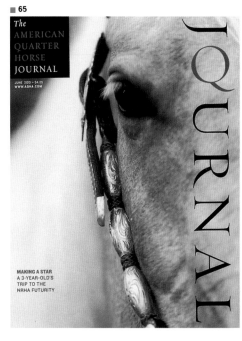

■ 62

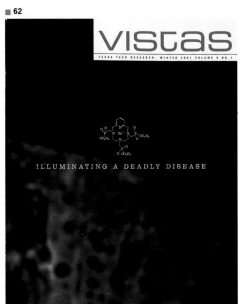

■ 64

■ 61
Publication The American Prospect
Art Director Alissa Levin
Designer Alissa Levin
Illustrator Brian Cronin
Studio Point Five Design
Publisher The American Prospect
Client The American Prospect
Issue December 3, 2001
Category Cover

■ 62
Publication Vistas: Texas Tech Research
Creative Director Artie Limmer
Art Directors Alyson Keeling, T.J. Tucker
Designers Alyson Keeling, T.J. Tucker
Photo Editor Artie Limmer
Photographer Artie Limmer
Studio Texas Tech University Creative Services
Publisher Texas Tech University
Client Texas Tech University
Issue Winter 2001
Category Cover

■ 63
Publication LA Weekly
Art Director Bill Smith
Illustrator Raymond Pettibon
Publisher Village Voice Media
Issue May 18, 2001
Category Cover

■ 64
Publication 64 Magazine
Creative Director Tyler Darden
Art Director Tyler Darden
Designer Tyler Darden
Illustrator Sterling Hundley
Publisher Shine Publications
Issue January/February 2001
Category Cover

■ 65
Publication The American Quarter Horse Journal
Creative Director D.J. Stout
Art Director Brian Smith
Designers D.J. Stout, Nancy McMillan
Photographer Jennifer Barron
Studio Pentagram Design, Austin
Publisher The American Quarter Horse Association
Client American Quarter Horse Association
Issue June 2001
Category Cover

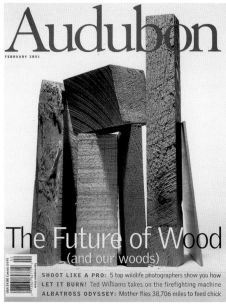

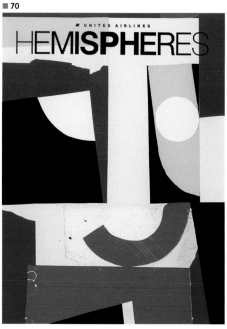

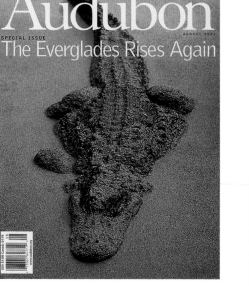

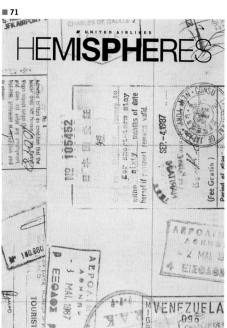

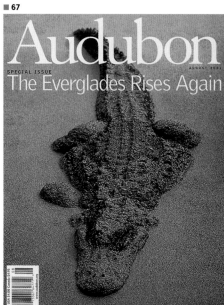

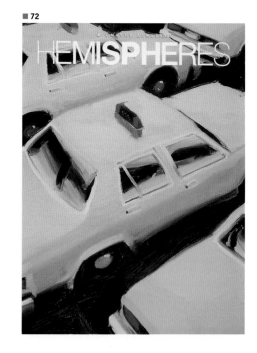

■ 73

■ 74

■ 75

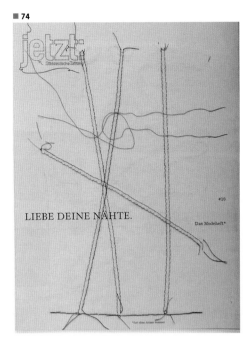

■ 86

■ 70
Publication Hemispheres
Art Directors Jaimey Easler, Jody Mustain,
Jennifer Hill
Illustrator Ivan Chermayeff
Publisher Pace Communications
Client United Airlines
Issue March 2001
Category Cover

■ 71
Publication Hemispheres
Art Directors Jaimey Easler, Jody Mustain,
Jennifer Hill
Illustrator Maïa James Müller
Publisher Pace Communications
Client United Airlines
Issue June 2001
Category Cover

■ 72
Publication Hemispheres
Art Directors Jaimey Easler, Jody Mustain,
Jennifer Hill
Illustrator Peter Sylvada
Publisher Pace Communications
Client United Airlines
Issue December 2001
Category Cover

■ 73
Publication Esquire
Design Director John Korpics
Photo Editor Fiona McDonagh
Photographer Fabrizio Ferri
Publisher The Hearst Corporation-Magazines Division
Issue February 2001
Category Cover

■ 74
Publication Jetzt
Art Director Mirko Borsche
Designer Sandra Eichler
Illustrator Sandra Eichler
Photo Editor Bettina Beust
Publisher Süddeutsche Zeitung
Issue March 05, 2001
Category Cover

■ 75
Publication Martha Stewart Kids
Creative Director Gael Towey
Art Director Deb Bishop
Designer Deb Bishop
Photo Editor Jodi Nakatsuka
Photographers Victoria Pearson, Stephen Lewis,
William Abranowicz, Sang An, Victor Schrager
Stylists Jodi Levine, Paige Norman, Stephana
Bottom, Mel Gomez, Ayesha Patel, Matthew
Gleason, Cyndi DiPrima
Publisher Martha Stewart Living Omnimedia
Issue Summer/Fall 2001
Category Cover

■ 76
Publication Martha Stewart Weddings
Creative Director Eric Pike
Art Director Ellen Burnie
Photo Editor Jodi Nakatsuka
Photographer Simon Watson
Stylist Page Marchese Norman
Publisher Martha Stewart Living Omnimedia
Issue Winter 2001
Category Cover

Shrek,
un ogro poco convencional
de un cuento
de hadas
poco convencional
en una película de animación poco convencional

ITALIANOS 2001 | LOS 25 MÁS AUTÉNTICOS

FINAL FANTASY SÓLO LA HUELLA DESCUBRE QUE ES UNA PELÍCULA DIGITAL

HAY CINES, TIENDAS, RESTAURANTES, DISCOTECAS, BOLERAS, BARE
DE COPAS, JUEGOS RECREATIVOS, HIPERMERCADOS, CENTROS D
BELLEZA, ZONAS INFANTILES... SON LAS 31 NUEVAS CATEDRALES DEL OCI

■ 77
Publication Metropoli
Design Director Carmelo Caderot
Art Director Rodrigo Sánchez
Designer Rodrigo Sánchez
Illustrator Rodrigo Sánchez
Photo Editor Rodrigo Sánchez
Publisher Unidad Editorial S.A.
Issue July 13, 2001
Category Cover

■ 78
Publication Metropoli
Design Director Carmelo Caderot
Art Director Rodrigo Sánchez
Designer Rodrigo Sánchez
Photo Editor Rodrigo Sánchez
Publisher Unidad Editorial S.A.
Issue August 24, 2001
Category Cover

■ 79
Publication Metropoli
Design Director Carmelo Caderot
Art Director Rodrigo Sánchez
Designer Rodrigo Sánchez
Illustrator Rodrigo Sánchez
Photo Editor Rodrigo Sánchez
Publisher Unidad Editorial S.A.
Issue November 16, 2001
Category Cover

■ 80
Publication Metropoli
Design Director Carmelo Caderot
Art Director Rodrigo Sánchez
Designer Rodrigo Sánchez
Illustrator Rodrigo Sánchez
Publisher Unidad Editorial S.A.
Issue December 28, 2001
Category Cover

■ 81
Publication MBA Jungle
Creative Director Matthew Guemple
Art Director Matthew Guemple
Designer Darren Tuozzoli
Photo Editor Ondrea Barbe
Photographer Tom Haynes
Publisher Jungle Media Group
Issue February 2001
Category Cover

■ 82
Publication MBA Jungle
Creative Director Matthew Guemple
Art Director Matthew Guemple
Designer Neil Russo
Photographer Tom Haynes
Publisher Jungle Media Group
Issue September 2001
Category Cover

■ 83

■ 84

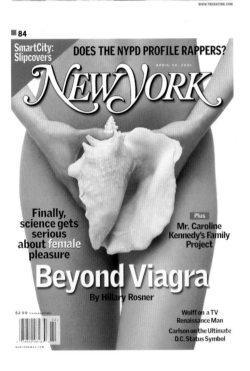

■ 85

■ 86

■ 87

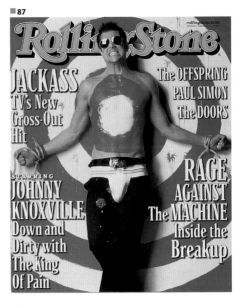

■ 88

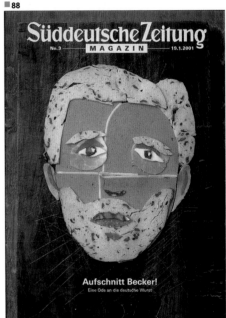

■ 83
Publication The Nation
Art Director Scott Stowell
Designers Scott Stowell, Susan Barber
Illustrators Susan Barber, Chad Roberts
Photographer Foodpix
Studio Open
Publisher The Nation Company L.P.
Client The Nation
Issue April 02, 2001
Category Cover

■ 84
Publication New York Magazine
Design Director Michael Picón
Photo Editor Chris Dougherty
Photographer Karen Kuehn
Publisher Primedia Magazines Inc.
Issues April 30, 2001
Category Cover

■ 85
Publication Real Simple
Creative Director Roland Bello
Art Director Eva Spring
Designer Roland Bello
Photo Editor Jean Herr
Photographer David Gubert
Publisher Time Inc.
Issue March 2001
Category Cover

■ 86
Publication Real Simple
Creative Director Roland Bello
Designer Roland Bello
Photo Editor Jean Herr
Photographer Paul Whicheloe
Publisher Time Inc.
Issue April 2001
Category Cover

■ 87
Publication Rolling Stone
Art Director Fred Woodward
Designer Fred Woodward
Photo Editors Fiona McDonagh, Audrey Landreth
Photographer Mark Seliger
Publisher Wenner Media
Issue February 01, 2001
Category Cover

■ 88
Publication Süddeutsche Zeitung Magazin
Art Director Michael Weies
Designer Anne Blaschke
Illustrators Olaf Hajek, Martin Haake
Publisher Magazin Verlagsges Süeddeutsche Zeitung mbH
Issue January 19, 2001
Category Cover

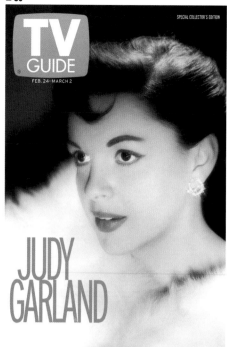

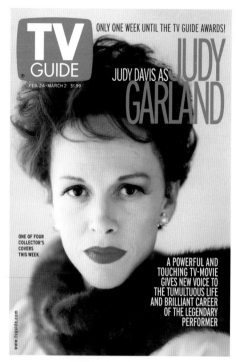

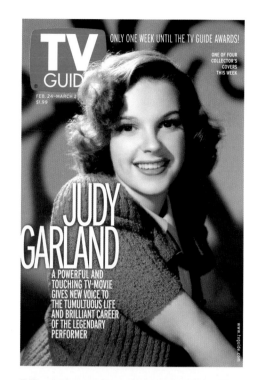

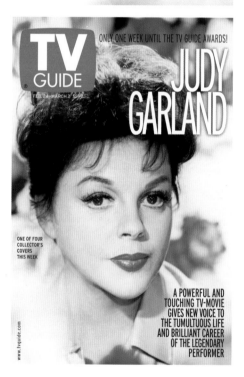

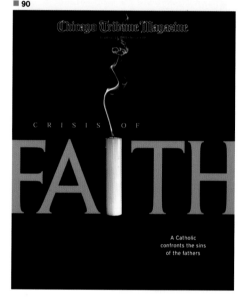

Publication TV Guide
Design Director Maxine Davidowitz
Art Director Theresa Griggs
Designer Maxine Davidowitz
Photo Editors Hazel Hammond, Nancy Schwartz
Photographers Bill Reitzel, Philippe Halsman,
Warner Brothers, MGM
Publisher TV Guide Inc.
Issue February 24, 2001
Category Cover

Publication Chicago Tribune Sunday Magazine
Art Directors David Syrek, Joe Darrow
Photographer Tom Schierlitz
Publisher Chicago Tribune Company
Issue February 11, 2001
Category Cover

■ 91

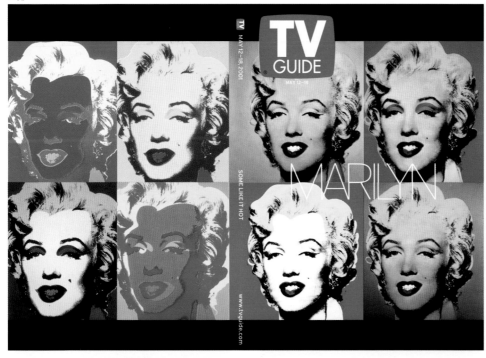

■ 94

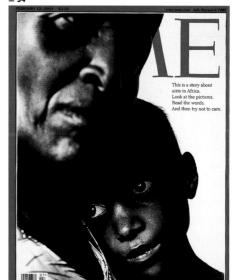

■ 92

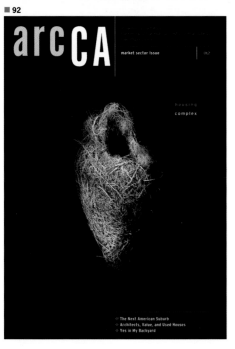

■ 93

■ 95

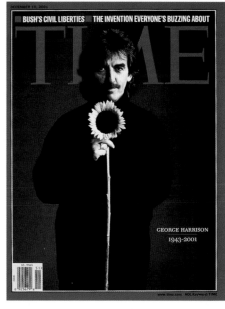

■ 91
Publication TV Guide
Design Director Maxine Davidowitz
Art Director Theresa Griggs
Designer Maxine Davidowitz
Illustrator Andy Warhol
Photo Editors Hazel Hammond, Nancy Schwartz
Publisher TV Guide Inc.
Issue May 12, 2001
Category Cover

■ 92
Publication arcCA
Design Director Bob Aufuldish
Designer Bob Aufuldish
Photographer Richard Barnes
Studio Aufuldish & Warinner
Publisher McGraw-Hill/AIACC
Client American Institute of Architects
California Council
Issue Vol. 1, No. 2 2001
Category Cover

■ 93
Publication arcCA
Design Director Bob Aufuldish
Designer Bob Aufuldish
Photographer Marc Phu
Studio Aufuldish & Warinner
Publisher McGraw-Hill/AIACC
Client American Institute of Architects
California Council
Issue Vol. 1, No. 3 2001
Category Cover

■ 94
Publication Time
Art Director Arthur Hochstein
Designer Arthur Hochstein
Photo Editors Robert Stevens, MaryAnne Golon
Photographer James Nachtwey
Publisher Time Inc.
Issue February 12, 2001
Category Cover

■ 95
Publication Time
Art Director Arthur Hochstein
Designer Arthur Hochstein
Photo Editor Marie Tobias
Photographer Mark Seliger
Publisher Time Inc.
Issue December 10, 2001
Category Cover

■ 98

■ 99

■ 100

96
Publication Vanity Fair
Design Director David Harris
Art Director Gregory Mastrianni
Photo Editors Susan White, Kathryn MacLeod
Photographer Annie Leibovitz
Publisher The Condé Nast Publications Inc.
Issue April 2001
Category Cover

97
Publication Vanity Fair
Design Director David Harris
Art Director Julie Weiss
Designers David Harris, Chris Mueller
Photo Editor Susan White
Photographer Jonas Karlsson
Publisher The Condé Nast Publications Inc.
Issue November 2001
Category Cover

98
Publication The New York Times Magazine
Art Director Janet Froelich
Designer Joele Cuyler
Photo Editor Kathy Ryan
Photographer Platon
Publisher The New York Times
Issue November 4, 2001
Category Cover

99
Publication The New York Times Magazine
Art Director Janet Froelich
Designer Janet Froelich
Photo Editors Kathy Ryan, Jody Quon
Photographer Mikako Koyama
Publisher The New York Times
Issue December 23, 2001
Category Cover

100
Publication Chicago Tribune Sunday Magazine
Art Director David Syrek
Illustrator David Syrek
Publisher Chicago Tribune Company
Issue April 29, 2001
Category Cover

■ 101

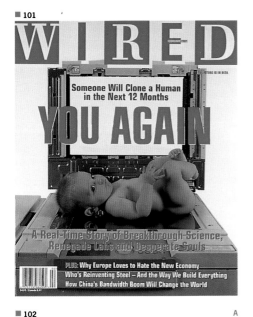

■ 102   A

ARCADE

■ 103

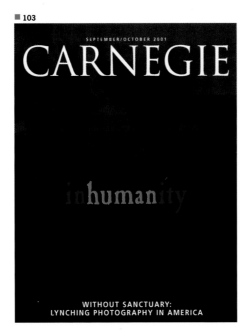

■ 104

■ 105

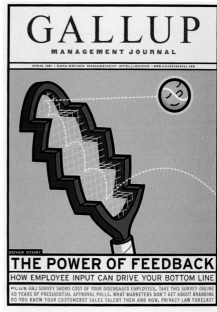

■ 106

■ 101
Publication Wired
Design Director Daniel Carter
Art Director Susana Rodriguez
Designer Daniel Carter
Photo Editor Christa Aboitiz
Photographer Jason Schmidt
Publisher The Condé Nast Publications Inc.
Issue February 2001
Category Cover

■ 102
Publication Arcade Journal of Architecture and Design
Design Director Karen Cheng
Designer Karen Cheng
Publisher Northwest Architectural League
Issue Winter 2001
Category Cover
    A **MERIT:** Design: Redesign

■ 103
Publication Carnegie Magazine
Creative Director Jim Bolander
Designer Bryan Brunsell
Studio Brady Communications
Publisher Carnegie Museums
Issue September 01, 2001
Category Cover

■ 104
Publication Commonfund Quarterly
Design Director Frank C. Lionetti
Designer Frank C. Lionetti
Photographer Bob Elsdale
Studio Frank C. Lionetti Design Inc
Publisher Commonfund
Issue Summer 2001
Category Cover

■ 105
Publication Gallup Management Journal
Creative Director Terry Koppel
Design Director Carin Goldberg
Art Director Kristina DiMatteo
Designers Carin Goldberg, Kristina DiMatteo, Rebecca Alden
Illustrator Christoph Niemann
Photo Editor Bess Hauser
Publisher Time Inc. Custom Publishing
Issue Spring 2001
Category Cover

■ 106
Publication Gallup Management Journal
Creative Director Terry Koppel
Design Director Carin Goldberg
Art Director Kristina DiMatteo
Designers Carin Goldberg, Kristina DiMatteo, Rebecca Alden
Photo Editor Bess Hauser
Photographer Michael Heiko
Publisher Time Inc. Custom Publishing
Issue Winter 2001
Category Cover

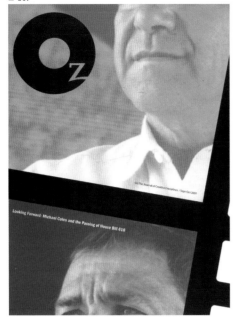

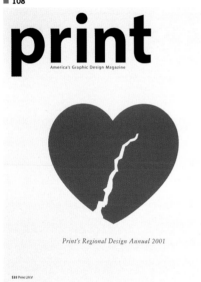

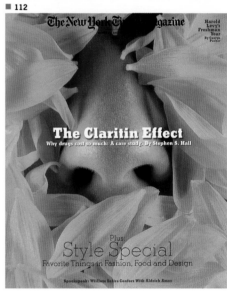

■ 107
Publication Oz
Creative Director Ted Fabella
Art Director Ted Fabella
Designer Ted Fabella
Photographer Ken Takata
Studio Office of Ted Fabella
Publisher Oz Publishing
Client OZ Publishing
Issue September/October 2001
Category Cover

■ 108
Publication Print
Art Director Steven Brower
Designer Steven Brower
Publisher RC Publications
Issue September/October 2001
Category Cover

■ 109
Publication The New York Times Book Review
Art Director Steven Heller
Illustrator Chris Ware
Publisher The New York Times
Issue June 3, 2001
Category Cover
   A MERIT: Design: Entire Issue

■ 110
Publication The Guardian G2
Creative Director Mark Porter
Art Director Roger Browning
Designer Fraser McDermott
Photo Editor Roger Tooth
Publisher Guardian Newspapers LTD.
Issue March 7, 2001
Category Cover

■ 111
Publication The New York Times Magazine
Art Director Janet Froelich
Designer Joele Cuyler
Photo Editor Kathy Ryan
Photographer Tyler Hicks
Publisher The New York Times
Issue February 18, 2001
Category Cover

■ 112
Publication The New York Times Magazine
Art Director Janet Froelich
Designer Joele Cuyler
Photo Editor Kathy Ryan
Photographer James Wojcik
Publisher The New York Times
Issue March 11, 2001
Category Cover

■ 113

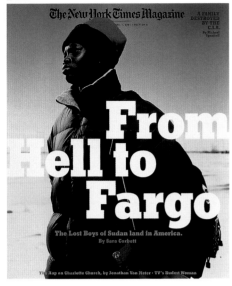

■ 115

■ 117

■ 114

■ 116

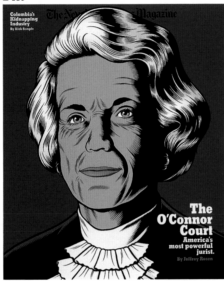

■ 118

■ 113
Publication The New York Times Magazine
Art Director Janet Froelich
Designer Claude Martel
Photo Editor Kathy Ryan
Photographer Jeff Riedel
Publisher The New York Times
Issue April 1, 2001
Category Cover

■ 114
Publication The New York Times Magazine
Art Director Janet Froelich
Designer Lisa Naftolin
Photo Editors Kathy Ryan, Jody Quon
Photographer Mary Ellen Mark
Publisher The New York Times
Issue October 14, 2001
Category Cover

■ 115
Publication The New York Times Magazine
Art Director Janet Froelich
Designer Joele Cuyler
Photo Editor Kathy Ryan
Photographer Andrew Eccles
Publisher The New York Times
Issue June 10, 2001
Category Cover

■ 116
Publication The New York Times Magazine
Art Director Janet Froelich
Designer Nancy Harris
Illustrator Charles Burns
Publisher The New York Times
Issue June 3, 2001
Category Cover

■ 117
Publication The Washington Post
Art Director Kelly Doe
Designer Kelly Doe
Illustrator Alex Williamson
Publisher The Washington Post Co.
Issue November 9, 2001
Category Front Page

■ 118
Publication Weekend Journal
Art Director Stephen Fay
Illustrators Pierre-Paul Pariseau, Randy Jones
Publisher Dow Jones & Co., Inc.
Issue May 11, 2001
Category Front Page

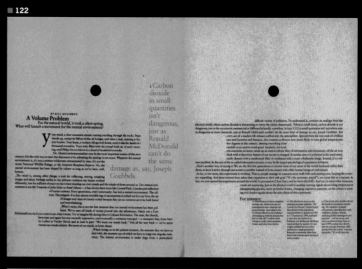

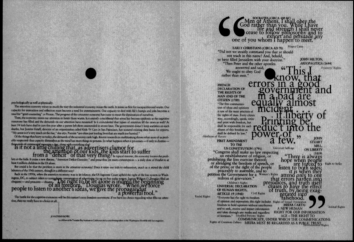

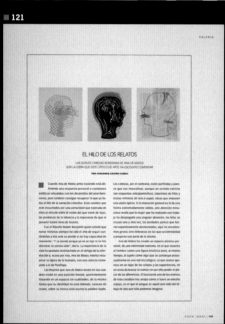

■ 120
Publication American Way
Design Directors Gilberto Mejia, Charles Stone
Designer Gilberto Mejia
Studio American Way Magazine
Publisher American Airlines Publishing
Client American Airlines
Issue April 15, 2001
Category Features: Spread

■ 121
Publication Casa Ideal
Creative Director Ricardo Feriche
Art Directors Pilar Velloso, Rocio Hidalgo
Designer Fernanda Ambrosio
Illustrator Ana Matos
Studio Feriche & Black, S.L.
Publisher RBA Editores
Issue May 2001
Category Department

■ 119
Publication American Way
Design Directors Gilberto Mejia, Charles Stone
Designer Marianne Dunn
Illustrator Jon Cannell
Studio American Way Magazine
Publisher American Airlines Publishing
Client American Airlines
Issue April 1, 2001
Category Features: Spread

■ 122
Publication Adbusters
Art Directors Tom Brown, Paul Shoebridge
Designer Tom Brown
Studio Tom Brown Art & Design
Publisher The Media Foundation
Client Adbusters
Issue October/November 2001
Category Features: Story

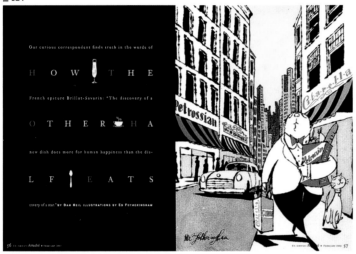

■ 123

Publication Adbusters
Art Director Tom Brown
Designer Tom Brown
Illustrator Aude Van Ryn
Studio Tom Brown Art & Design
Publisher The Media Foundation
Client Adbusters
Issue June/July 2001
Category Features: Spread

■ 124

Publication Attaché
Art Director Holly Holliday
Designer Holly Holliday
Illustrator EdwinFotheringham
Publisher Pace Communications
Client US Airways
Issue February 2001
Category Features: Spread

■ 125

Publication Attaché
Art Director Holly Holliday
Designer Holly Holliday
Photographer Terry Heffernan
Publisher Pace Communications
Client US Airways
Issue July 2001
Category Features: Spread

■ 126

Publication Attaché
Art Director Holly Holliday
Designer Holly Holliday
Photographer Hope Sandrow
Publisher Pace Communications
Client US Airways
Issue October 2001
Category Features: Spread

■ 127

Publication Expansion
Creative Director Guillermo Caballero
Art Director Ricardo Peña
Illustrator Jorge Del Angel
Publisher Grupo Editorial Expansion
Issue November 28, 2001
Category Features: Spread

This England

The Great Escape

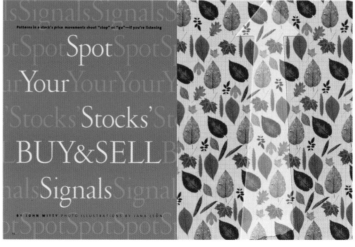

LIVE FREE OR MOVE

■ 128
Publication Big
Creative Director Marcelo Jünemann
Art Director Daren Ellis
Publisher Big Magazine, Inc.
Issue April 1, 2001
Category Entire Issue

■ 129
Publication Bloomberg Personal Finance
Art Director Frank Tagariello
Designer Frank Tagariello
Photo Editors Mary Shea, Carrie Guenther
Photographer Richard Misrach
Publisher Bloomberg L.P.
Issue May 2001
Category Features: Spread

■ 130
Publication Bloomberg Personal Finance
Art Director Frank Tagariello
Designer Frank Tagariello
Photo Editor Mary Shea
Photographer Ethan Hill
Publisher Bloomberg L.P.
Issue July/August 2001
Category Features: Spread

■ 131
Publication Bloomberg Personal Finance
Art Director Frank Tagariello
Designer Anna Kula
Photo Editor Mary Shea
Photographer Jana León
Publisher Bloomberg L.P.
Issue December 2001
Category Features: Spread

a LIFE IN LIMBO
BY TRACEY MIRKIN PHOTOGRAPHS BY STEFFEN THALEMANN

a. manette
ansay

What happens if you strip a writer bare? What happens if, like a grade-schooler wielding a soft pink eraser, you rub away the penciled-in curlicues of a writer's life? Get rid of physical trappings? Take away the safaris, the drunken fountain cavortings, the quiet garden tending? What if you distill the writer to such an extent that even the writing itself—the small-gestured and yet intensely corporeal act of putting down the words—is no longer the ritual morning spent writing longhand on ledger sheets, or the late afternoon banging on a near-antique Royal typewriter, or even the postmidnight session tapping quietly in the intimate, alien glow of a monitor screen?

GO FOR IT—
IN BROWNIES,
SPECIAL-OCCASION CAKES
AND MORE

CHOCOLATE
TO
THE
MAX

BY CAROLE BLOOM
PHOTOGRAPHY BY LEO GONG

JIMMY CARTER
Man
of his
Words

America's thirty-ninth president figured out what it takes to be a farmer, a businessman, a naval officer, a global peacemaker, a diplomat and a champion of the poor and hungry. So how does he make a living? He's a writer.

LAZY DAYS ON
PRINCE
EDWARD
ISLAND

WHEN JINX AND JEFFERSON MORGAN SET OUT FOR A HOLIDAY IN CANADA'S SMALLEST PROVINCE, THEY ENCOUNTER QUAINT TOWNS, COZY INNS, TERRIFIC SEAFOOD—AND ANNE OF GREEN GABLES, WELL, SORT OF.

PHOTOGRAPHY BY ERICKA McCONNELL

Arte digital

Vedova
dei Fiori

ANTONIO GARCÍA APREA

■ 132
Publication Book
Design Director Timothy Jones
Designer Jeremy Wortsman
Photo Editor Lila Garnett
Photographer Steffen Thalemann
Publisher West Egg Publications
Issue September/October 2001
Category Features: Spread/Single Page

■ 133
Publication Book
Design Director Timothy Jones
Photo Editor Lila Garnett
Photographer Platon
Publisher West Egg Publications
Issue November/December 2001
Category Features: Spread

■ 134
Publication Bon Appétit
Creative Director Campion Primm
Art Director Giuliana Schwab
Photo Editor Elizabeth Mathews
Photographer Leo Gong
Publisher The Condé Nast Publications Inc.
Issue February 2001
Category Features: Spread

■ 135
Publication Bon Appétit
Creative Director Campion Primm
Art Director Giuliana Schwab
Photo Editor Elizabeth Mathews
Photographer Ericka McConnell
Publisher The Condé Nast Publications Inc.
Issue June 2001
Category Features: Spread

■ 136
Publication Max, Todo el hombre
Creative Director Gerardo Balderas Luna
Designers Alejandro Ortiz López, Sol Vázquez Falcón
Illustrator Antonio García Aprea
Photo Editors Edgar Alamill Ávilla, Rodrigo Aceves Vázquez
Publisher Editorial Premiere, S.A. de C.V.
Issue September 2001
Category Features: Spread

design MERIT

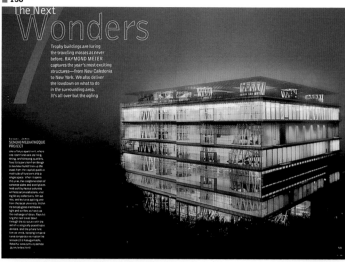

■ 138
Publication Condé Nast Traveler
Design Director Robert Best
Art Director Kerry Robertson
Designer Robert Best
Photo Editors Kathleen Klech, Esin Goknar
Photographer Raymond Meier
Publisher The Condé Nast Publications Inc.
Issue March 2001
Category Features: Story

■ 139
Publication Country Home
Art Director Paul Zimmerman
Designer Susan Uedelhofen
Photographer Jeff McNamara
Publisher Meredith Corp.
Issue May 2001
Category Features: Spread

■ 137
Publication Gastronomica: The Journal of Food and Culture
Creative Directors Frances Baca, Lee Friedman
Design Directors Frances Baca, Lee Friedman
Designers Frances Baca, Lee Friedman
Publisher Universtiy of California Press Journals
Issue February 2, 2001
Category Entire Issue

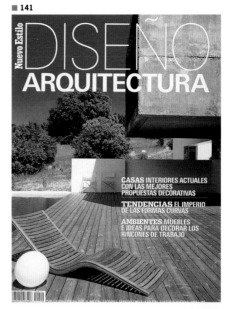

■ 140
Publication City
Creative Director Fabrice Frere
Design Director Fabrice Frere
Art Directors Mariana Ochs, Adriana Jacoud
Illustrator Anabelle Verhoye
Photo Editor Piera Gelardi
Photographers Anne Menke, Martyn Thompson
Publisher City NY Publishing LLC
Issue September 1, 2001
Category Entire Issue

■ 141
Publication Diseno Arquitectura
Creative Directors MaryJane Fahey, David O'Connor
Designers MaryJane Fahey, David O'Connor
Photo Editors Blanca Miguel, Beatriz Perez De Arminan
Photographer Maria Gorbena
Studio MaryJane Fahey/David O'Connor Editorial Design
Publisher Axel Springer, Madrid, Spain
Issue May 2001
Category Entire Issue

PITCH PERFECT

MUSIC GREAT QUINCY JONES TELLS HOW HE HAS REINVENTED HIMSELF AND SPOTTED KEY TRENDS FOR FIVE DECADES.

JACK POT!

HARRAH'S wins big by taking an unconventional approach to luring customers.
BY JOANNE KELLEY

> Stravinsky said that OBSERVATION is the key responsibility for creative people. He thought it was important to watch the forces of nature. That's why African music is so POWERFUL.

> We're working to make SILICON VALLEY out of South Africa. It's the world's most AMBITIOUS idea but could be incredible.

PERSONAL INFORMATION ABOUT EVERYTHING FROM A CUSTOMER'S AGE TO HIS FAVORITE DRINK ARE RECORDED IN Harrah's DATAbase.

Ray Gelato's **MAMBO ITALIANO**

BY LESLIE ROSENBERG PHOTOGRAPHY BY TODD BURRIS

"WHEN YOU PLAY THIS MUSIC you can't do a complete original album, because there are always things people want to hear, otherwise they're not going to buy the record."

■ 142

Publication Context
Creative Director Mark Maltais
Design Director Mark Maltais
Art Directors Mark Maltais, Gretchen Kirchner
Designers Mark Maltais, Gretchen Kirchner
Photographer Patrick Demarchelier
Publisher Diamond Cluster International Inc.
Issue April/May 2001
Category Features: Story

■ 143

Publication Context
Creative Director Mark Maltais
Design Director Mark Maltais
Art Directors Mark Maltais, Gretchen Kirchner
Designers Mark Maltais, Gretchen Kirchner
Publisher Diamond Cluster International Inc.
Issue October/November 2001
Category Features: Story

■ 144

Publication Atomic
Creative Director Jeff Griffith
Art Director Jeff Griffith
Designer Jeff Griffith
Photographer Todd Burris
Publisher Atomic Magazine, Inc.
Issue Fall/Winter 2001
Category Features: Story

Mr coffee

Starbucks
Chairman Howard Schultz says building a brand now is harder than ever.

The proprietor of a *sushi* restaurant in Tokyo finished the meal by putting me in my car and *thanking me* for coming to his restaurant.

Around the world, Starbucks has become an *oasis*. Internally, we call it 'the third place,' between home and the office.

Ewan McGregor treks to Morocco and the Moulin Rouge. 94
He drank shots but fired few: Hungary's dashing outlaw. 100
Christina Ricci has evolved from sulker to siren—and she's just 21. 116
Jesse Jackson keeps hope alive amid hints and allegations. 122
Paris launches its best-dressed season in many moons. 144

details

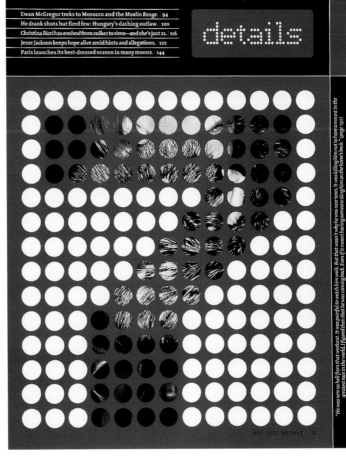

The Cheap Seats

■ 145
Publication Context
Creative Director Mark Maltais
Design Director Mark Maltais
Art Directors Mark Maltais, Gretchen Kirchner
Designers Mark Maltais, Gretchen Kirchner
Photographer Marc Baptiste
Publisher Diamond Cluster International Inc.
Issue August/September 2001
Category Features: Story

■ 146
Publication Details
Creative Director Dennis Freedman
Design Director Edward Leida
Art Director Rockwell Harwood
Photo Editors Alice Rose George, Amy Steigbigel, Jeannine Foeller
Publisher The Condé Nast Publications Inc.
Issue May 2001
Category Contents/Department

■ 147
Publication Details
Creative Director Dennis Freedman
Design Director Edward Leida
Art Director Rockwell Harwood
Photo Editors Alice Rose George, Amy Steigbigel, Jeannine Foeller
Publisher The Condé Nast Publications Inc.
Issue May 2001
Category Department

■ 148
Publication Details
Creative Director Dennis Freedman
Design Director Edward Leida
Art Director Rockwell Harwood
Photo Editors Alice Rose George, Amy Steigbigel, Jeannine Foeller
Publisher The Condé Nast Publications Inc.
Issue October 2001
Category Department

design MERIT

TO GEL AND BACK WITH THE VOYAGER NEST CHAIR,
THE ULTIMATE SOFT-CORE EXPERIENCE.

92   DETAILS AUGUST 2001

■ 151

■ 152

■ 149
Publication Details
Creative Director Dennis Freedman
Design Director Edward Leida
Art Director Rockwell Harwood
Photo Editors Alice Rose George, Amy Steigbigel, Jeannine Foeller
Photographer Nathaniel Goldberg
Publisher The Condé Nast Publications Inc.
Issue August 2001
Category Features: Story

■ 150
Publication Details
Creative Director Dennis Freedman
Design Director Edward Leida
Art Director Rockwell Harwood
Photo Editors Alice Rose George, Amy Steigbigel, Jeannine Foeller
Photographer Bill Steele
Publisher The Condé Nast Publications Inc.
Issue August 2001
Category Department

■ 151
Publication Details
Creative Director Dennis Freedman
Design Director Edward Leida
Art Director Rockwell Harwood
Photo Editors Alice Rose George, Amy Steigbigel, Jeannine Foeller
Photographer Doug Dubois
Publisher The Condé Nast Publications Inc.
Issue June 2001
Category Department

■ 152
Publication Details
Creative Director Dennis Freedman
Design Director Edward Leida
Art Director Rockwell Harwood
Photo Editors Alice Rose George, Amy Steigbigel, Jeannine Foeller
Publisher The Condé Nast Publications Inc.
Issue August 2001
Category Department

POWER

J
{the joker}
By Sean Elder

Photographs by Michael Thompson

Nur für Junge

Nur für Mädchen:

Sex #1
Worte finden.

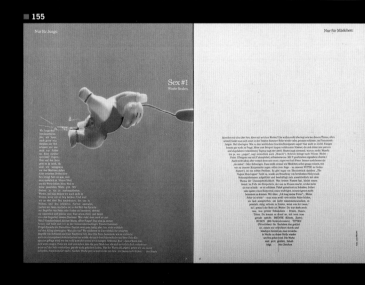

■ 154
Publication Details
Creative Director Dennis Freedman
Design Director Edward Leida
Art Director Rockwell Harwood
Photo Editors Alice Rose George, Amy Steigbigel, Jeannine Foeller
Photographer Michael Tompson
Publisher The Condé Nast Publications Inc.
Issue December 2001
Category Features: Story

■ 155
Publication Jetzt
Art Director Mirko Borsche
Designer Sandra Eichler
Photo Editor Bettina Beust
Photographer Julia Meister
Publisher Süddeutsche Zeitung
Issue April 2, 2001
Category Department

■ 153
Publication Details
Creative Director Dennis Freedman
Design Director Edward Leida
Art Director Rockwell Harwood
Photo Editors Alice Rose George, Amy Steigbigel, Jeannine Foeller
Photographer Michael Thompson
Publisher The Condé Nast Publications Inc.
Issue September 2001
Category Features: Story

design MERIT

the cat in the hat

by nick compton
photographs by tom munro

After all the tattoos, booze, and hotel mount-la-television clothes, the dark prince of Hollywood has a brand new bag: playing papa to a 2-year-old daughter on a farm in the south of France. The miraculous mellowing of Johnny Depp.

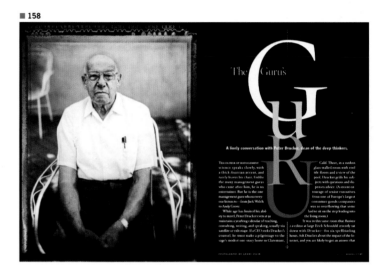

FIG:1

BONEHEAD SAFARI

My Hunt *for* America's dumbest VC

By Ralph King

ILLUSTRATIONS BY DAVID HUGHES

So

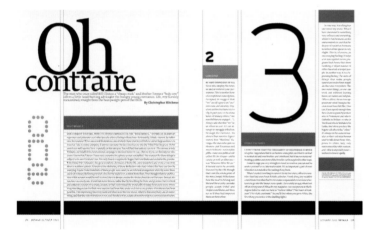

The Guru's

GURU

A lively conversation with Peter Drucker, dean of the deep thinkers.

Oh contraire

The men who once called Bill Clinton a "cheap crook" and Mother Teresa a "holy cow" offers a little head-butting advice after the humpty-young contrarian. Life, they harshly reexamined, straight from the heavyweight pen of the Hitch.

By Christopher Hitchens

2

3

■ 157
Publication Business 2.0
Creative Director Susan Scandrett
Art Directors Tim J Luddy, Carolyn Perot
Designer Carolyn Perot
Illustrator David Hughes
Photo Editor Susan B. Smith
Publisher Time Inc.
Issue January/February 2001
Category Features: Spread

■ 158
Publication Business 2.0
Creative Director Susan Scandrett
Art Directors Tim J Luddy, Carolyn Perot
Designer Susan Scandrett
Photo Editor Susan B. Smith
Photographer Grant Delin
Publisher Time Inc.
Issue October 2001
Category Features: Spread

■ 156
Publication Details
Creative Director Dennis Freedman
Design Director Edward Leida
Art Director Rockwell Harwood
Photo Editors Alice Rose George, Amy Steigbigel, Jeannine Foeller
Photographer Tom Munro
Publisher The Condé Nast Publications Inc.
Issue October 2001
Category Entire Issue

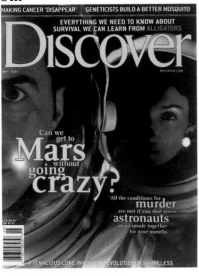

■ 159
Publication Discover
Design Director Michael Mrak
Art Director John Seeger Gilman
Designers Michael Mrak, John Seeger Gilman, Ian Brown
Photo Editors Maisie Todd, Monica Bradley
Photographers Larry Fink, Kai Wiechmann, Grant Delin, Justine Parsons, Eric Weeks, James Smolka, Joe Toreno, John Kotlowski
Publisher Disney Publishing Worldwide
Issue May 2001
Category Entire Issue

■ 160
Publication Discover
Design Director Michael Mrak
Art Director John Seeger Gilman
Designer John Seeger Gilman
Photo Editor Maisie Todd
Photographer Brent Humphreys
Publisher Disney Publishing Worldwide
Issue July 2001
Category Features: Spread

■ 161
Publication Discover
Design Director Michael Mrak
Art Director John Seeger Gilman
Designer John Seeger Gilman
Photo Editors Maisie Todd, Monica Bradley
Photographer Richard Barnes
Publisher Disney Publishing Worldwide
Issue October 2001
Category Features: Spread

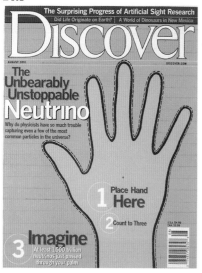

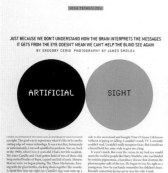

Fairs

DOMOTECHNICA '01
March 7–10, 2001

Books

☐ **SuperDutch: New Architecture in the Netherlands**
By Bart Lootsma
Princeton Architectural Press, $45

☐ **Portfolio of Contemporary Gardens**
By Stephen Woodhams
Writers Digest Books, $40

Birthdays

3/9/1902 Edward Durell Stone
3/16/1918 Aldo Van Eyck
3/21/1887 Eric Mendelsohn
3/27/1886 Mies van der Rohe

Exhibitions

CARLOS GARAICOA: THE RUINS, THE UTOPIA
October 12, 2000–March 4, 2001

ANDREAS GURSKY
March 4–May 15, 2001

COMFORT: RECLAIMING PLACE IN A VIRTUAL WORLD
March 9, 2000–May 20, 2001

NOMADIC CONNECTIONS
March 12–April 7, 2001

UNNATURAL SCIENCE
June 3, 2000–March 15, 2001

BITSTREAMS: ART IN THE DIGITAL AGE
March 22–June 10, 2001

VISION, TECHNOLOGY, AND COMMERCE: ONE HUNDRED YEARS OF INDUSTRIAL DESIGN
July 28, 2000–March 24, 2001

CUSTOM BUILT: A 20-YEAR SURVEY OF WORK BY ALLAN WEXLER
March 30–June 24, 2001

dwell

CALENDAR March 2001

Products

☐ **Modular Day Bed**
By Parma Lilac
London

☐ **Gondola Sofa**
By Russell Baker
Bombast
Vancouver

☐ **Martinsell Chair**
By Rachel Hutchinson
Rachel Hutchinson Furniture

☐ **Magazine Stand**
By Monika Piatkowski
and Mark Dyson
Hive

Vocabulary

CONTROLLED ENVIRONMENT: A factory where assembly lines fabricate houses, safe from rain, pilferers, and scheduling hang-ups—everything but excess control.

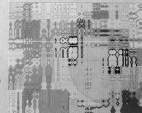

■ 162
Publication Discover
Design Director Michael Mrak
Art Director John Seeger Gilman
Designers Michael Mrak, John Seeger Gilman, Ian Brown
Photo Editors Maisie Todd, Monica Bradley
Photographers Dan Winters, Thomas Mangold, Grant Delin, James Smolka, Andrea Modica, Greg Miller, Ferit Kuyas, Eric Weeks
Publisher Disney Publishing Worldwide
Issue August 2001
Category Entire Issue

■ 163
Publication Dwell
Creative Director Jeanette Hodge Abbink
Designer Shawn Hazen
Photo Editor Maren Levinson
Publisher Pixie Communiications
Issue April 2001
Category Contents

2wice

Parr

ONE HOUSE.
TWO FAMILIES. THREE CHILDREN.
FOUR LAST NAMES.

THE KIDS FIT RIGHT IN

"It's easy to see that we have kids living here and we're not telling them to get out of the living room," says Stacy Fong of the Venice, California, house that her husband, architect David Hertz, designed for them and their three young children. "We don't want to make anything off-limits to them. If you don't want the kids around, what's the use in having them?"

■ 164
Publication 2wice
Art Director J. Abbott Miller
Designer Roy Brooks
Studio Pentagram
Publisher 2wice Arts Foundation
Issue Fall 2001
Category Entire Issue

■ 165
Publication Dwell
Creative Director Jeanette Hodge Abbink
Designers Shawn Hazen, Jeanette Hodge Abbink
Illustrators Arthur Mount, Jed Morfit
Photo Editor Maren Levinson
Photographers William Howard, Dwight Eschliman, Dewey Nicks, Peter Marlow, Kristine Larsen, Jock McDonald, Robert Cardin, Kreg Holt, Olivier Laude, Robert Ziebell, Jonan Light, Emily Nathan
Publisher Pixie Commuinications
Issue December 2001
Category Entire Issue

■ 166
Publication Entertainment Weekly
Design Director Geraldine Hessler
Art Director Tamaye Perry
Illustrator Edwin Fotheringham
Publisher Time Inc.
Issue February 16, 2001
Category Features: Spread/Single Page

■ 164
Publication Entertainment Weekly
Design Director Geraldine Hessler
Art Director Tamaye Perry
Publisher Time Inc.
Issue September 7, 2001
Category Features: Story

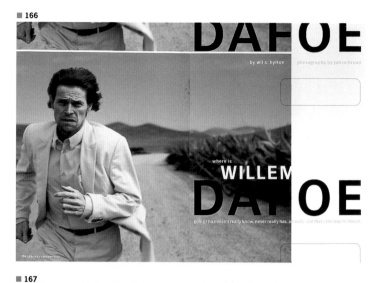

■ 165
Publication Entertainment Weekly
Design Director Geraldine Hessler
Art Directors John Walker, Jennifer Procopio,
Tamaye Perry, Robert Festino, Jennie Chang
Designers Sara Osten, Lee Berresford, Amy Won
Photo Editors Sarah Rozen, Denise Sfraga, Michael Kochman,
Michele Romero, Luciana Chang, Richard B. Maltz, Suzanne Reagan,
Fredya C. Tavin, Nola Tully, Marian Isel Barragn
Photographers Nigel Parry, Martin Schoeller,
Dan Winters, Firooz Zahedi, Sheryl Nields
Publisher Time Inc.
Issue October 5, 2001
Category Enitre Issue

■ 166
Publication Esquire
Design Director John Korpics
Photo Editor Fiona McDonagh
Photographer Julian Broad
Publisher The Hearst Corporation-Magazines Division
Issue February 2001
Category Features: Spread

■ 167
Publication Esquire
Design Director John Korpics
Photo Editor Fiona McDonagh
Photographer Michael Lewis
Publisher The Hearst Corporation-Magazines Division
Issue February 2001
Category Features: Spread

■ 168

Who Owns This Body ?

■ 169

■ 170

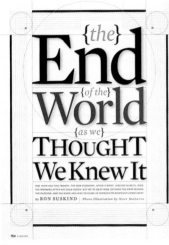

{the} End {of the} World {as we} THOUGHT We Knew It

■ 171

The Digital Man 2003

Body Tech

Rome Again

■ 168
Publication Esquire
Design Director John Korpics
Photo Editor Nancy Jo Iacoi
Photographer Matt Jones
Publisher The Hearst Corporation-Magazines Division
Issue June 2001
Category Features: Spread

■ 169
Publication Esquire
Design Director John Korpics
Art Director Hannah McCaughey
Illustrator Roberto Parada
Publisher The Hearst Corporation-Magazines Division
Issue April 2001
Category Features: Spread

■ 170
Publication Esquire
Design Director John Korpics
Illustrator Matt Mahurin
Publisher The Hearst Corporation-Magazines Division
Issue April 2001
Category Features: Spread

■ 171
Publication Esquire
Design Director John Korpics
Designers Hannah McCaughey, Todd Albertson, Erin Whelan, Kim Forsberg
Illustrators Roberto Parada, John Craig, Matt Mahurin
Photo Editor Nancy Jo Iacoi
Photographers Martin Schoeller, Peggy Sirota,
Noe Dewitt, Chris Buck, Gerald Forster
Publisher The Hearst Corporation-Magazines Division
Issue April 2001
Category Entire Issue

■ 172
Publication Esquire
Design Director John Korpics
Photo Editor Nancy Jo Iacoi
Photographer Bruce Davidson
Publisher The Hearst Corporation-Magazines Division
Issue July 2001
Category Features: Spread

■ 173
Publication Esquire
Design Director John Korpics
Photo Editor Nancy Jo Iacoi
Publisher The Hearst Corporation-Magazines Division
Issue July 2001
Category Features: Spread

■ 174
Publication MBA Jungle
Creative Director Matthew Guemple
Art Director Matthew Guemple
Designer Matthew Guemple
Photo Editor Ondrea Barbe
Photographer Tom Haynes
Publisher Jungle Media Group
Issue May 2001
Category Features: Spread

■ 175
Publication Esquire
Design Director John Korpics
Photo Editor Fiona McDonagh
Photographer Christian Witkin
Publisher The Hearst Corporation-Magazines Division
Issue January 2001
Category Features: Story

WHAT'S NEXT FOR THE NET?

IT'S CRUNCH TIME. ON WALL STREET AND IN THE POPULAR IMAGINATION, THE NEW ECONOMY IS FACING ITS FIRST BIG TEST. WE GATHERED SOME OF SILICON VALLEY'S BRIGHTEST THINKERS AND TOUGHEST EXECUTIVES TO SORT THROUGH THE CRITICAL ISSUES THAT ARE FACING COMPANIES AND THEIR LEADERS. JUST WHAT DOES IT MEAN TO HAVE AN "INTERNET STRATEGY" THESE DAYS? WHICH IDEAS ARE VENTURE CAPITALISTS STILL PREPARED TO FUND? HOW DO ORGANIZATIONS ATTRACT AND RETAIN THE BEST PEOPLE IN A BRUTAL BUSINESS CLIMATE? LISTEN UP: HERE IS TOUGH TALK FROM A FAST CROWD ABOUT THE CHANGING FUTURE OF THE INTERNET ECONOMY.

MODERATED BY GEORGE ANDERS AND POLLY LABARRE ILLUSTRATIONS BY STEVE BRODNER

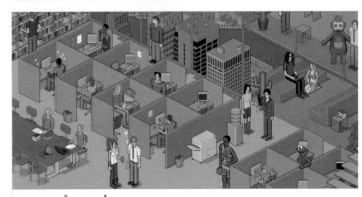

peoplepalooza Yes, you need a n Internet strategy. Sure, you've got to stay on the good side of Wall Street. But when it comes to building great companies, the most urgent business challe nge is finding and keeping great people. In an economy driven by ideas and charged by the Web, brainpower is the real source of competitive advantage. H ere is the ultimate collection of bold ideas, killer systems, and cutting-edge Internet tools to help companies win the battle for talent—and to help people m ake the most of their jobs. CREATED BY BILL BREEN AND ANNA MUOIO ILLUSTRATION BY NANA RAUSCH

■ 176
Publication Esquire
Design Director John Korpics
Photo Editor Nancy Jo Iacoi
Photographer Dan Winters
Publisher The Hearst Corporation-Magazines Division
Issue September 2001
Category Features: Spread

■ 177
Publication Esquire
Design Director John Korpics
Photo Editor Catriona NiAolain
Photographer Guzman
Publisher The Hearst Corporation-Magazines Division
Issue September 2001
Category Features: Spread

■ 178
Publication Fast Company
Design Director Patrick Mitchell
Designers Emily Crawford, Julia Moburg, Kristin Fitzpatrick, Melanie deForest
Illustrator Christoph Neiman
Photo Editors Alicia Jylkka, Lauren Bollettino
Publisher Gruner & Jahr USA Publishing
Issue January 2001
Category Entire Issue

Creative Space

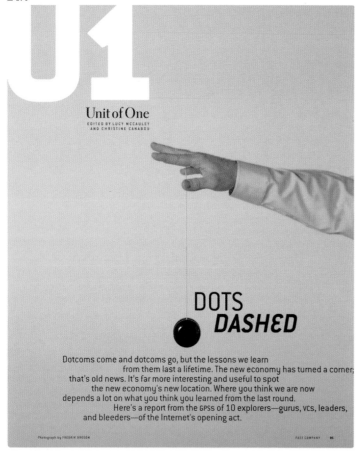

■ 179
Publication Fast Company
Design Director Patrick Mitchell
Designer Julia Moburg
Photo Editor Alicia Jylkka
Photographer Fredrik Brodén
Publisher Gruner & Jahr USA Publishing
Issue February 2001
Category Contents/Department

■ 180
Publication Fast Company
Design Director Patrick Mitchell
Designer Julia Moburg
Photo Editor Alicia Jylkka
Photographer Fredrik Brodén
Publisher Gruner & Jahr USA Publishing
Issue April 2001
Category Contents/Department

■ 181
Publication Fast Company
Design Director Patrick Mitchell
Designer Julia Moburg
Photo Editor Alicia Jylkka
Photographer Fredrik Brodén
Publisher Gruner & Jahr USA Publishing
Issue August 2001
Category Contents/Department

■ 182
Publication Fast Company
Design Director Patrick Mitchell
Designer Kristin Fitzpatrick
Illustrator Mark Matcho
Publisher Gruner & Jahr USA Publishing
Issue August 2001
Category Contents/Department

Business Fights Back

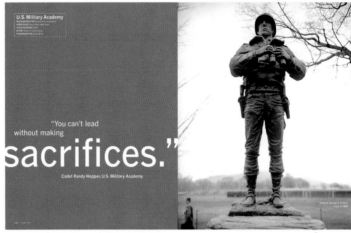

Business
Fights
Back

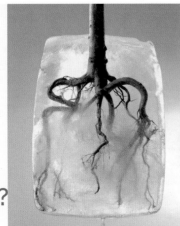

183
Publication Fast Company
Design Director Patrick Mitchell
Designers Emily Crawford, Julia Moburg, Kristin Fitzpatrick
Illustrators Brian Cronin, Milton Glaser, Kirsten Ulve, Christoph Niemann
Photo Editors Alicia Jylkka, Lauren Bollettino
Photographers Antonin Kratochvil, Chris Buck, David Barry, Fredrik Brodén, Jana Leon, Steve Pyke
Publisher Gruner & Jahr USA Publishing
Issue December 2001
Category Entire Issue

184
Publication Fast Company
Design Director Patrick Mitchell
Designers Patrick Mitchell, Emily Crawford
Photo Editor Alicia Jylkka
Photographers Fredrik Brodén, Daniela Stallinger, Grant Delin, Eric Tucker
Publisher Gruner & Jahr USA Publishing
Issue June 2001
Category Features: Story

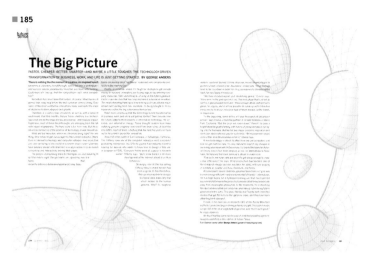

The Big Picture

FASTER, CHEAPER, BETTER, SMARTER—AND MAYBE A LITTLE TOUGHER: THE TECHNOLOGY-DRIVEN TRANSFORMATION OF BUSINESS, WORK, AND LIFE IS JUST GETTING STARTED. **BY GEORGE ANDERS**

eBay
Learns to
Trust Again

The world's most successful Internet company is based on two pillars of growth: the global spread of Internet-style capitalism and confidence in the basic goodness of the people who do business on the site. Both ideas came under attack on September 11.

By George Anders
Illustrations by Brian Cronin

future tense
INNOVATION

On the Verge
Five technologies that are poised to reshape business, work, and life

Illustrations by CHRISTOPH NIEMANN

Fast Company **129**

Continental's
Turnaround
Pilot

Before September 11, Bonnie Reitz was a central figure in the transformation that saved Continental Airlines. Now, in the aftermath of terror, she gets to do it all over again: "This is our time to lead. How we respond can set us apart."

By Keith H. Hammonds
Photographs by Chris Buck

Pamela Porter and her colleagues at Crisis Management International are the National Guard of therapists—called to duty at a moment's notice to respond to disaster. Here's the remarkable story of their response to September 11.

By Charles Fishman
Photographs by Antonin Kratochvil

Crisis
and Confidence
at Ground Zero

What's Next for the Net?

Nothing but Net

■ 185
Publication Fast Company
Design Director Patrick Mitchell
Designer Julia Moburg
Illustrator Christoph Niemann
Publisher Gruner & Jahr USA Publishing
Issue October 2001
Category Features: Story

■ 186
Publication Fast Company
Design Director Patrick Mitchell
Designer Emily Crawford
Illustrator Brian Cronin
Photo Editor Alicia Jylkka
Photographers Chris Buck, Antonin Kratochvil
Publisher Gruner & Jahr USA Publishing
Issue December 2001
Category Features: Story

THE YEAR IN BUSINESS

the top
10
Business Stories

Talk about a bad-news pileup. In one short year, the longest economic expansion in U.S. history screeched to a halt, the seventh-largest company in the nation self-destructed, and our world changed irrevocably when a few zealots stepped onto some airplanes. What follows are FORTUNE's picks for the most important business stories of an unforgettably tumultuous 2001. *By Alynda Wheat*

December 24, 2001 FORTUNE · 113

THE YEAR IN BUSINESS

2. The Recession
With the market melting down, consumer confidence evaporating, and joblessness rising, not even Alan Greenspan's ten rate cuts—and another expected this month—could stave off recession. At least you lived to see the biggest boom ever. Now wave bye-bye.

3. The Enron Implosion
Thanks to the energy trader's dubious bookkeeping, Ken Lay went from running a $101 billion company to presiding over the biggest bankruptcy in history.

4. California's Energy Crisis
As energy became scarce, the state instituted rolling blackouts and spent $11 billion to bail out PG&E and SoCal Edison. While conservation stabilized soaring prices, the crisis—plus the Enron collapse—left the deregulation movement in tatters.

118 · FORTUNE

THE MONEY HUNT

stormy weather ahead?

by kenneth klee
with maceable montandan

Credit crunch? No credit crunch? It really doesn't matter. Here's our advice on how to raise money for your business in all kinds of weather.

illustration by richard beards

FORTUNE

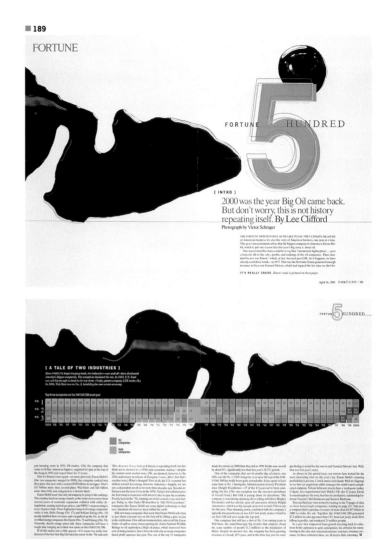

FORTUNE 5 HUNDRED

[INTRO]

2000 was the year Big Oil came back. But don't worry, this is not history repeating itself. By Lee Clifford

Photograph by Victor Schrager

April 16, 2001 FORTUNE · 101

FORTUNE 5 HUNDRED

[A TALE OF TWO INDUSTRIES]

April 16, 2001 FORTUNE · 103

■ 187
Publication Fortune
Art Director Blake Taylor
Designer Nai Lee Lum
Photo Editors Michele F. McNally, Mia Dehl, Courtenay Dolan, William Nabers, Janene Outlaw, Scott Thode
Photographers James Nachtwey, Martin Simon, Greg Smith, Michael Llewellyn
Publisher Time Inc.
Issue December 24, 2001
Category Features: Story

■ 188
Publication Fortune Small Business
Art Director Scott A. Davis
Designer Anna Christian
Illustrator Richard Beards
Publisher Time Inc.
Issue April 2001
Category Features: Spread/Single Page

■ 189
Publication Fortune
Art Director Blake Taylor
Designer Blake Taylor
Photo Editors Michele F. McNally, Alix Colow
Photographer Victor Schrager
Publisher Time Inc.
Issue April 16, 2001
Category Features: Story

HAVE YOU SEEN THIS MAN?

PHILIP SEYMOUR HOFFMAN HAS BECOME THE MOST UBIQUITOUS MAN IN MOVIES. IN THE PAST FEW YEARS, HE HAS STOLEN VIRTUALLY EVERY FILM HE HAS APPEARED IN, FROM *MAGNOLIA* TO *THE TALENTED MR. RIPLEY* TO *ALMOST FAMOUS*. NOW, AS THE ACTOR STEPS CENTER STAGE IN THE POLITICAL DOCUMENTARY *LAST PARTY 2000*, DAVID KAMP REVEALS JUST WHO HE IS

It didn't happen off the coast of Yemen, with the world watching and CNN doing live shots. But nineteen men died in the skies over Arizona last spring, in an aircraft some say shouldn't fly. Why did they die? Because as any marine can tell you, peace is hell

Crash of the Osprey
by Peter Richmond

Driven Wild:
THE SAD TALE OF THE REAL CROCODILE DUNDEE
ROD ANSELL WAS A TOUGH AUSSIE WHO COULD SURVIVE ANYTHING: CROCODILES, THE OUTBACK, DAYS WITHOUT FOOD AND WATER. HE BECAME A LIVING LEGEND—AN INSPIRATION FOR MEN AND MOVIES. THEN THEY TOOK HIS STORY AWAY BY MATTHEW TEAGUE

THE LOVE MACHINE
BY JOHN SEDGWICK

HEATH LEDGER
IS WISE TO YOU, HOLLYWOOD
THE CAMERA LOVES HIM. SO DOES HEATHER GRAHAM. THE AUSSIE SIPS WATERMELON MARTINIS WITH THE STAR WHO HAS NO ILLUSIONS
PHOTOGRAPHS BY ROBERT ERDMANN

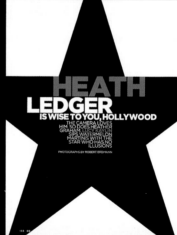

■ 190
Publication Gentlemen's Quarterly
Design Director Arem Duplessis
Art Director Paul Martinez
Designer Arem Duplessis
Photo Editor Jennifer Crandall
Photographer Michael Thompson
Publisher The Condé Nast Publications Inc.
Issue January 2001
Category Features: Spread

■ 191
Publication Gentlemen's Quarterly
Design Director Arem Duplessis
Art Director Paul Martinez
Designer Paul Martinez
Photo Editors Jennifer Crandall, Catherine Talese
Photographer Tom Tavee
Publisher The Condé Nast Publications Inc.
Issue January 2001
Category Features: Spread

■ 192
Publication Gentlemen's Quarterly
Design Director Arem Duplessis
Art Director Paul Martinez
Designer Paul Martinez
Photo Editors Jennifer Crandall, Michael Norseng
Photographer Clive Hide
Publisher The Condé Nast Publications Inc.
Issue April 2001
Category Features: Spread

■ 193
Publication Gentlemen's Quarterly
Design Director Arem Duplessis
Art Director Paul Martinez
Designer Matthew Lenning
Photo Editors Jennifer Crandall, Catherine Talese
Photographers Dan Winters, Gary Tanhauser
Publisher The Condé Nast Publications Inc.
Issue February 2001
Category Features: Spread

■ 194
Publication Gentlemen's Quarterly
Design Director Arem Duplessis
Art Director Paul Martinez
Designer Arem Duplessis
Photo Editor Jennifer Crandall
Photographer Robert Goodman
Publisher The Condé Nast Publications Inc.
Issue June 2001
Category Features: Spread

■ 195

■ 196

■ 197

■ 198

■ 199

■ 197
Publication Gentlemen's Quarterly
Design Director Arem Duplessis
Art Director Paul Martinez
Designer Arem Duplessis
Photo Editors Jennifer Crandall, Cathrine Talese
Photographer Robert Maxwell
Publisher The Condé Nast Publications Inc.
Issue July 2001
Category Features: Spread

■ 198
Publication Gentlemen's Quarterly
Design Director Arem Duplessis
Art Director Paul Martinez
Designer Paul Martinez
Photo Editors Jennifer Crandall, Kristen Schaefer
Photographer Antoine Le Grand
Publisher The Condé Nast Publications Inc.
Issue September 2001
Category Department

■ 199
Publication Gentlemen's Quarterly
Design Director Arem Duplessis
Art Director Paul Martinez
Designer Arem Duplessis
Photo Editor Jennifer Crandall
Photographer Norman Jean Roy
Publisher The Condé Nast Publications Inc.
Issue October 2001
Category Features: Spread

■ 195
Publication Gentlemen's Quarterly
Design Director Arem Duplessis
Art Director Paul Martinez
Designer Paul Martinez
Photo Editors Jennifer Crandall, Cathrine Talese
Photographer Judson Baker
Publisher The Condé Nast Publications Inc.
Issue June , 2001
Category Features: Spread

■ 196
Publication Gentlemen's Quarterly
Design Director Arem Duplessis
Art Director Paul Martinez
Designer Arem Duplessis
Photo Editors Jennifer Crandall, Cathrine Talese
Photographer Sacha Waldman
Publisher The Condé Nast Publications Inc.
Issue June 2001
Category Features: Spread

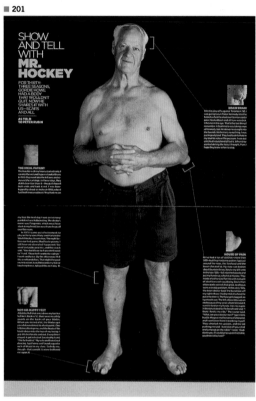

Publication Gentlemen's Quarterly
Design Director Arem Duplessis
Art Director Paul Martinez
Designer Arem Duplessis
Photo Editor Jennifer Crandall
Photographer Norman Jean Roy
Publisher The Condé Nast Publications Inc.
Issue December 2001
Category Features: Spread

■ 201
Publication Gentlemen's Quarterly
Design Director Arem Duplessis
Art Director Paul Martinez
Designer Matthew Lenning
Photo Editors Jennifer Crandall, Catherine Talese
Photographer Dan Winters
Publisher The Condé Nast Publications Inc.
Issue December 2001
Category Features: Spread

■ 202
Publication Inc.
Design Director Patrick Mitchell
Designers Patrick Mitchell, Kristin Fitzpatrick, Linda Koury, Daigo Fujiwara
Illustrator Greg Clarke
Photo Editors Alicia Jylkka, Stephan Jacobs
Photographers David Barry, Chris Buck
Publisher Gruner & Jahr USA Publishing
Issue October 16, 2001
Category Redesign

housebeautiful

Living with Style

LusciousColors TimelessChic ComfyModern

photographer JOHN COOLIDGE
writer MARTIN FILLER
producer MIGUEL FLORES-VIANNA

l.a. confident

With graphic assurance, **Blair Belcher** jazzes up Beverly Hills

e
elements of style

photographer STEPHEN LEWIS   producer ELIZABETH MAYHEW & PROSPER/JE PAGANI

photographer
PIETER ESTERSOHN
writer
CAROL PRISANT

open house

{A skillful and amiable trio makes visual music on Long Island}

Rosy Future
People say that when the gardener is gone, so is the garden, but Chatwood is a happy exception. Its new owner, Susan Lueck, lovingly maintains Helen Blake Watkins's famous collection of old roses

photographer
JOHN HALL
writer and producer
ELIZABETH G. HUNTER

{GIANTS of DESIGN}

[JACQUES GRANGE]   [SUSAN WEBER SOROS]   [IAN SCHRAGER]

[RICHARD GLUCKMAN]   [KELLY LYNCH & MITCH GLAZER]   [LOUIS OLIVER GROPP]

They're talented, driven, and deeply original. House Beautiful's seven 2001 Giants of Design Award winners epitomize excellence in all the fields we care about: decoration, architecture, design, historic preservation, decorative arts education, and design journalism. On the following eighteen pages, we salute Jacques Grange, Susan Weber Soros, Ian Schrager, Richard Gluckman, Kelly Lynch and Mitch Glazer, and Louis Oliver Gropp for making our lives better, richer, and infinitely more beautiful. Bravo!

photographer TIMOTHY GREENFIELD-SANDERS   producer HOWARD GREENBERG

■ 203
Publication House Beautiful
Creative Director Nora Sheehan
Design Director Nora Sheehan
Art Director Howard Greenberg
Designers Nora Sheehan, Kristin Smith
Photo Editor Howard Greenberg
Publisher The Hearst Corporation-Magazines Division
Issue February 2001
Category Entire Issue

■ 204
Publication House Beautiful
Creative Director Nora Sheehan
Design Director Nora Sheehan
Art Director Howard Greenberg
Designers Nora Sheehan, Kristin Smith
Photo Editor Howard Greenberg
Publisher The Hearst Corporation-Magazines Division
Issue June 2001
Category Entire Issue

design MERIT

Publication Latina Magazine
Creative Director Irasema Rivera
Art Director Ebelinda Antigua
Designer Judy Wong
Photo Editor Adrienne Aurichio
Photographer Gentl + Hyers
Publisher Latina Media Ventures
Issue July 2001
Category Features: Story

■ 206
Publication Los Angeles Magazine
Art Directors Joe Kimberling, Lisa M. Lewis
Photo Editor Kathleen Clark
Photographer Joseph Rodriguez
Publisher Emmis Communications
Issue May 2001
Category Features: Spread/Single Page

■ 207
Publication InStyle
Design Director Paul Roelofs
Designer Rob Hewitt
Photo Editors Carla Popenfus,
Rosaliz Jimenez
Photographer Troy Word
Publisher Time Inc.
Issue Fall 2001
Category Features: Spread/Single Page

■ 208
Publication InStyle
Design Director Paul Roelofs
Art Director Rob Hewitt
Designer Rob Hewitt
Illustrator 500 Gls/Unit
Photo Editors Carla Popenfus, Rosaliz Jimenez
Publisher Time Inc.
Issue Spring 2001
Category Contents/Department

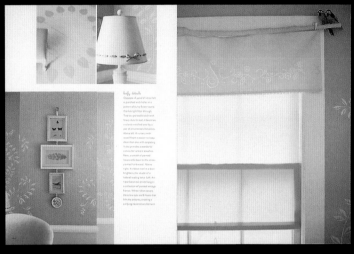

■ 209
Publication Los Angeles Magazine
Art Director Joe Kimberling
Designer Lisa M. Lewis
Photo Editor Kathleen Clark
Publisher Emmis Communications
Issue Spring 2001
Category Entire Issue

■ 210
Publication Martha Stewart Baby
Creative Director Gael Towey
Art Director Deb Bishop
Designer Deb Bishop
Photo Editor Jodi Nakatsuka
Photographer William Abranowicz
Stylists Melanio Gomez, Cyndi DiPrima
Publisher Martha Stewart Living Omnimedia
Issue Spring 2001
Category Features: Story

■ 211
Publication My Generation
Art Director Jennifer Gilman
Designer Jennifer Gilman
Photo Editor Jessica De Witt
Photographer Peggy Sirota
Publisher AARP
Issue September/October 2001
Category Features: Spread/Single Page

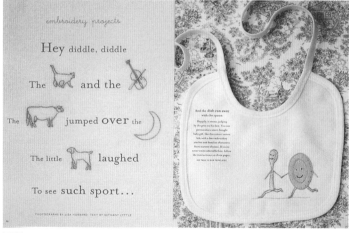

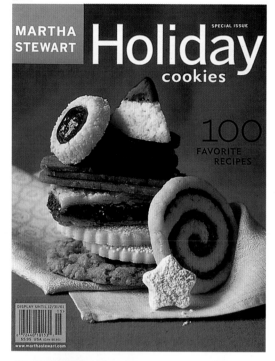

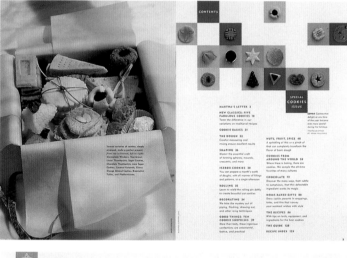

■ 212
Publication Martha Stewart Baby
Creative Director Gael Towey
Art Director Deb Bishop
Designer Deb Bishop
Photo Editor Jodi Nakatsuka
Photographer Gentl + Hyers
Stylist Jodi Levine
Publisher Martha Stewart Living Omnimedia
Issue Fall 2001
Category Features: Story

■ 213
Publication Martha Stewart Baby
Creative Director Gael Towey
Art Director Deb Bishop
Designer Jennifer Wagner
Photo Editor Jodi Nakatsuka
Photographer Lisa Hubbard
Stylist Jodi Levine
Publisher Martha Stewart Living Omnimedia
Issue Spring 2001
Category Features: Spread/Single Page

■ 214
Publication Martha Stewart Living
Creative Director Eric Pike
Art Director Brooke Hellewell
Designers Brooke Hellewell, Jenny Hoitt
Photographers Anna Williams, Richard Gerhard Jung, Sang An
Publisher Martha Stewart Living Omnimedia
Issue Holiday 2001
Category Entire Issue

■ 215
Publication Martha Stewart Kids
Creative Director Gael Towey
Art Director Deb Bishop
Designer Jennifer Wagner
Photo Editor Jodi Nakatsuka
Photographer Stephen Lewis
Stylist Stephana Bottom
Publisher Martha Stewart Living Omnimedia
Issue Summer/Fall 2001
Category Features: Story
　　　　　A MERIT: Design: Features: Spread

■ 216
Publication Martha Stewart Living
Design Director Barbara de Wilde
Art Director James Dunlinson
Designer James Dunlinson
Photo Editor Mary Dail
Photographer Christopher Baker
Stylists Fritz Karch, Brian Harter Andriola
Publisher Martha Stewart Living Omnimedia
Issue May 2001
Category Features: Story

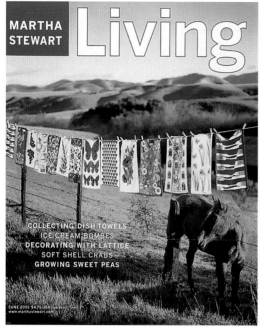

■ 217
Publication Martha Stewart Living
Design Director Barbara de Wilde
Art Directors Scot Schy, James Dunlinson, Brooke Hellewell, Alexa Mulvihill,
Timothy Hsu, Jill Groeber, Jenny Hoitt, Cheryl Molnar
Photo Editor Mary Dail
Publisher Martha Stewart Living Omnimedia
Issue June 2001
Category Entire Issue

■ 218
Publication Martha Stewart Kids
Creative Director Gael Towey
Art Director Deb Bishop
Designer Jennifer Wagner
Photo Editor Jodi Nakatsuka
Photographer Gentl + Hyers
Stylist Jodi Levine
Publisher Martha Stewart Living Omnimedia
Issue Holiday 2001
Category Features: Story

MARTHA STEWART Living

CHESTNUTS, FROM
STUFFING TO STRUDEL
NAPKIN FOLDING
FLOWERING BULBS
CHINESE EXPORT
PORCELAIN
SHRIMP COCKTAIL 101
DECORATING WITH RED

Thanksgiving

NOVEMBER 2001 $4.75 USA (CAN. $5.75)
www.marthastewart.com

Napkin Folding

Chestnuts

ADVENTURE

thirteen ways of looking at a

void

The Sahara's Ténéré
is a chunk of the
planet gone dead.
154,000 square miles
of nothing—except
faith, war, salt, beer,
speed . . . and an
urgent sense of
what it is to be alive

By Michael Finkel
Photography by Chris Anderson

"Cameras," says Mustafa.

"Beer," says Grace.

INHALE

EKOLU∞3

stories + departments

design MERIT

Publication Martha Stewart Living
Design Director Barbara de Wilde
Art Directors Scot Schy, James Dunlinson, Alexa Mulvihill, Angela Gubler, Jill Groeber, Alanna Jacobs, Jenny Hoitt, Timothy Hsu, Yu Mei Tam Compton, Brooke Hellewell
Publisher Martha Stewart Living Omnimedia
Issue November 2001
Category Entire Issue

Publication National Geographic Adventure
Design Director Julie Curtis
Art Director Mike Bain
Designer Julie Curtis
Photo Editor Sabine Meyer
Photographer Chris Anderson
Publisher National Geographic Society
Issue September/October 2001
Category Features: Story

Publication Hawaii Skin Diver
Art Director Clifford Cheng
Designer Clifford Cheng
Studio Voice
Publisher Hawaii Skin Diver Publishing
Issue Fall 2001
Category Contents/Department

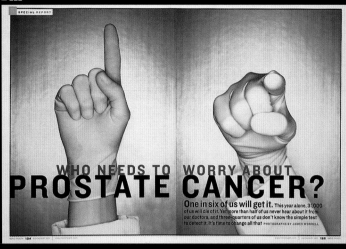

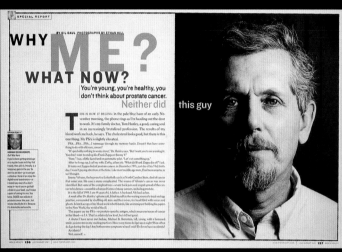

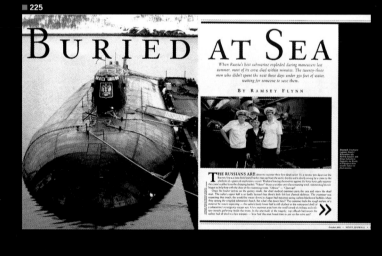

■ 222
Publication Men's Health
Art Directors George Karabotsos, Wilbert Gutierrez
Designer Wilbert Gutierrez
Photo Editors Marianne Butler, Axel Kessler
Photographers James Worrell, Ethan Hill
Publisher Rodale Inc.
Issue July/August 2001
Category Features: Story

■ 223
Publication Men's Health
Art Directors George Karabotsos, Wilbert Gutierrez
Designer Wilbert Gutierrez
Illustrator Drew Friedman
Publisher Rodale Inc.
Issue September 2001
Category Features: Spread/Single Page

■ 224
Publication Men's Journal
Art Director Michael Lawton
Designers Robert Perino, Michael Lawton
Photo Editor Deborah Edelstein
Photographer Baron Wolman
Publisher Wenner Media LLC
Issue May 2001
Category Features: Spread/Single Page

■ 225
Publication Men's Journal
Art Director Michael Lawton
Designers Keith Campbell, Michael Lawton
Photo Editor Deborah Edelstein
Photographer AP/Wide World Photos
Publisher Wenner Media LLC
Issue October 2001
Category Features: Spread/Single Page

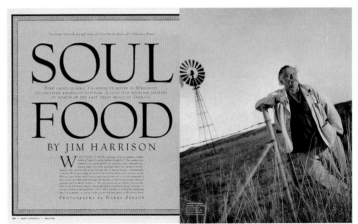

■ 226
Publication Men's Journal
Art Director Michael Lawton
Designers Thomas Alberty, Michael Lawton
Photo Editor Deborah Edelstein
Photographer Giorgia Fiorio
Publisher Wenner Media LLC
Issue August 2001
Category Features: Story

■ 227
Publication Men's Journal
Art Director Michael Lawton
Designers Robert Perino, Keith Campbell, Thomas Alberty, Michael Lawton
Photo Editors Ian Spanier, Carin Pearce, Naomi Nista, Laurel Wassner
Photographers Mark Shapiro, Viktor Koen, Harry Benson
Publisher Wenner Media LLC
Issue March 2001
Category Entire Issue

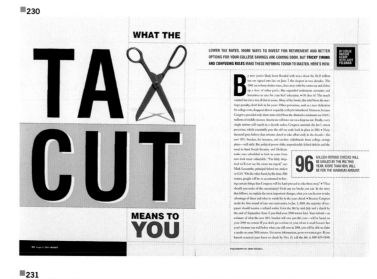

228
Publication Money
Art Director Syndi Becker
Designer Marc Whalen
Photo Editors Jane Clark, Betsy Keating
Photographer Jonathan Barkat
Publisher Time Inc.
Issue February 2001
Category Features: Spread/Single Page

229
Publication Money
Art Director Syndi Becker
Designer MaryAnn Salvato
Photo Editors Jane Clark, Betsy Keating
Photographer Michael Llewellyn
Publisher Time Inc.
Issue June 2001
Category Features: Spread/Single Page

230
Publication Money
Art Director Syndi Becker
Designer MaryAnn Salvato
Photo Editors Jane Clark, Cathy Mather
Photographer John Kuczuca
Publisher Time Inc.
Issue August 2001
Category Features: Spread/Single Page

231
Publication My Generation
Art Director Jennifer Gilman
Designer Jennifer Gilman
Photo Editor Katherine Bourbeau
Photographer Greg Gorman
Publisher AARP
Issue March/April 2001
Category Features: Spread/Single Page

232
Publication Navigator
Art Director Kevin de Miranda
Photographer David Turner
Publisher Pace Communications
Client Holiday Inn Express
Issue January 2001
Category Features: Spread/Single Page

2001: A Face Odyssey
PHOTOGRAPHED BY FRANK W. OCKENFELS 3

The story of a city—its happiness,
its creativity, its passion, its drama, its pain—is
written in its faces. And on the following
pages is the New York epic—in 54 portraits.

LET'S GO, TOKYO

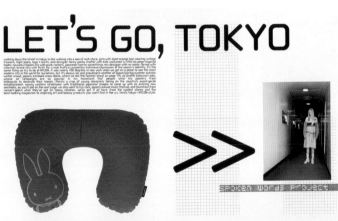

■ 233
Publication New York Magazine
Design Director Michael Picón
Photo Editor Chris Dougherty
Photographer Frank W. Ockenfels 3
Publisher Primedia Magazines Inc.
Issue January 8, 2001
Category Entire Issue

■ 234
Publication Nylon
Art Director Lina Kutsovskaya
Designers Kathleen McGowan, Jason Engdahl
Designer Jason Engdahl
Publisher Nylon LLC
Issue October 2001
Category Entire Issue

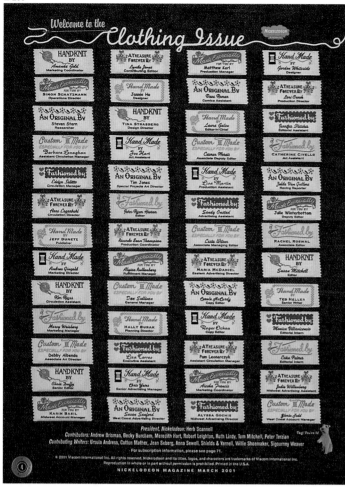

EL HOMBRE TRANQUILO

LE SOBRAN QUILATES DE TALENTO, PERO MUY POCOS SE ACUERDAN DE SU
NOMBRE. LEJOS DE LAS LUMINARIAS CENTRALES DE HOLLYWOOD, LOS FOCOS LE
DESIGNAN COMO ETERNO SECUNDARIO. AHORA, SE PONE DETRÁS Y DELANTE DE LA
CÁMARA EN "POLLOCK", UN PROTAGONISTA GENIAL, CON NOMINACIÓN AL OSCAR.

EL ROSTRO DEL BIOTERROR

EN UNA COMPARECENCIA EN EL CONGRESO ESTADOUNIDENSE EL
MES PASADO, KEN ALIBEK, COMO CONSEJERO DE DEFENSA
BACTERIOLÓGICA, RECOMENDABA PLANCHAR EL CORREO PARA
ANULAR EL ÁNTRAX. EL CONSEJO PODÍA PARECER RUDIMENTARIO,
PERO PROVENÍA DE UN HOMBRE QUE DIRIGIÓ EL SOFISTICADO
PROGRAMA DE ARMAMENTO BIOLÓGICO DE LA UNIÓN SOVIÉTICA
Y QUE UN DÍA SE LLAMÓ CORONEL KANATJAN ALIBEKOV.

El corazón
salvaje de
Peter Beard

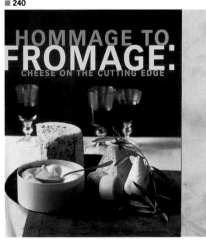

joe d'eve

Eve Ensler keeps going into scary territory. And when she does, stars like Calista Flockhart, Alanis Morissette, Phylicia Rashad, Winona Ryder, and Susan Sarandon—along with audiences all over the world—are happy to follow. How a smart, funny playwright raises eyebrows, self-esteem, and millions of dollars to end violence against women. BY JUDITH STONE

Photograph by ETHAN HILL

WILL POWER

BY FRED SCHRUERS

Getting the story of Muhammad Ali onto the screen was an epic battle. But a muscled-up Will Smith and pugnacious director Michael Mann managed to overcome all obstacles—including 27,000 overeager extras.

PHOTOGRAPHS BY JAKE CHESSUM

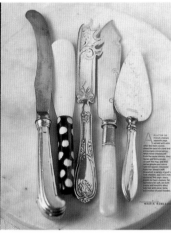

HOMMAGE TO FROMAGE:
CHEESE ON THE CUTTING EDGE

design MERIT

being john lee
by christopher shulgan
photography by chris buck

Publication O, The Oprah Magazine
Design Director Carla Frank
Designer Ed Mann
Photo Editor Karen Frank
Photographer Ethan Hill
Publisher The Hearst Corporation-Magazines Division
Issue January 2001
Category Features: Spread

Publication O, The Oprah Magazine
Design Director Carla Frank
Designer Erika Oliveira
Photo Editors Karen Frank, Kim Gougenheim
Photographer Maria Robledo
Publisher The Hearst Corporation-Magazines Division
Issue March 2001
Category Features: Spread

Publication Premiere
Art Director Richard Baker
Designer Richard Baker
Photo Editor Doris Brautigan
Photographer Jake Chessum
Publisher Hachette Filipacchi Media U.S.
Issue December 1, 2001
Category Features: Story

Publication Shift
Art Director Antonio Enrico De Luca
Designer Jaspal Riyait
Photographer Chris Buck
Publisher Multi-Vision Publishing
Issue October 1, 2001
Category Features: Spread

■ 243
Publication Reader's Digest
Creative Director Hannu Laakso
Art Director Dean Abatemarco
Designer Dean Abatemarco
Photo Editor Bill Black
Photographer Macduff Everton
Publisher Readers Digest
Issue June 1, 2001
Category Features: Story

■ 244
Publication Savoy
Creative Directors Lance Pettiford, Mimi Park
Designer Lance Pettiford
Publisher Vanguarde Media Inc.
Issue February 2001
Category Features: Spread/Single Page

■ 245
Publication Saveur
Art Director Julie Pryma
Designer Julie Pryma
Illustrator Oliver Williams
Photo Editor Maya Kaimal
Photographer Joshua Paul
Publisher World Publications
Issue December 2001
Category Features: Story

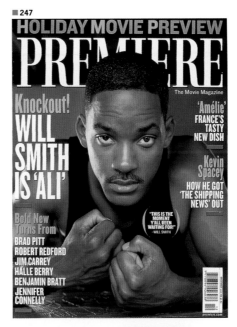

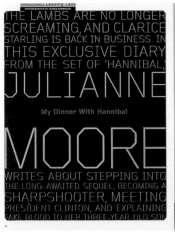

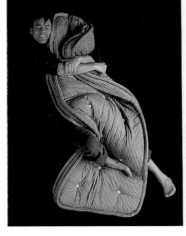

■ 246
Publication Premiere
Art Director Richard Baker
Designers Richard Baker, Bess Wong, Christine Cucuzza, Katherine Bigelow
Illustrators Tim Bauer, Robert deMichiell, Owen Smith, Roberto Parada, Blair Drawson
Photo Editor Nancy Jo Iacoi
Photographers Ruven Afanador, Michael O'Neill, Martin Schoeller, Jake Chessum, Christian Witkin, Stephen Danelian, Michael Lavine, Alison Dyer, Dan Chaukin, Dana Menussi, Chris Buck, Michael Lewis
Publisher Hachette Filipacchi Media U.S.
Issue February 2001
Category Entire Issue

■ 247
Publication Premiere
Art Director Richard Baker
Designers Richard Baker, Christine Cucuzza, Katherine Bigelow
Illustrators Dan Adel, Chip Wass, Matt Mahurin, Robert deMichiell
Photo Editor Doris Brautigan
Photographers Jake Chessum, Chris Buck, Mark Heithoff, Gerald Forster, Patrick Cariou, Rankin
Publisher Hachette Filipacchi Media U.S.
Issue December 1, 2001
Category Entire Issue

LIVING WITH BOOKS

Think of them as roommates, companions who dress up your home with their beauty, wit, and warmth. Be kind to them

Remember the days when a few cinder blocks and a couple of pieces of plywood made a bookshelf? It was cheap, it was functional, and not much in the way of assembly was required. In the context of a college dorm room, it looked pretty good, too.

But grown-ups need more interesting options for living with books. Whether you've acquired a large collection of art books, hundreds of paperback mysteries, or a serious set of first editions, you need a place to put them, preferably in a style that befits your home's decor and your reading habits. And bookshelves aren't the only option. Books can be lined up on a mantel, piled on the floor (gracefully), and stacked on tables. They can reside in the kitchen, the bedroom, the dining room—anywhere you like to read.

WRITTEN BY JEAN GORMAN   PRODUCED BY KELLY TAGORE   PHOTOGRAPHS BY SARAH MAINGOT

winning looks

[SEVEN STUNNING OLYMPIANS SHARE THEIR HEALTH AND BEAUTY SECRETS]

Whoever said "Look good, feel good" had it backward. It is not about perception but participation, and never was this simple truth more apparent than when we saw these seven Olympic medalists last summer in Sydney—drenched in sweat, caked with dirt, dripping wet—and never looking better.

If you do not recognize them, it may be because you are not used to seeing them out of uniform. But what sports fan can forget how these athletes positively glowed, radiating from deep within at the moment when mind, body, and spirit converged and they emerged, not unlike new mothers, from their grueling ordeal absolutely spent? And absolutely beautiful. The picture of perfect health.

WRITTEN BY SCOTT GUMMER   PHOTOGRAPHS BY GERALD FORSTER

adventures in eating

SIX EASY DINNERS FROM AROUND THE WORLD

TEXT AND FOOD STYLING BY RORI SPINELLI-TROVATO   PHOTOGRAPHS BY SUSIE CUSHNER

china

instant gardens

YOUR PLANT-BY-NUMBER GUIDE TO A FAST—AND LUSH—PAVILION OF POTTED GREENERY

Plants come in thousands of species; people who garden come in just two. True devotees spend hours poring over the tiny print of seed catalogs in the dark of winter and debate hostas versus ferns with a passion usually reserved for election-year politics. And then there is everyone else. Many of us long to step into a private Eden at the end of the day, but the mere idea of creating one makes us throw in the trowel and run the other way. Even without an army of professional gardeners, a lush green space is within your grasp: You can plant a container garden more quickly and maintain it more easily than a flower bed. It's flexible (small enough to fit on a tabletop or large enough to sprawl under a favorite tree), and by massing containers and choosing mature plants, you can create a dramatic garden in a weekend instead of a season.

To make container gardening as effortless as possible, we've dreamed up four versions and provided detailed how-to's. If you tailor the plant lists to your zone with the help of your local garden center, this is as close to immediate garden gratification as you can get.

PRODUCED AND WRITTEN BY KELLY TAGORE   PHOTOGRAPHS BY MINH + WASS   STYLED BY MARALINE SZABO   GARDEN DESIGN BY RICHARD HAYDEN AND ROBERT ROSEN

the little house that could

HOW ONE FAMILY TOOK A WEE HOUSE ON A SMALL LOT IN LOS ANGELES AND MADE IT WORK—BEAUTIFULLY

WRITTEN BY JENNY ALLEN   PRODUCED BY KELLY TAGORE   PHOTOGRAPHS BY JOSHUA PAUL

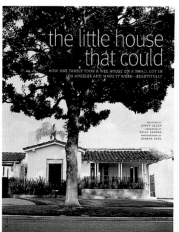 

■ 248
Publication Real Simple
Creative Director Roland Bello
Art Director Eva Spring
Designers Roland Bello, Millie Rossman Kidd, Eva Spring
Photo Editor Jean Herr
Photographers David Gubert, Sarah Maingot, Gerald Forster, Susie Cushner
Publisher Time Inc.
Issue March 2001
Category Entire Issue

■ 249
Publication Real Simple
Creative Directors Roland Bello, Michael Grossman
Design Director Jill Armus
Art Director Eva Spring
Designers Jill Armus, Roland Bello, Millie Rossman Kidd, Eva Spring
Photo Editor Jean Herr
Photographers Ellen Silverman, Minh+Wass, Joshua Paul, Susie Cushner
Publisher Time Inc.
Issue May 2001
Category Entire Issue

TIMELINE

JENNIFER GRANT

bask in bed

take back your morning

These five women start the day their way: meditating, socializing, dog walking, doing a headstand, even staying in bed

WRITTEN BY MARTHA TAY
PHOTOGRAPHED BY DEBORAH JAFFE

A DAY AT THE BEACH

leg lengthener

satisfying salads

Grilled-Tuna Salad

REAL SIMPLE
life/home/body/soul

Secrets of a stress-free holiday

50 gifts under $50
Fix-ahead **party** food
The easiest **tree** ever
Treats to make and give
Resolutions you'll keep

DECEMBER 2001/JANUARY 2002

It's a
wonderful life

When she was diagnosed with terminal cancer, Janet Lasley found joy fast

WRITTEN BY JEAN HANFF KORELITZ
PHOTOGRAPHED BY JOHN DOLAN

SPORTS

DIAMONDS ARE FOREVER

IN CAPE COD'S 44-GAME SUMMER BASEBALL LEAGUE, TOP COLLEGE PROSPECTS HONE THEIR SKILLS, HOPING FOR A SHOT AT THE SHOW. ONE WAY OR ANOTHER, THE EXPERIENCE TOUCHES THEIR LIVES — PERMANENTLY. BY KEN McALPINE

PHOTOGRAPHY BY DOUGLAS MERRIAM

SOUTHWEST AIRLINES SPIRIT   JULY 2001

■ 250
Publication Real Simple
Creative Directors Roland Bello, Michael Grossman
Design Director Jill Armus
Art Director Eva Spring
Designers Jill Armus, Roland Bello, Millie Rossman Kidd, Eva Spring
Photo Editor Jean Herr
Photographers Jim Franco, Deborah Jaffe, Coppola & Grande, Antoine Bootz
Publisher Time Inc.
Issue June/July 2001
Category Entire Issue

■ 251
Publication Real Simple
Creative Directors Michael Grossman, Robert Newman
Art Directors Chalkley Calderwood-Pratt, Eva Spring
Designers Chalkley Calderwood-Pratt, Robert Newman, Eva Spring, Chad Tomlinson
Photo Editors Jean Herr, Naomi Nista
Photographers William Waldron, John Dolan, William Meppem
Publisher Time Inc.
Issue December 2001/January 2002
Category Entire Issue

■ 252
Publication Southwest Airlines Spirit
Design Director J.R. Arebalo, Jr.
Designer J.R. Arebalo, Jr.
Photographer Douglas Merriam
Publisher American Airlines Publishing
Client Southwest Airlines
Issue July 2001
Category Features: Spread

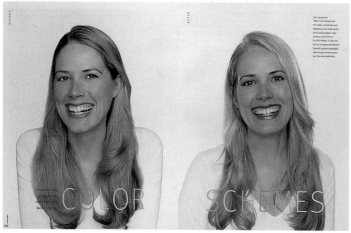

■ 254
Publication Nerve
Creative Director Michael Grossman
Designer Andrea Dunham
Photo Editor Genevieve Field
Photographer Nola Lopez
Publisher Nerve.com
Issue January 2001
Category Features: Single page

■ 253
Publication Real Simple
Creative Director Michael Grossman
Design Director Jill Armus
Art Directors Chalkley Calderwood-Pratt, Eva Spring
Photo Editors Jean Herr, Naomi Nista
Photographers William Waldron, Cedric Angeles, Perry Hagopian, Bob Heimstra
Publisher Time Inc.
Issue September 2001
Category Entire Issue

■ 255
Publication Switch
Creative Director Gerardo Balderas Luna
Designers Apolo Castrejón Torres, Alejandro Toboada Martinez-Sotomayor
Photo Editors Edgar Alamill Ávilla, Rodrigo Aceves Vázquez
Photographer Danny Clinch
Publisher Editorial Premiere, S.A. de C.V.
Issue September 1, 2001
Category Features: Spread/Single Page

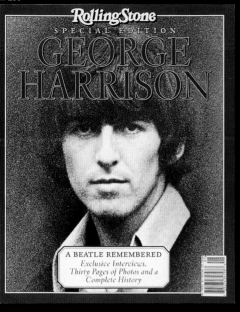

The Mystery Inside George

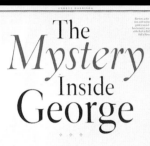

1980~2001

The Quiet Years

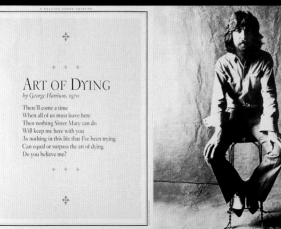

Art of Dying
by George Harrison, 1970

There'll come a time
When all of us must leave here
Then nothing Sister Mary can do
Will keep me here with you
As nothing in this life that I've been trying
Can equal or surpass the art of dying
Do you believe me?

■ 256
Publication Rolling Stone
Art Director Gail Anderson
Designers Gail Anderson, Ken DeLago, Siung Tjia
Photo Editors Fiona McDonagh, Audrey Landreth
Photographers Robert Freeman, Mark Seliger
Publisher Wenner Media
Client Rolling Stone
Category Entire Issue

■ 257
Publication Rolling Stone
Art Director Fred Woodward
Designers Fred Woodward, Gail Anderson
Photo Editor Fiona McDonagh
Photographer Mark Seliger
Publisher Wenner Media
Client Rolling Stone
Issue March 29, 2001
Category Features: Story

■ 258
Publication Rolling Stone
Art Director Fred Woodward
Designer Ken DeLago
Photo Editors Fiona McDonagh, Audrey Landreth
Photographer Mark Seliger
Publisher Wenner Media
Client Rolling Stone
Issue January 18, 2001
Category Features: Spread

■ 259
Publication Rolling Stone
Art Director Fred Woodward
Designer Siung Tjia
Photo Editor Fiona McDonagh
Photographer Lee Jenkins
Publisher Wenner Media
Client Rolling Stone
Issue August 2, 2001
Category Features: Spread

■ 260
Publication Rolling Stone
Art Director Fred Woodward
Designer Siung Tjia
Photo Editor Fiona McDonagh
Photographer Sam Jones
Publisher Wenner Media
Client Rolling Stone
Issue August 16, 2001
Category Features: Spread

■ 261
Publication Rolling Stone
Art Director Fred Woodward
Designer Gail Anderson
Photo Editor Fiona McDonagh
Photographer Mark Seliger
Publisher Wenner Media
Client Rolling Stone
Issue November 8, 2001
Category Features: Spread

■ 262
Publication Sports Illustrated
Creative Director Steven Hoffman
Designer Linda Root
Publisher Time Inc.
Issue October 29, 2001
Category Features: Spread

make room

FALL FASHION

■ 263
Publication Smock
Creative Director Kristin Johnson
Designer Kristin Johnson
Photographer Howard Huang
Studio Kristin Johnson Design
Publisher Smock Magazine, Inc.
Issue Spring 2001
Category Features: Story

■ 264
Publication Smock
Creative Director Kristin Johnson
Designer Kristin Johnson
Photographer Zack Gold
Studio Kristin Johnson Design
Publisher Smock Magazine, Inc.
Issue Winter 2001
Category Features: Story

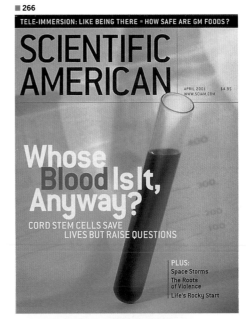

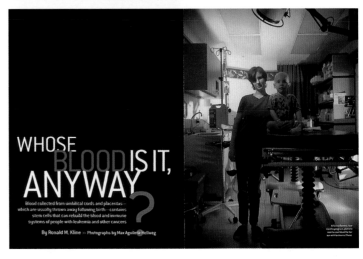

■ 265
Publication Smock
Creative Director Kristin Johnson
Designer Kristin Johnson
Photographers Samantha Rapp, Mark Squires
Studio Kristin Johnson Design
Publisher Smock Magazine, Inc.
Issue Spring 2001
Category Features: Story

■ 266
Publication Scientific American
Design Director Amy Rosenfeld
Art Directors Donna Agajanian, Gretchen Smelter
Designers Donna Agajanian, Gretchen Smelter,
Amy Rosenfeld, Edward Bell, Jana Brenning
Photo Editors Alison Morley, Bridget Gerety
Publisher Scientific American Inc.
Issue April 2001
Category Redesign

MUT ZUM MUSTER

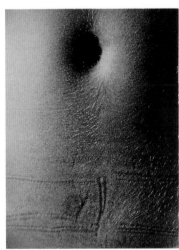

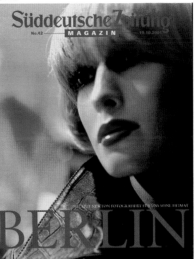

Süddeutsche Zeitung MAGAZIN

BERLIN

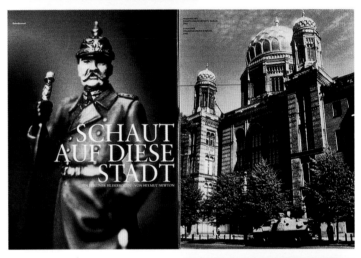

SCHAUT AUF DIESE STADT

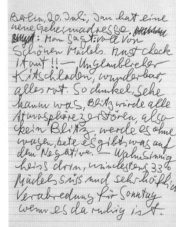

■ 267
Publication Süddeutsche Zeitung Magazin
Art Director Michael Weies
Designers Michael Weies, Friederike Gauss
Photo Editor Claudia Bingemann
Photographer Helmut Newton
Publisher Magazin Verlagsges Süddeutsche Zeitung mbH
Issue October 19, 2001
Category Entire Issue

■ 268
Publication Süddeutsche Zeitung Magazin
Art Directors Michael Weies, Friederike Gauss
Designer Friederike Gauss
Photo Editor Eva Fischer
Photographer Joachim Baldauf
Publisher Magazin Verlagsges Süddeutsche Zeitung mbH
Issue December 14, 2001
Category Features: Story

■ 270

■ 271

■ 272

■ 269
Publication Süddeutsche Zeitung Magazin
Art Directors Michael Weies, Friederike Gauss
Designer Florin Preussler
Photo Editor Eva Fischer
Photographers Manfred Jarisch, Ulrike Myrzik
Publisher Magazin Verlagsges. Sueddeutsche Zeitung mbH
Issue December 4, 2001
Category Features: Story

■ 270
Publication Texas Monthly
Art Director Scott Dadich
Designer Scott Dadich
Illustrator Matt Mahurin
Publisher Emmis Communications Corp.
Issue June 2001
Category Features: Spread/Single Page

■ 271
Publication Texas Monthly
Art Director Scott Dadich
Designer Scott Dadich
Photo Editor Scott Dadich
Photographer Dan Winters
Publisher Emmis Communications Corp.
Issue August 2001
Category Features: Spread

■ 272
Publication Technology Review
Art Director Eric Mongeon
Designer Eric Mongeon
Photographer Angela Wyant
Publisher Massachusetts Institute of Technology
Issue March 2001
Category Features: Single Page

The Devil and Mr. Jones

by Gary Cartwright

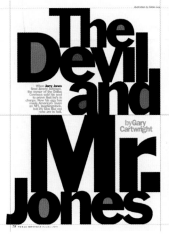

Hogs and heifers, wildflowers and prairie dogs, bowling alleys and one-room schoolhouses—it doesn't get more honest-to-good-ness than Iowa. Gini Alhadeff explores the state's discreet charms

the heart of the heartland

photographed by aldo rossi

Following the stumbling and

I'VE ALWAYS KEPT PIGS. IN IOWA, I LEARNED TO CALL THEM HOGS, OR HAAHÖS, AS IT IS PRONOUNCED

Angel in the Backfield

Confession: I've been a Cowboys

Emmit Smith enters his twelfth season with the Cowboys looking as fresh as a rookie. That's a good thing, because the star running back is carrying the weight of his team—and history—on his shoulder pads. by Gary Cartwright

In an obscure corner of a practice

Perhaps sweets, steaks, and country air are the recipe for a good life. I could see myself at age 100, sitting out in a field, listening to the corn grow

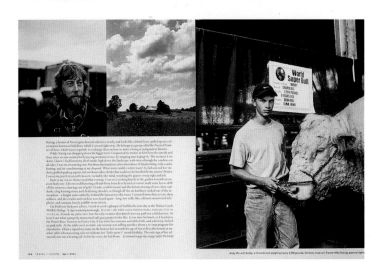

■ 273
Publication Texas Monthly
Art Director Scott Dadich
Designer Scott Dadich
Illustrators Eddie Guy, Philip Burke, Johanna Goodman
Photo Editor Scott Dadich
Publisher Emmis Communications Corp.
Issue October 2001
Category Features: Story

■ 274
Publication Travel & Leisure
Creative Director Pamela Berry
Art Director Laura Gharrity
Designers Stephanie Achar, Jae Han
Photo Editor Heidi Posner
Photographer Aldo Rossi
Publisher American Express Publishing Co.
Issue April 2001
Category Features: Story

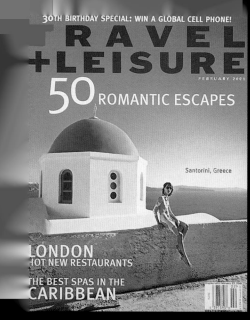

TRAVEL +LEISURE

FEBRUARY 2001

50 ROMANTIC ESCAPES

Santorini, Greece

LONDON
HOT NEW RESTAURANTS

THE BEST SPAS IN THE CARIBBEAN

it's not easy being
greenland

BY NATHAN LUMP · PHOTOGRAPHED BY ANDERS OVERGAARD

BY GINI ALHADEFF
PHOTOGRAPHED BY CEDRIC ANGELES

LEIPZIG WAKES UP

Goethe, Schiller, and Bach slept here, but there's not much sleeping
going on these days. Since the wall came down, Leipzig has retained
its old-world flavor while becoming one of Germany's liveliest cities

The Player's Clubs

NEW STICKS FOR THE GOLFER WITH AN A-GAME

PRO shop
EDITED BY P. HAHN LIVINGSTON

FINE GEAR—CUSTOM-FITTED

Big gray guns:
The new 300 Series
drivers create the
highest ball speed
ever produced by a
TaylorMade wood.

b etter players are clamoring for better sticks—and club makers are listening. For two decades manufacturers have mainly focused on game-improvement clubs, introducing high-tech enhancements such as perimeter weighting and ultrathin-metal club faces with higher-handicap players in mind. Now the single-digit crowd is getting its due in the form of clubs designed with feedback from Tour pros. Here are some tasty new treats.

RETAILORING TAYLORMADE

Say good-bye to the distinctive copper tone and welcome more gunmetal gray to the pro shop. With the introduction of the titanium 300 Series of drivers, TaylorMade has signaled a significant change of pace in its product lines and marketing strategy, going after the advanced player first and hoping higher handicappers will follow. This move not only introduces a new, bolder color but a stronger logo as well.

"Over the last few years, the better player did

PHOTOGRAPHS BY SHIN OHIRA

T&LGolf | 43

JOE MESI: PORTRAIT OF A BOXER
by Thad Weitz

■ 278
Publication Travel & Leisure
Creative Director Pamela Berry
Art Director Laura Gharrity
Designers Stephanie Achar, Jae Han
Photo Editor Heidi Posner
Publisher American Express Publishing Co.
Issue June 2001
Category Entire Issue

■ 279
Publication Travel & Leisure Family
Creative Director Pamela Berry
Art Director Laura Gharrity
Designers Stephanie Achar, Jae Han
Photo Editor Heidi Posner
Publisher American Express Publishing Co.
Issue Fall /Winter 2001
Category Entire Issue

design MERIT

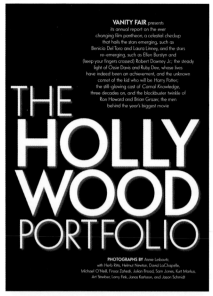

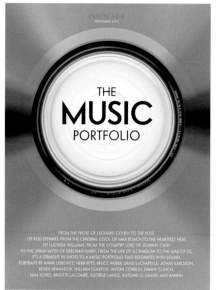

■ 280
Publication Vanity Fair
Design Director David Harris
Art Directors Gregory Mastrianni, Julie Weiss, Lisa Meipala Kennedy
Designers Adam Bookbinder, Lee Ruelle
Photo Editor Susan White
Photographer Annie Leibovitz
Publisher The Condé Nast Publications Inc.
Issue April 2001
Category Entire Issue

■ 281
Publication Vanity Fair
Design Director David Harris
Art Director Julie Weiss
Designer Christopher Israel
Photo Editor Susan White
Publisher The Condé Nast Publications Inc.
Issue November 2001
Category Features: Story

■ 282

■ 283

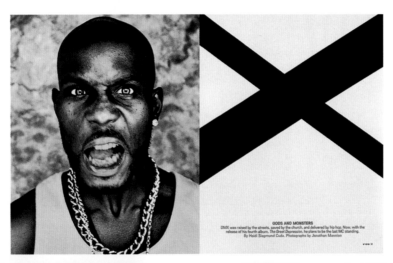

■ 282
Publication Vanity Fair
Design Director David Harris
Art Director Julie Weiss
Designer Chris Mueller
Photo Editor Susan White
Photographer Jonas Karlsson
Publisher The Condé Nast Publications Inc.
Issue November 2001
Category Department

■ 283
Publication Vibe
Design Director Florian Bachleda
Art Director Brandon Kavulla
Designer Alice Alves
Illustrators Matt Mahurin, Carlos Aponte, David Navascues
Photo Editors George Pitts, Dora Somosi
Photographers Jonathan Mannion, Larry Sultan, Kevin Westenberg, Ajamu
Publisher Miller Publishing Group
Issue October 2001
Category Entire Issue

the cheese of meaux

■ 284
Publication Wegmans Menu
Creative Director Emma Ross
Art Director Wendy Scofield
Designer Wendy Scofield
Photographer Johnathan Gregson
Publisher John Brown Publishing
Issue Holiday 2001
Category Features: Story

■ 285
Publication Vibe
Design Director Florian Bachleda
Art Director Brandon Kavulla
Designers Alice Alves, Michael Friel
Illustrators Carlos Aponte, Alex Ostroy, Luba Lukova
Photo Editors George Pitts, Dora Somosi
Photographers Matthias Vriens, Christopher Kolk, Suzanne Karsters
Publisher Miller Publishing Group
Issue December 2001
Category Entire Issue

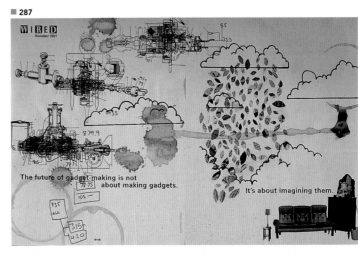

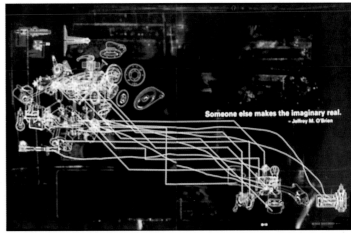

■ 286
Publication Wired
Design Director Susana Rodriguez
Art Directors Federico Gutiérrez, Eric Siry
Designers Federico Gutiérrez, Van Burnham, Eric Siry, Becky Hui
Photo Editor Christa Aboitiz
Photographer Morten Kettel
Publisher The Condé Nast Publications Inc.
Issue May 2001
Category Features: Story

■ 287
Publication Wired
Design Director Susan Rodriguez
Art Director Susan Rodriguez
Illustrator Shynola
Publisher The Condé Nast Publications Inc.
Issue November 2001
Category Contents/Department

■ 288
Publication Wine Spectator
Art Director David Bayer
Designer David Bayer
Illustrator Stefano Vitale
Publisher M. Shanken Communications Inc.
Issue March 31, 2001
Category Features: Spread

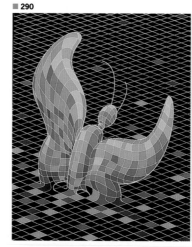

MY OWN PRIVATE TOKYO
BY WILLIAM GIBSON

■ 289

Publication Wired
Design Director Susana Rodriguez
Art Director Federico Gutiérrez
Designers Federico Gutiérrez, Chad Kloepfer, Susana Rodriguez, Becky Hui, Stefan Belavy
Photo Editor Christa Aboitiz
Publisher The Condé Nast Publications Inc.
Issue September 2001
Category Features: Story

■ 290

Publication Worth
Design Director Deanna Lowe
Art Director Dirk Barnett
Designer Dirk Barnett
Illustrator Christoph Niemann
Publisher Worth Media
Issue June 2001
Category Features: Spread

■ 291

Publication Worth
Design Director Deanna Lowe
Art Director Dirk Barnett
Designer Dirk Barnett
Photo Editors Marianne Butler, Victoria Rich
Photographer Joe Pugliese
Publisher Worth Media
Issue June 2001
Category Features: Spread

■ 292

■ 294

■ 295

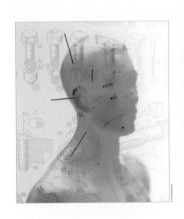

■ 293

■ **292**
Publication Yahoo! Internet Life
Design Director Gail Ghezzi
Art Director Robert Priest
Designers Robert Priest, Peter B. Curry
Photo Editor Gail Henry
Publisher Ziff-Davis, Inc.
Issue May 2001
Category Redesign

■ **293**
Publication Yahoo! Internet Life
Design Director Gail Ghezzi
Designer Jose G. Fernandez
Photo Editor Gail Henry
Photographer Micheal McLaughlin
Publisher Ziff-Davis, Inc.
Issue December 2001
Category Features: Spread

■ **294**
Publication @issue
Creative Director Kit Hinrichs
Art Director Maria Wenzel
Designers Maria Wenzel, Amy Chan
Studio Pentagram Design, Inc.
Publisher Corporate Design Foundation
Issue Winter 2001
Category Features: Spread

■ **295**
Publication Yahoo! Internet Life
Design Director Gail Ghezzi
Designer Jose G. Fernandez
Photo Editor Gail Henry
Photographer Plastock/Photonica
Publisher Ziff-Davis, Inc.
Issue August 2001
Category Features: Spread

Emoticons Quiz ?-)

In 1982, Carnegie Mellon researcher Scott Fahlman was a participant in some of the earliest online newsgroups. The exchange revealed its limitations since online participants lacked the benefit of vocal cues and facial expressions to tell them whether a poster was being ironic, humorous or serious. Frustrated by the lack of feedback, Fahlman proposed that posters express their feelings through the use of self-invented ASCII hieroglyphs, using keyboard characters to draw digital "smiley" faces. The rest is history. Now known as "emoticons," these faces (presented sideways) have become the emotional language of online chat rooms, email and instant messaging, with new icons being invented every day. See if you can guess what these emoticons mean.

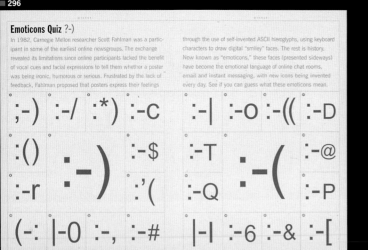

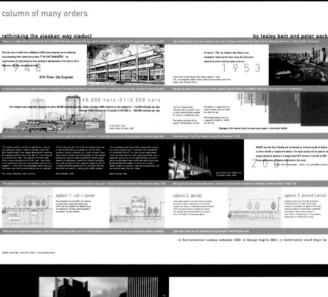

column of many orders

rethinking the alaskan way viaduct
by lesley bain and peter sackett

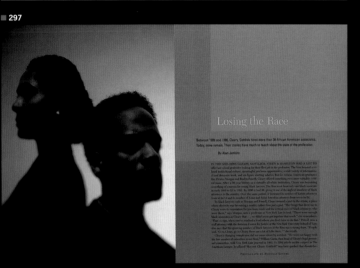

Losing the Race

Between 1895 and 1995, Cleary, Gottlieb hired more than 30 African American associates. Today, none remain. Their stories have much to teach about the state of the profession.

By Alan Jenkins

on public and private realms

296
Publication @issue
Creative Director Kit Hinrichs
Designer David Asari
Studio Pentagram Design, Inc.
Publisher Corporate Design Foundation
Issue Winter 2001
Category Features: Spread

297
Publication The American Lawyer
Art Director Joan Ferrell
Designer Joan Ferrell
Photo Editor T. L. Litt
Photographer Douglas Levere
Publisher American Lawyer Media
Issue October 2001
Category Features: Spread

298
Publication Arcade Journal of Architecture and Design
Design Director Karen Cheng
Designer Karen Cheng
Publisher Northwest Architectural League

June 2001

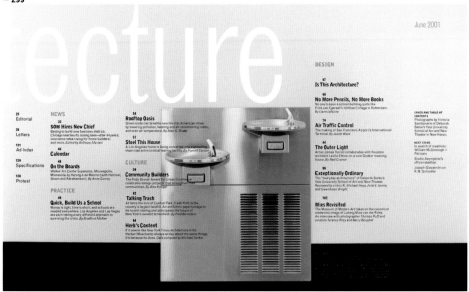

NEWS

23 Editorial

26 Letters

121 Ad Index

129 Specifications

138 Protest

33 SOM Hires New Chief
Beijing to build new business district; Chicago rewrites its zoning laws—after 44 years; insurance rates rising for home builders; and more. Edited by Anthony Mariani

Calendar

46 On the Boards
Walker Art Center Expansion, Minneapolis, Minnesota, by Herzog & de Meuron (with Hammel, Green and Abrahamson). By Anne Guiney

PRACTICE

49 Quick, Build Us a School
Money is tight, time is short, and schools are needed everywhere. Los Angeles and Las Vegas are each taking a very different approach to surviving the crisis. By Bradford McKee

54 Rooftop Oasis
Green roofs can breathe new life into American cities by lowering pollution, heating and air conditioning costs, and even air temperature. By Alan G. Brake

58 Steel This House
A Los Angeles home is being converted into a sprawling, steel-clad antimicrobial housing facility. By Purcell Carson

CULTURE

38 Community Builders
The Rudy Bruner Award for Urban Excellence rewards urban design projects that strengthen their communities. By Alex Krieger

42 Talking Trash
At Fresh Kills is the star of Central Park, Fresh Kills is the nation's largest landfill. An exhibition pays homage to its recent closing and anticipates the future of New York's newest brownfield. By Fred Bernstein

64 Herb's Content
If it seems like New York Times architecture critic Herbert Muschamp always writes about the same things, it's because he does. Data compiled by Michael Sorkin

DESIGN

67 Is This Architecture?

68 No More Pencils, No More Books
No one's been a school building quite like Erick van Egeraat's Ichthus College in Rotterdam. By Liane Lefaivre

74 Air Traffic Control
The making of San Francisco Airport's International Terminal. By Jacob Ward

78 The Outer Light
Artist James Turrell collaborates with Houston architect Leslie Elkins on a new Quaker meeting house. By Ned Cramer

96 Exceptionally Ordinary
The "everyday architecture" of Deborah Berke's Yale University School of Art and New Theater. Reviewed by critics K. Michael Hays, Joan I. Levine, and Gwendolyn Wright.

102 Mies Revisited
The Museum of Modern Art takes on the canonical modernist image of Ludwig Mies van der Rohe. An interview with photographer Thomas Ruff and curators Terence Riley and Barry Bergdoll

COVER AND TABLE OF CONTENTS
Photographs by Victoria Sambunaris

NEXT ISSUE:
In search of creativity; William McDonough + Partners

Studio Asymptote's office rebellion

Joseph Giovannini on R.M. Schindler

WHERE'S THE

HOW-TO
BY LOUISE WITT

EXIT?

Everyone knows start-ups rarely make it into the IPO pipeline. So what are other ways you can get a return?

PHOTOGRAPHS BY PETE McARTHUR

"Angel investors could drive harder bargains. They don't focus on how they can be hurt and how to exit the company."

Entrepreneurs have lawyers representing their interests, so hire your own lawyer to review the term sheets.

To Each His Own

THANKS TO HUNGRY MONEY MANAGERS, THE SEARCH FOR A SEPARATE-ACCOUNT MANAGER IS NOW A MORE MANAGEABLE TASK

It was the dark ages of money management—say, about 1997—in Overland Park, Kan., and the Legacy Trust Co. was routinely servicing its six-figure clients by investing their assets in mutual funds, just as astute financial advisers had done for some 70 years. Only through mutual funds went the conventional wisdom in those primitive times, could an investor with a mere $250,000 or so enjoy the twin benefits of professional management and portfolio diversification. Any personalized money management for an investor of such modest wealth was out of the question altogether. BY DAN ROTTENBERG

ILLUSTRATIONS BY ISTVAN BANYAI

■ 299

Publication Architecture
Art Director Lisa Naftolin
Designer Adam Michaels
Photo Editor Alexandra Brez
Photographer Victoria Sambunaris
Publisher VNU, Inc.
Issue June 2001
Category Contents

■ 300

Publication Bloomberg Angel Advisor
Art Director Carol Layton
Designer Carol Layton
Photographer Pete McArthur
Studio CL Design
Publisher Bloomberg L.P.
Client Bloomberg L.P.
Issue January/February 2001
Category Features: Story
   A **MERIT:** Design: Features: Spread

■ 301

Publication Bloomberg Wealth Manager
Art Director Laura Zavetz
Designer Laura Zavetz
Illustrator Istvan Banyai
Publisher Bloomberg L.P.
Issue May 2001
Category Features: Spread

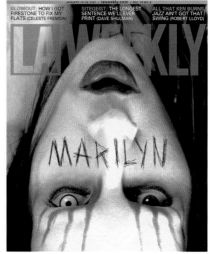

■ 308

the new

Putting a digital spin on an old economy company is no easy task. These CFOs have the knack.

BY RUSS BANHAM

■ 309

BEHIND THE GREEN DOOR

With a Web portal, finance employees can go where they've never gone before.

BY TIM REASON

■ 306
Publication CMYK Magazine
Creative Director Geneviéve Astrelli
Art Directors Tom Finnegan, Arturo Samayoa
Designer Amy Chang
Studio Nimbus Design
Publisher Aroune-Freigen Publishing Co.
Issue November 2001
Category Redesign

■ 307
Publication LA Weekly
Art Director Bill Smith
Photographer P.R. Brown
Publisher Village Voice Media
Issue January 12, 2001
Category Features: Spread

■ 308
Publication eCFO
Design Director Robert Lesser
Art Directors Laura McFadden, Paul M. Lee
Designer Laura McFadden
Photo Editor Carol Lieb
Photographer Lynne Siler
Publisher CFO Publishing Corp
Issue Summer 2001
Category Features: Spread

■ 309
Publication eCFO
Design Director Robert Lesser
Art Directors Laura McFadden, Paul M. Lee
Designer Paul M. Lee
Illustrator Craig Frazier
Photo Editor Carol Lieb
Publisher CFO Publishing Corp
Issue Fall 2001
Category Features: Spread

WALK THIS WAY

For most of us, walking is akin to breathing, an activity so banal that we take it for granted. But behind the scenes, the feet are a factory of productivity; the body, a machine of well-calibrated complexity. Even a simple stroll is a biomechanical wonder.

When the foot strikes the ground, it absorbs about one and a half times the body's weight, then pushes off the ground with a similar amount of force. That force is then dispersed through the knees, hips, and torso. Yet all the while, the body never buckles beneath the strain.

BY ELIZABETH WALLACE
ILLUSTRATIONS BY ULLA PUGGAARD

earth's edge

A grueling trek through Chile   becomes a sentimental journey.

BY DAVID HOWARD

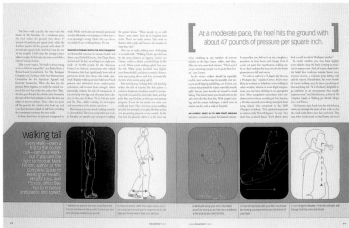

[At a moderate pace, the heel hits the ground with about 47 pounds of pressure per square inch.]

walking tall

The landscape keeps us hungry for the next   bend. Cows and sheep far outnumber people

bundle up

happy trails

On Location

■ 310

Publication Feat
Creative Director Robb Allen
Art Directors Jennifer Napier, Eugene Wang
Designers Jennifer Napier, Eugene Wang
Illustrator Ulla Puggaard
Photo Editors Danielle Place, Tracy Thompkins
Publisher Hachette Filipacchi Custom Publishing
Client Rockport
Issue Fall/Winter 2001
Category Features: Story

■ 311

Publication Feat
Creative Director Robb Allen
Art Directors Jennifer Napier, Eugene Wang
Designers Jennifer Napier, Eugene Wang
Photo Editors Danielle Place, Tracy Thompkins
Publisher Hachette Filipacchi Custom Publishing
Client Rockport
Issue Fall/Winter 2001
Category Features: Story

Ed.

DOUBLE CLICK: JOHN MERROW
ON TECHNOLOGY IN EDUCATION

KIDS TELL PRINCIPALS
WHERE TO GO

PEERING INTO THE FUTURE
OF HUMAN DEVELOPMENT

THE MAGAZINE OF THE HARVARD GRADUATE SCHOOL OF EDUCATION | SPRING 2001 | VOL. XLV. NO. 1

**REDREAM-
ING
OAKLAND
SCHOOLS**
recovering, redreaming, and reinvigorating an urban district

REDREAM-ING OAKLAND SCHOOLS

BY JESSICA SIEGEL PHOTOGRAPHS BY KEN LIGHT

Tacked on to a bare wall on the third floor of the Oakland (CA) Unified School District headquarters is a crayon drawing by a third-grader named Boris titled "School Land." The finely detailed picture imagines classrooms, a meeting room, a copy room, offices, lockers, a restroom, a preschool, and a lunchroom filling the spacious building, next to spaces for art, yoga, and karate. Outside, a path lined with flowers leads from a playground to a big lake. The drawing is a "redreaming," as Jose Martinez puts it, of what the schools could be—grounded in reality but lifted by the imagination of a child.

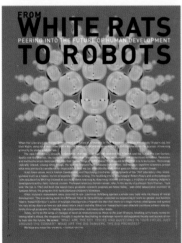

FROM WHITE RATS TO ROBOTS
PEERING INTO THE FUTURE OF HUMAN DEVELOPMENT

THE BIG
idea

BY DEIRDRE R. SCHWIESOW
PHOTOGRAPHY BY ROCKY THIES

To Jack Donahue, innovation and government needn't be mutually exclusive. He should know—this Harvard professor has spent most of his career studying how one affects the other.

E-GOVERNMENT

KING

KNIGHTS

■ 312
Publication Ed.
Creative Director Fritz Klaetke
Designers Fritz Klaetke, Ian Varrassi
Illustrator John Hersey
Photo Editor Jane Buchbinder
Photographers Ken Light, Lionel DeLevingne, Susie Fitzhugh
Studio Visual Dialogue
Publisher Harvard Graduate School of Education
Issue Spring 2001
Category Redesign

■ 313
Publication Federal Catalyst
Art Director Sylvia Gashi
Photographer Rocky Thies
Studio The Magazine Group/TMG Web
Client American Management Systems
Issue Spring 2001
Category Features: Spread/Single Page

■ 314
Publication Food Arts
Art Director Nancy Karamarkos
Designer Nancy Karamarkos
Photo Editor Melissa Malinowsky
Photographer Bill Milne
Publisher M. Shanken Communications Inc.
Issue April 2001
Category Features: Spread/Single Page

design MERIT

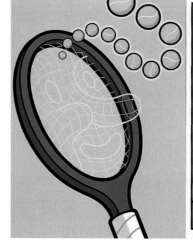

■ 316

Publication Independent School
Art Director Glenn Pierce
Illustrator Whitney Sherman
Studio The Magazine Group/TMG Web
Client National Association of Independent Schools
Issue Fall 2001
Category Features: Spread

■ 317

Publication Gallup Management Journal
Creative Director Terry Koppel
Design Director Carin Goldberg
Art Director Kristina DiMatteo
Designers Carin Goldberg, Kristina DiMatteo, Rebecca Alden
Photo Editor Bess Hauser
Photographer Jessica Wecker
Publisher Time Inc. Custom Publishing
Issue Spring 2001
Category Department

■ 318

Publication Gallup Management Journal
Creative Director Terry Koppel
Design Director Carin Goldberg
Art Director Kristina DiMatteo
Designers Carin Goldberg, Kristina DiMatteo, Rebecca Alden
Illustrator Christoph Niemann
Publisher Time Inc. Custom Publishing
Issue Spring 2001
Category Features: Spread

■ 315

Publication Gallup Management Journal
Creative Director Terry Koppel
Design Director Carin Goldberg
Art Director Kristina DiMatteo
Designers Carin Goldberg, Kristina DiMatteo, Rebecca Alden
Illustrator Jeffrey Fisher
Photo Editor Bess Hauser
Photographer Nathaniel Welch
Publisher Time Inc. Custom Publishing
Issue Spring 2001
Category Features: Story
        A MERIT: Design: Features: Spread

design MERIT

THE "SATISFIED" CUSTOMER WHO BUYS BAGFULS OF YOUR BRAND TODAY MIGHT FLEE TO A COMPETITOR TOMORROW.

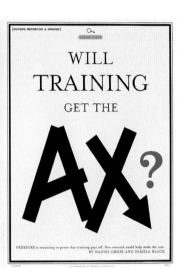

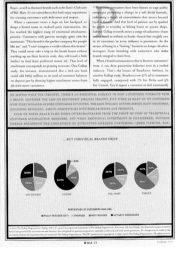

Publication Gallup Management Journal
Creative Director Terry Koppel
Design Director Carin Goldberg
Art Director Kristina DiMatteo
Designers Carin Goldberg, Kristina DiMatteo, Rebecca Alden
Publisher Time Inc. Custom Publishing
Issue Summer 2001
Category Contents/Department

Publication Gallup Management Journal
Creative Director Terry Koppel
Design Director Carin Goldberg
Art Director Kristina DiMatteo
Designers Carin Goldberg, Kristina DiMatteo, Rebecca Alden
Photo Editor Bess Hauser
Photographer Fredrik Brodén
Publisher Time Inc. Custom Publishing
Issue Summer 2001
Category Features: Story

Publication Gallup Management Journal
Creative Director Terry Koppel
Design Director Carin Goldberg
Art Director Kristina DiMatteo
Designers Carin Goldberg, Kristina DiMatteo, Rebecca Alden
Illustrator Steven Guarnaccia
Photo Editor Bess Hauser
Publisher Time Inc. Custom Publishing
Issue Summer 2001
Category Features: Spread

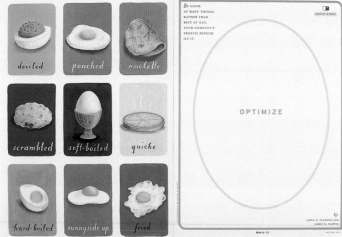

A

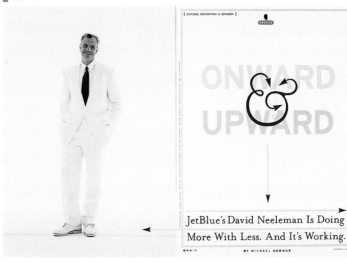

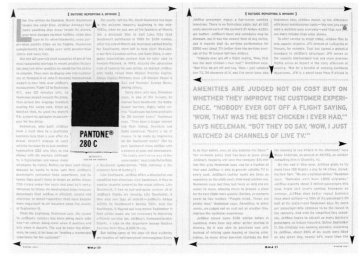

■ 322
Publication Gallup Management Journal
Creative Director Terry Koppel
Design Director Carin Goldberg
Art Director Kristina DiMatteo
Designers Carin Goldberg, Kristina DiMatteo, Rebecca Alden
Illustrator Sarah Wilkins
Photo Editor Bess Hauser
Publisher Time Inc. Custom Publishing
Issue Winter 2001
Category Features: Spread

■ 323
Publication Gallup Management Journal
Creative Director Terry Koppel
Design Director Carin Goldberg
Art Director Kristina DiMatteo
Designers Carin Goldberg, Kristina DiMatteo, Rebecca Alden
Illustrator Philippe Weisbecker
Photo Editor Bess Hauser
Publisher Time Inc. Custom Publishing
Issue Winter 2001
Category Features: Spread

■ 324
Publication Gallup Management Journal
Creative Director Terry Koppel
Design Director Carin Goldberg
Art Director Kristina DiMatteo
Designers Carin Goldberg, Kristina DiMatteo, Rebecca Alden
Illustrator Neil Flewellen
Photo Editor Bess Hauser
Photographer Chris Callis
Publisher Time Inc. Custom Publishing
Issue Winter 2001
Category Features: Story
　　A MERIT: Design: Features: Spread

■ 325
Publication Gallup Management Journal
Creative Director Terry Koppel
Design Director Carin Goldberg
Art Director Kristina DiMatteo
Designers Carin Goldberg, Kristina DiMatteo, Rebecca Alden
Publisher Time Inc. Custom Publishing
Issue Winter 2001
Category Contents

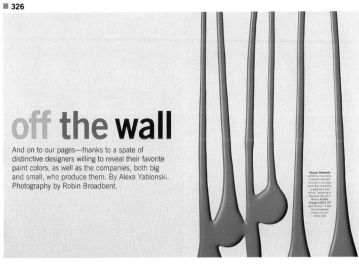

off the wall

And on to our pages—thanks to a spate of distinctive designers willing to reveal their favorite paint colors, as well as the companies, both big and small, who produce them. By Alexa Yablonski. Photography by Robin Broadbent.

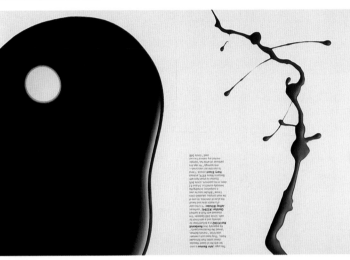

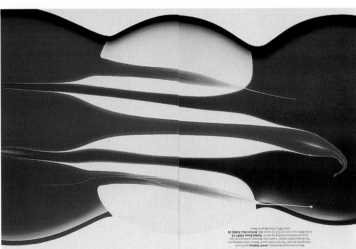

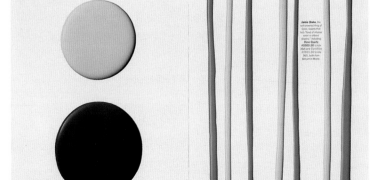

■ 326

Publication Interior Design
Art Director Miranda Dempster
Designer Miranda Dempster
Photographer Robin Broadbent
Publisher Cahners
Issue October 31, 2001
Category Features: Story

■ 327

Publication IQ
Creative Director Robb Allen
Art Directors Jennifer Napier, Grace Lee
Designer Grace Lee
Illustrator Mark Tellok
Photo Editor Danielle Place
Publisher Hachette Filipacchi Custom Publishing
Client Cisco Systems
Issue January/February 2001
Category Features: Story

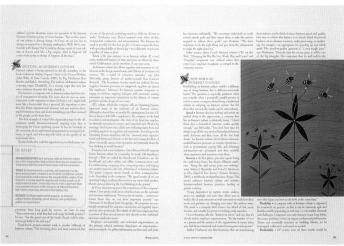

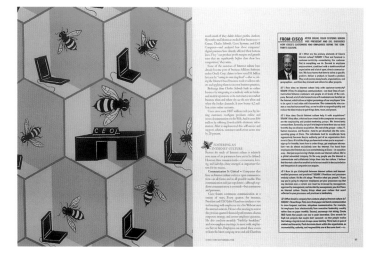

RAGNAR AXELSSON

Gelebte Märchen

Bilder aus einer anderen Welt: Der Isländer Ragnar Axelsson, beim diesjährigen Oskar-Barnack-Preis mit einer Honourable Mention ausgezeichnet, dokumentiert traditionelles Leben auf den Nordatlantikinseln.

RAGNAR AXELSSON

BRUCE GILDEN

Einladung zur Geisterbahn

Neues von Bruce Gilden. Bei Nacht und von ganz unten nähert sich der Magnum-Fotograf der postmodernen japanischen Gesellschaft.

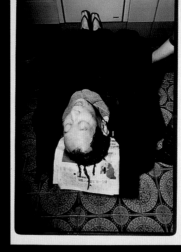

BRUCE GILDEN

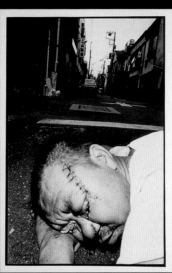

■ 331
Publication Leica World
Creative Director Horst Moser
Designers Horst Moser, Sabine Krohberger
Photo Editors Michael Koetzle, Horst Moser
Photographer Ragnar Axelsson
Studio Independent-Medien-Design
Publisher Leica Camera AG
Issue September 1, 2001
Category Features: Story

■ 332
Publication Leica World
Creative Director Horst Moser
Designers Horst Moser, Sandra Jessica Gramisci
Photo Editors Michael Koetzle, Horst Moser
Photographer Bruce Gilden
Studio Independent-Medien-Design
Publisher Leica Camera AG
Issue September ,1 2001
Category Features: Story

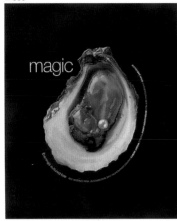

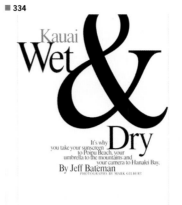

Splash & Dash

We

Sea & Sky

QUIET CHAOS

SITUATED SOMEWHERE ON THE MARGINS, GARY PANTER SLIPS INTO AND OUT OF THE MAINSTREAM WITH A ZEN-LIKE GRACE.

PANTER REVELS IN ESOTERIC INSPIRATION, FROM JAPANESE MOVIE MONSTERS AND MEXICAN MAGAZINE ADS TO BOCCACCIO, DANTE, JOYCE, AND DICK (PHILIP K., THAT IS).

■ 333
Publication Oasis
Art Director Carol Moskot
Designer Carol Moskot
Photographers Gabor Jurina, Shun Sasabuchi
Publisher Multi-Vision Publishing
Issue November 1, 2001
Category Features: Story

■ 334
Publication Travel Etc.
Art Director Tom Brown
Designer Tom Brown
Photo Editor Tom Brown
Photographer Mark Gilbert
Studio Tom Brown Art & Design
Publisher Uniglobe Travel International
Client Uniglobe Travel International
Issue Fall 2001
Category Features: Story

■ 335
Publication Metropolis
Art Director Criswell Lappin
Designer Damian Chadwick
Illustrator Gary Panter
Photographer Kristine Larsen
Publisher Bellerophon Publications
Issue April 2001
Category Features: Story

■ 336

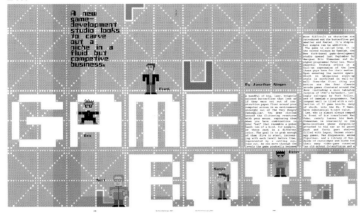

■ 338

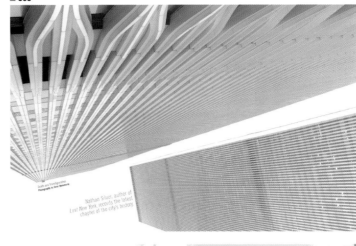

■ 337

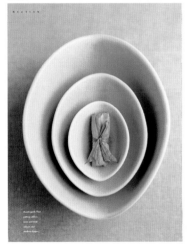

■ 339

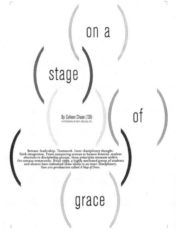

■ 336
Publication Metropolis
Art Director Criswell Lappin
Designer Damian Chadwick
Illustrator Peter Lee
Publisher Bellerophon Publications
Issue July 2001
Category Features: Story

■ 337
Publication Sawasdee
Creative Director John Boyer
Art Director Teresita Khaw
Designer Connie Chu
Photo Editor Jennifer Spencer
Photographer Formula z/s
Publisher Emphasis Media Ltd.
Issue September 2001
Category Features: Spread

■ 338
Publication Metropolis
Art Director Criswell Lappin
Designer Damian Chadwick
Photo Editor Sara Barrett
Photographer Sean Hemmerle
Publisher Bellerophon Publications
Issue December 2001
Category Features: Story

■ 339
Publication Trinity Western
Art Director Tom Brown
Designer Tom Brown
Photographer Mike Rathjen
Studio Tom Brown Art & Design
Publisher Trinity Western University
Client Trinity Western University
Issue Summer 2001
Category Features: Spread

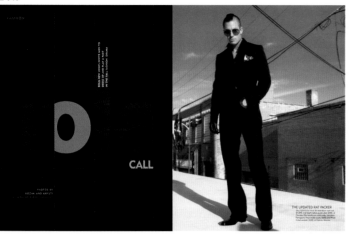

■ 340
Publication Chicago Tribune Sunday Magazine
Art Director David Syrek
Photographer Kozak & Krysti
Publisher Chicago Tribune Company
Issue September 9, 2001
Category Features: Spread

■ 342
Publication Trinity Western
Art Director Tom Brown
Designer Tom Brown
Photographer Carmen Tomé
Studio Tom Brown Art & Design
Publisher Trinity Western University
Client Trinity Western University
Issue Fall 2001
Category Features: Spread

■ 341
Publication Trinity Western
Art Director Tom Brown
Designer Tom Brown
Photographer James Labounty
Studio Tom Brown Art & Design
Publisher Trinity Western University
Client Trinity Western University
Issue Fall 2001
Category Features: Spread

■ 343
Publication Vistas: Texas Tech Research
Creative Director Artie Limmer
Art Directors T.J. Tucker, Alyson Keeling
Designer T.J. Tucker
Photo Editor Artie Limmer
Photographer Melissa Goodlett
Studio Texas Tech University Creative Services
Publisher Texas Tech University
Client Texas Tech University
Issue Summer 2001
Category Features: Spread

Contents

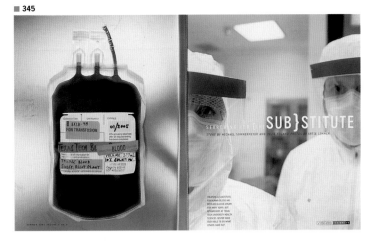

■ 344
Publication Wesleyan University Magazine
Design Director Robert J. George
Photo Editor Bill Burkhart
Photographer Bill Burkhart
Studio R & R Creative
Publisher Wesleyan University
Issue Winter 2001
Category Redesign

■ 345
Publication Vistas: Texas Tech Research
Creative Director Artie Limmer
Art Director T.J. Tucker
Designer T.J. Tucker
Photographer Artie Limmer
Studio Texas Tech University Creative Services
Publisher Texas Tech University
Client Texas Tech University
Issue Summer 2001
Category Features: Spread

■ 346
Publication Vistas: Texas Tech Research
Creative Director Artie Limmer
Art Director T.J. Tucker
Designer T.J. Tucker
Illustrator T.J. Tucker
Photo Editor Artie Limmer
Studio Texas Tech University Creative Services
Publisher Texas Tech University
Client Texas Tech University
Issue Summer 2001
Category Features: Spread

■ 347
Publication Vistas: Texas Tech Research
Creative Director Artie Limmer
Art Directors Alyson Keeling, T.J. Tucker
Designer T.J. Tucker
Photo Editor Artie Limmer
Studio Texas Tech University Creative Services
Publisher Texas Tech University
Client Texas Tech University
Issue Winter 2001
Category Features: Spread

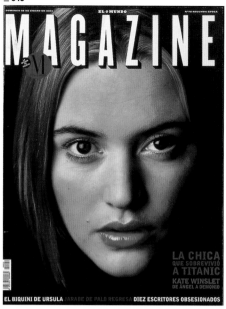

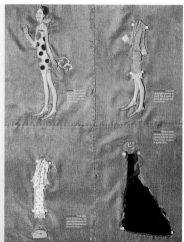

■ 348
Publication Magazine El Mundo
Design Director Carmelo Caderot
Art Director Rodrigo Sánchez
Designers Rodrigo Sánchez, Maria González, Javier Sanz
Photo Editor Rodrigo Sánchez
Photographer Jason Dell
Publisher Unidad Editorial S.A.
Issue January 28, 2001
Category Entire Issue

■ 349
Publication Magazine El Mundo
Design Director Carmelo Caderot
Art Director Rodrigo Sánchez
Designers Rodrigo Sánchez, Maria González, Javier Sanz
Illustrator Paula Sanz
Photo Editor Rodrigo Sánchez
Publisher Unidad Editorial S.A.
Issue October 14, 2001
Category Entire Issue

MAGAZINE

96 PAGINAS NÚMERO EXTRAORDINARIO
EL MUNDO

VIVA LA NAVIDAD

Merluza de Namibia, no del Cantábrico. Cuidado con las falsificaciones de la China. Test: quizás sea alérgico a estas fiestas y no lo sepa. MODA. Elegantísima, con y sin marca. El club de los cinco guapos. El bazar de las sorpresas. Menús para los más raritos.

OLVIDE LA CRISIS

MODA LA ESTRELLA DE LA FIESTA

M
EXTRA NAVIDAD

DISFRUTAR EN TIEMPOS DE CRISIS

Cómo vestir con estrella sin estrellarse — Entrevista distendida con Bimba Bosé, la última sensación de las pasarelas — El club de los cinco: Carmelo Gómez, Daniele Liotti, Juan Carlos Fresnadillo, Carlos Baute y Miguel Ángel Nicolás se saltan todas las normas de etiqueta — El gran bazar de las sorpresas: aquí están los regalos más buscados del año — Cuatro formas atípicas de poner una buena mesa: metal, madera, plástico y loza — Seis menús para los más caprichosos de la casa: vegetariano, de fusión, precocinado, italiano, infantil y artesano — Las Navidades empiezan con una buena cesta: así son los regalos de empresa que reciben millones de españoles junto a la paga extra

ENTREVISTABIMBABOSÉ

Garden Party
The first lady who'd prefer to be Mrs. Bush.
Photograph by Jessica Wynne
Text by Doris Kearns Goodwin

In Sync
Only one girl can sing lead.
Photographs by Gillian Laub
Text by Diane Cardwell

Hard Time
Behind bars with 1,000 male convicts.
Photographs by Brenda Ann Kenneally
Text by Ted Conover

design MERIT

■ 350
Publication Magazine El Mundo
Design Director Carmelo Caderot
Art Director Rodrigo Sánchez
Designers Rodrigo Sánchez, Maria González, Javier Sanz
Photo Editor Rodrigo Sánchez
Publisher Unidad Editorial S.A.
Issue December 9, 2001
Category Entire Issue

■ 351
Publication The New York Times
Art Director Janet Froelich
Designer Joele Cuyler
Photo Editors Kathy Ryan, Jody Quon, Evan Kriss, Kira Pollack, Cavan Farrell,
Photographers Sally Mann, Mary Ellen Mark, Gillian Laub, Jessica Wynne, Justine Kurland, Diana Walker, Nan Goldin, Tina Barney, Lauren Greenfield, Joyce Tenneson, Brenda Ann Kenneally
Publisher The New York Times
Issue September 9, 2001
Category Entire Issue

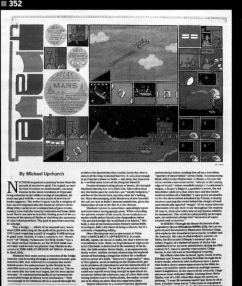

By Michael Upchurch

By Verlyn Klinkenborg

Books for Summer Reading

Go-Go Chic
To model these Courrèges inspired baby-doll coats and dresses, we went looking for a real doll. Marley Shelton to the rescue.
Photographs by Marcus Mâm · Styled by Elizabeth Stewart

The New York Times Magazine

12.9.01 · In this week's issue...

The Year in
Ideas

Continued on Page 10

Publication The New York Times
Art Director Steven Heller
Illustrator Chris Ware
Publisher The New York Times
Issue June 3, 2001
Category Entire Issue

Publication The New York Times
Art Director Janet Froelich
Designer Claude Martel
Photographer Marcus Mâm
Producer Elizabeth Stewart
Publisher The New York Times
Issue July 15, 2001
Category Features: Story

Publication The New York Times
Art Director Janet Froelich
Designer Joele Cuyler
Photo Editors Kathy Ryan, Kira Pollack
Publisher The New York Times
Issue December 9, 2001
Category Contents

■ 355

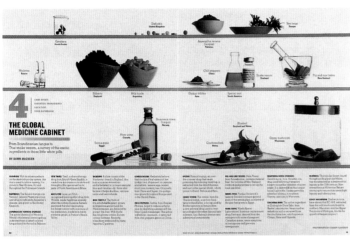

■ 356

■ 357

■ 355
Publication The New York Times
Art Director Janet Froelich
Designers Andrea Fella, Claude Martel
Photo Editor Kathy Ryan
Photographers Lendon Flanagan,
Katy Grannan, Catherine Chalmers
Publisher The New York Times
Issue May 6, 2001
Category Entire Issue

■ 356
Publication The New York Times
Art Director Janet Froelich
Designer Nancy Harris
Photo Editor Kathy Ryan
Publisher The New York Times
Issue April 8, 2001
Category Contents

■ 357
Publication The New York Times
Art Director Janet Froelich
Designer Claude Martel
Photo Editors Kathy Ryan, Jody Quon
Photographers Justine Kurland, Bill Jacobson,
Marcia Lippman, Barbel Schmidt
Publisher The New York Times
Issue November 11, 2001
Category Features: Story

The New York Times Magazine · OCTOBER 14, 2001

LOVE

In the 21st Century

*At a time when everything feels unmoored, the desire to anchor
one life to another is stronger than ever.*
By Matthew Klam

It was Saturday, four days after the World Trade Center attack. It was a
new world. My wife, Lara, and I, for better or worse, were the same old
us, doing what we typically do when the world shakes us up — we were
ignoring each other. Lara is a psychologist, and it had obviously been a
big week for feeling crazy, and she was worn out, she had that excuse.
As for me, I had been throwing out everything I had ever written and
was uselessly, ceaselessly revising. Through overwork and now tragedy, we

The New York Times Magazine · NOVEMBER 11, 2001

The Return Of New York

Out of the haze of grief, we can see more clearly than ever what our city is and what it could become. BY JACOB WEISBERG

Dealing with what happened to our city on Sept. 11
has involved a kind of progression, and for many of us, the initial
phase included some level of incomprehension. One of the
stranger images left in my head from that terrible morning is of a
woman standing on my corner in TriBeCa, laughing into her
cellphone. Survivors, many of them coated head to toot with ash,
were processing mutely up Church Street. My wife and I had
run outside to determine whether we should evacuate the
children from our apartment. And this nicely dressed woman was
chatting with a friend as if New York were the same city it had

Love In the Time of Coloring

For Sarah and Sean, commitment starts early.
By Denby Dolan

Photograph by Judith Joy Ross

When Debbie Met Christina, Who Then Became Chris

Does a sex change mean the end of the relationship?
By Nan Corbett

Photographs by Mary Ellen Mark

Let Us Count the Ways [1-9]

1. LENA DUNHAM
ST. ANN'S STUDENT

2. HAL SIROWITZ
POET LAUREATE OF QUEENS

3. MOBY, MUSICIAN

St. Ann's students under the Brooklyn Bridge. Photograph by Justine Kurland

[1-9]

4. ERNESTO QUIÑONEZ
WRITER

5. ANDRÉ ACIMAN, WRITER

6. DIANE SAWYER
NEWS ANCHOR

7. ALEKS ROSENBERG
POET

8. DAVID SCHICKLER
WRITER

9. AMY SEDARIS, ACTOR

The 5s Urban on a Saturday morning. Photograph by Bill Jacobson

[rethink]

New Yorkers are happy to subordinate their lives to getting and spending money if they are surrounded by other people doing the same thing.

Times Square
BRING BACK
NEW YORKERS — AND SEX
By Frank Rich

Let all Broadway ticket prices float to their true market value, but require the top draws to underwrite cheaper tickets to the same hits.

ILLUSTRATIONS BY LAURENT CILLUFFO

■ 358
Publication The New York Times
Art Director Janet Froelich
Designer Lisa Naftolin
Photo Editors Kathy Ryan, Jody Quon
Photographers Mary Ellen Mark, Judith Joy Ross, Bill Jacobson
Publisher The New York Times
Issue October 14, 2001
Category Entire Issue

■ 359
Publication The New York Times
Art Director Janet Froelich
Designers Claude Martel, Nancy Harris
Illustrator Laurent Cilluffo
Photo Editors Kathy Ryan, Jody Quon, Evan Kriss, Kira Pollack, Cavan Farrell
Photographers Raymond Meier, Justine Kurland, Bill Jacobson
Publisher The New York Times
Issue November 11, 2001
Category Entire Issue
A **MERIT:** Design: Features: Story

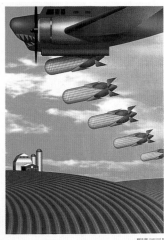

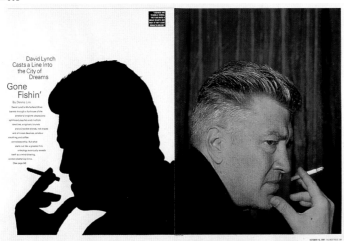

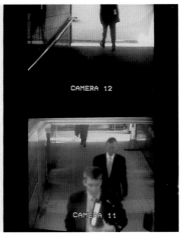

■ 362
Publication The New York Times
Art Director Janet Froelich
Designer Claude Martel
Photo Editor Kathy Ryan
Photographer Stephen Gill
Publisher The New York Times
Issue October 9, 2001
Category Features: Story

■ 363
Publication The Village Voice
Design Director Ted Keller
Art Director Minh Uong
Designer Michaelann Zimmerman
Illustrator Lloyd Miller
Publisher Village Voice Media
Issue May 22, 2001
Category Features: Spread

■ 360
Publication The Village Voice
Design Director Ted Keller
Art Director Minh Uong
Designer Kimberly Hall
Illustrator Max Grafe
Publisher Village Voice Media
Issue October 16, 2001
Category Features: Spread

■ 361
Publication The Village Voice
Design Director Ted Keller
Art Director Minh Uong
Designer Michaelann Zimmerman
Photo Editor Staci Schwartz
Photographer Robin Holland
Publisher Village Voice Media
Issue October 16, 2001
Category Features: Spread

■ 364
Publication The Village Voice
Design Director Ted Keller
Art Director Minh Uong
Designer Michaelann Zimmerman
Illustrator Lloyd Miller
Publisher Village Voice Media
Issue July 24, 2001
Category Features: Spread

GOLD online

■ 365
Publication Utah Carol.com
Creative Director The Speared Peanut
Designer The Speared Peanut
Illustrators The Speared Peanut, Eun-ha Paek
Photo Editor The Speared Peanut
Photographer Utah Carol
Online Address www.utahcarol.com
Category Self Promotion

MoMA
WHITNEY

MIES IN BERLIN
MIES IN AMERICA

The career of Ludwig Mies van der Rohe (1886-1969), one of the greatest architects of the

twentieth century, was divided into two periods: the first thirty years spent in Germany, the last thirty in America.

This summer, The Museum of Modern Art and the Whitney Museum of American Art host

concurrent exhibitions that explore the entirety of the architect's work.

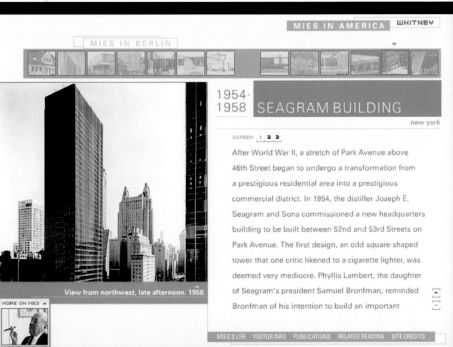

MIES IN AMERICA **WHITNEY**

MIES IN BERLIN

1954-1958 SEAGRAM BUILDING
new york

SCREEN 1 **2 3**

After World War II, a stretch of Park Avenue above 46th Street began to undergo a transformation from a prestigious residential area into a prestigious commercial district. In 1954, the distiller Joseph E. Seagram and Sons commissioned a new headquarters building to be built between 52nd and 53rd Streets on Park Avenue. The first design, an odd square-shaped tower that one critic likened to a cigarette lighter, was deemed very mediocre. Phyllis Lambert, the daughter of Seagram's president Samuel Bronfman, reminded Bronfman of his intention to build an important

View from northwest, late afternoon. 1958.

MORE ON MIES ▲

MIES'S LIFE VISITOR INFO PUBLICATIONS RELATED READING SITE CREDITS

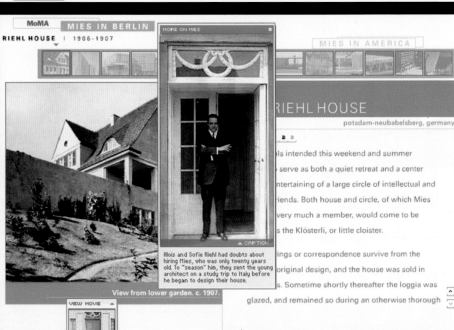

MoMA MIES IN BERLIN

RIEHL HOUSE | 1906-1907

MORE ON MIES ✕

MIES IN AMERICA

RIEHL HOUSE
potsdam-neubabelsberg, germany

2 3

...ls intended this weekend and summer

...serve as both a quiet retreat and a center

...ntertaining of a large circle of intellectual and

...riends. Both house and circle, of which Mies

...very much a member, would come to be

...s the Klösterli, or little cloister.

...ings or correspondence survive from the

...original design, and the house was sold in

...s. Sometime shortly thereafter the loggia was

glazed, and remained so during an otherwise thorough

▲ CAPTION

Alois and Sofie Riehl had doubts about hiring Mies, who was only twenty years old. To "season" him, they sent the young architect on a study trip to Italy before he began to design their house.

View from lower garden. c. 1907.

VIEW MOVIE ▲

MIES'S LIFE VISITOR INFO PUBLICATIONS RELATED READING SITE CREDITS

online SILVER

■ 366
Publication MoMA.org and Whitney.org
Creative Directors Warren Corbitt, Matt Owens
Designers Warren Corbitt, Lee Misenheimer
Studio one9ine
Publisher The Museum of Modern Art,
The Whitney Museum of American Art
Online Address www.MoMA.org/Mies
Category Information Design

■ 367
Publication Olympics.com
Creative Director Greg Hollobaugh
Design Director Denise Trabona
Designers Krista Fleming, Alan Urdan,
Jason Hollifield, Alix Han, Ed Mitchell
Photo Editors Andrew Locke, Brian Storm
Publisher MSNBC Interactive
Online Address www.olympics.com
Category Information Design

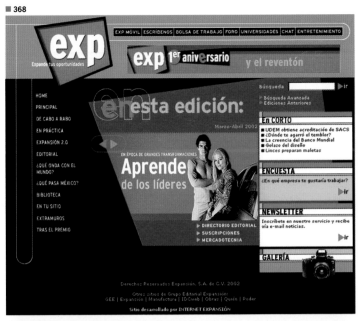

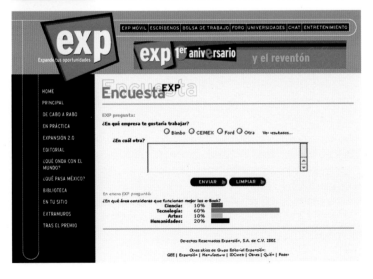

■ 368

Publication Exp.com
Creative Director Guillermo Caballero
Art Director María Soledad Martínez
Designers Roberto Ugalde, Georgina Enriquez
Publisher Grupo Editorial Expansión
Online Address www.Exp.com.mx
Category News/Education/Corporate

■ 369

Publication PopSci.com
Creative Directors Warren Corbitt, Matt Owens
Designers Warren Corbitt, Lee Misenheimer
Studio one9ine
Publisher Time4 media
Online Address www.PopSci.com
Category Website Redesign

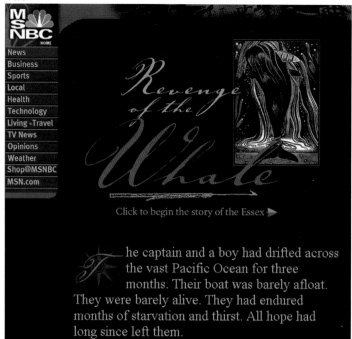

Click to begin the story of the Essex ▶

he captain and a boy had drifted across the vast Pacific Ocean for three months. Their boat was barely afloat. They were barely alive. They had endured months of starvation and thirst. All hope had long since left them.

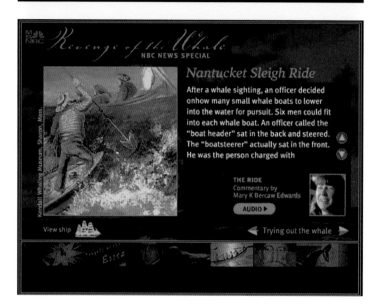

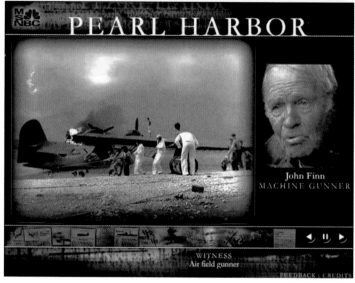

■ 370
Publication MSNBC.com
Creative Director Greg Hollobaugh
Art Director Paul Segner
Designer Tom Loftus
Publisher MSNBC Interactive
Online Address www.MSNBC.com/modules/tvnews/whalerevenge/
Category News/Education/Corporate

■ 371
Publication MSNBC.com
Creative Director Greg Hollobaugh
Art Director Paul Segner
Designer Ashley Wells
Photo Editor Meredith Birkett
Publisher MSNBC Interactive
Online Address www.MSNBC.com/news/pearlharbor_front.asp
Category News/Education/Corporate

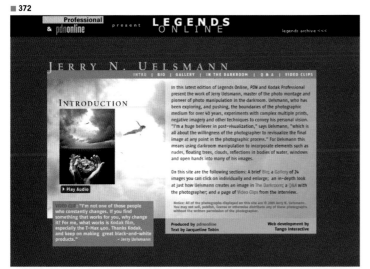

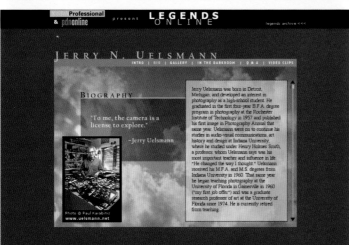

Bomb photographed for
Corbis Images

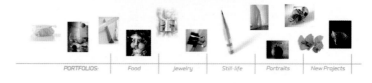

■ 372
Publication PDNOnline.com
Creative Director Lauren Wendle
Designer Tango Interactive
Publisher Jeff Roberts, VNU Business Publications USA
Client Kodak Professional
Online Address www.pdonline.com/legends/uelsmann
Category News/Education/Corporate

■ 373
Publication MoMA.org
Creative Directors Warren Corbitt, Matt Owens
Designers Matt Owens, Lee Misenheimer
Studio one9ine
Online Address www.MoMA.org/exhibitions/giacometti/
Category Information Design

■ 374
Publication MatthewKlein.com
Creative Director Matthew Klein
Designer Matthew Klein
Photographer Matthew Klein
Online Address www.MatthewKlein.com
Category Self Promotion

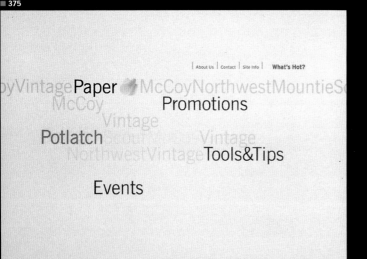

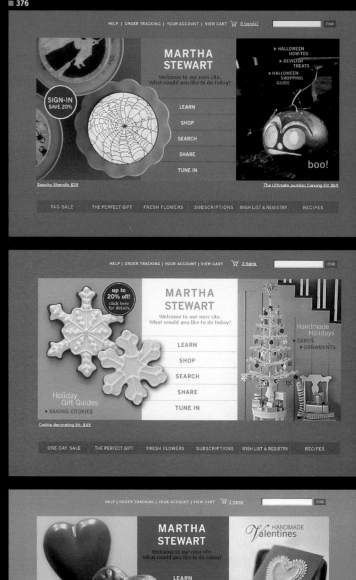

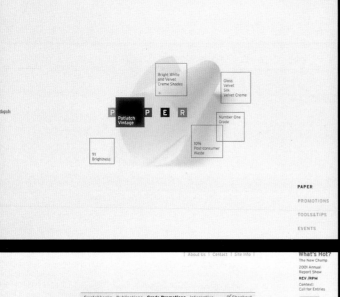

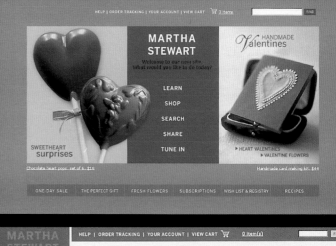

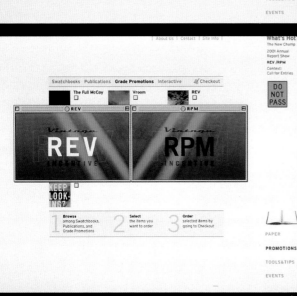

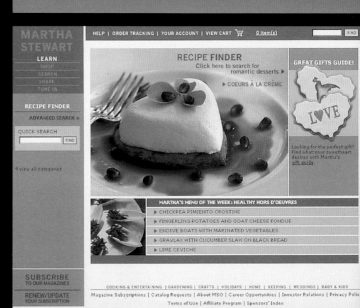

■ 375
Publication potlatchpaper.com
Design Director Kit Hinrichs
Designers Brian Jacobs, Douglas McDonald, Holger Struppek, Brian Cox
Photographer Terry Heffernan
Studio Pentagram Design, Inc.
Online Address www.potlatchpaper.com
Category Advertising/Catalog/Internal

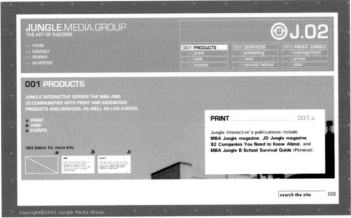

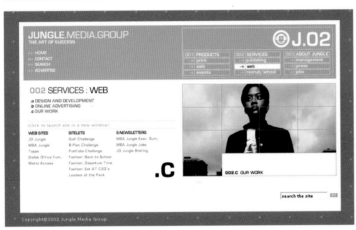

■ 376
Publication MarthaStewart.com
Creative Director Gael Towey
Design Director Colleen Stokes
Art Directors Amanda Vine, Christina Vicente
Designer Daniel Boguszewski
Photographers Beatriz De Costa, Gentl + Hyers, Anna Williams,
Sang An, William Abranowicz, Chris Baker
Publisher Martha Stewart Living Omnimedia
Online Address www.MarthaStewart.com
Category Website Redesign

■ 377
Publication JungleMediaGroup.com
Creative Director Courtney Skulley
Design Directors Ken Fassman, Joe Carbe
Publisher Jungle Media Group
Online Address www.JungleMediaGroup.com
Category Self Promotion

■ 378
Publication JDJungle.com
Creative Director Courtney Skulley
Design Directors Ken Fassman, Joe Carbe
Publisher Jungle Media Group
Online Address www.JDJungle.com
Category News/Education/Corporate

The Next
Wonders

Trophy buildings are luring the traveling masses as never before. RAYMOND MEIER captures the year's most exciting structures—from New Caledonia to New York. We also deliver the lowdown on what to do in the surrounding area. It's all over but the ogling

SENDAI, JAPAN
SENDAI MEDIATHEQUE PROJECT

Like a Tokyo apartment, where one room functions as living, dining, and sleeping quarters, Toyo Ito's partition-free design (a two-hour bullet train up the coast from the capital) packs a multitude of functions into a single space. When it opens this year, the conglomeration of concrete slabs and steel plates held aloft by helical columns will host art installations, visiting library collections, film series, and lectures spilling over from the local university. Within its two-ply glass membrane, light and air flow as freely as the exchange of ideas. Rays hitting the roof travel down through the structure with the aid of strategically placed optic devices, and the pillars function as vents, keeping temperatures temperate no matter the season (2-1 Kasuga-machi, Aoba-Ku; www.smt.city.sendai .jp/en/index.html).

VALENCIA, SPAIN
City of Arts and Sciences

BORDEAUX
Tribunal de Grande Instance

Places & Prices

Publication Condé Nast Traveler
Design Director Robert Best
Art Director Kerry Robertson
Designer Robert Best
Photo Editors Kathleen Klech, Esin Goknar
Photographer Raymond Meier
Publisher Condé Nast Publications, Inc.
Issue March 2001
Category Reportage: Story

Summer Squash

OPPOSITE: The squash gardener can provide her summer table with exotic varieties the grocery store rarely offers, such as 'Zucchetta Rampicante' (left) and 'Sundrop' (right). Harvesting squash means rummaging among spiny leaves and stems, so wear long sleeves.

PHOTOGRAPHS BY GENTL & HYERS TEXT BY DORA GALITZKI

177

■ 380
Publication Martha Stewart Living
Design Director Barbara de Wilde
Art Director Helen Sanematsu
Photo Editor Mary Dail
Photographer Gentl + Hyers
Stylists Ayesha Patel, Jennifer Hitchcox
Publisher Martha Stewart Living Omnimedia
Issue March 2001
Category Still Life/Interiors: Spread

photography GOLD

The Swimmer

Like Burt Lancaster before him, David Hasselhoff plays the part of the charming and winsome Neddy Merrill, who pool-hops his way home as a cast of backstabbing neighbors lounge around in the season's hottest resort clothes.

Photographs by Jeff Riedel
Styled by Robert Bryan and Mimi Lombardo
Styling by Mid-Desert at Bald

Credits on Page 86

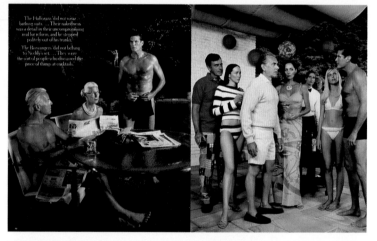

■ 381
Publication The New York Times Magazine
Art Director Janet Froelich
Designer Claude Martel
Photographer Jeff Riedel
Producers Robert Bryan, Mimi Lombardo
Publisher The New York Times
Issue November 25, 2001
Category Fashion/Beauty: Story

While the masses
may scream for ice cream,
the true fashion diva
sets her sights on Aaron
Basha's 18-karat gold,
diamond and aquamarine
baby shoe charm, opposite.
$2,400. At Aaron Basha,
680 Madison Avenue.
The diamond and platinum
bracelet, this page, and
10-carat diamond ring are
from Harry Winston,
718 Fifth Avenue.

Even without
these dazzling
jewels, you've
got your finger
on the pulse.

You've
Got
Nails

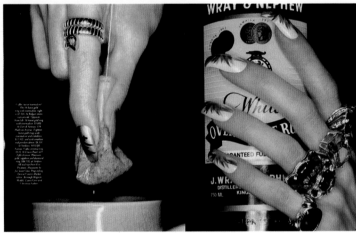

■ 382
Publication The New York Times Magazine
Art Director Janet Froelich
Designer Claude Martel
Photographer Carlton Davis
Producer Anne Christensen
Publisher The New York Times
Issue February 11, 2001
Category Fashion/Beauty: Story

photography **GOLD**

hallelujah

it's collection time again. sunday
fashions, how great thou art.
photographed by marcelo krasilcic

STYLIST: HAIDEE FINDLAY-LEVIN
HAIR DENNIS LANIN FOR BUMBLE AND BUMBLE NYC
MAKEUP: DEVRA KINERY AT FRAME
MODEL: OLUCHI AT ELITE
STYLING ASSISTANT: RENATA ABRADE
PHOTOGRAPHY ASSISTANT: JONATHAN RAGLE

HAIR BAND BY FUTURE, PLANET OF STYLE, SHIRT BY BALENCIAGA LE DIX.
OPPOSITE: HAIR FLOWERS BY CONCORD, SHIRTDRESS AND JACKET BY UNITED BAMBOO. PEARL TIE FROM CHELSEA FLEA MARKET.

■ 383
Publication Nylon
Art Director Lina Kutsovskaya
Designers Kathleen McGowan, Jason Engdahl
Photographer Marcelo Krasilcic
Publisher Nylon LLC
Issue April 2001
Category Fashion/Beauty: Story

SHOCKING FAMILY SECRETS!

"I'm a neurotic mess. I'm really basically just like a sleeped-up Woody Allen."
— JAMES GANDOLFINI

Sopranos Stars Tell All

By Chris Heath

"In my mind, I started thinking about it as 'Twin Peaks' in the Jersey meadowlands."
— DAVID CHASE

"To win an award over the girl from 'Dark Angel' is not where it's at for me." — EDIE FALCO

"I don't like audience that much. I don't mind playing it, but I don't like watching it." MICHAEL IMPERIOLI

"I'm such a shy person, and people think I'm really snotty because I'm shy but I'm not. I'm just shy." — DREA DE MATTEO

"You gotta go slow. When you get shot, you don't go right away. You never die right away." — TONY SIRICO

"I had to do a sex scene – that's not easy. I've never had a sex scene before. I was scared shit." — AIDA TURTURRO

"I don't know how people do it who look like themselves. If I looked in the mirror and saw me, I'm fucked." — STEVEN VAN ZANDT

ON THE SET OF "THE Sopranos," nobody takes any notice of the noises. Perhaps when you're working on the finest TV show around, you have too much else to think about. But perhaps it's more that, over time, the strangest distractions come to seem normal. Sometimes they are basic yelps, bellows, shouts, hollers and roars. Sometimes, loud animal noises. David Chase, *The Sopranos*' creator, remembers the first day's filming on the show's pilot episode. "I kept hearing these chicken noises," he says. "And you think, 'OK, what is this?' I never said anything."

All these noises are made by one man, James Gandolfini, and they can usually be heard just before a director shouts, "Action!" and Gandolfini fully slips into the guise that has made him famous, the role of Tony Soprano. "Oh, yeah," acknowledges Gandolfini when the subject is brought up. He

suggests that his habit's roots might lie in something he once learned in an acting class, about how a sharp noise can release tension. "It's almost like, you are about to make a fool of yourself, so you might as well make a fool of yourself right away," he reasons, "and then making a fool of yourself on camera is a little easier."

When asked whether different animal noises conjure up different moods, he insists otherwise – "No, totally random," he says – but he does concede that he is still trying to expand his menagerie. "I've been trying to do a pig noise for a very long time," he says, "and I can't seem to master it." For him, the gold standard in this field is Gérard Depardieu's splendid porcine snort in the movie *Green Card*. "I don't have anything that would even come close to

Doctor-patient confidentiality: James Gandolfini and Lorraine Bracco

PHOTOGRAPHS *by* MARK SELIGER

HBO thought *The Sopranos* would confuse people. They were insistent that the show be called *Family Man.*

"We have not done a politically correct show," says Chase. "And I'm not going to start now."

By Nick Compton

girl-inter-rupted

Christina Ricci was just visiting Prozac Nation, but the side effects were brutal. Now she's easing off the fruitcake for a taste of romantic-comedy flummery.
Photographs by Malerie Marder

DRESS BY ANNA MOLINARI, SHOES BY NARCISO

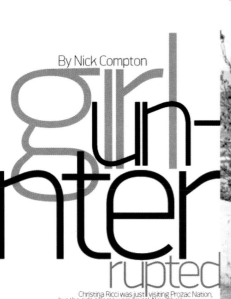

HERE SHE ISN'T going off and her reaction is horrific and Christina Ricci, the former only-only little hot-faced girl, is staging goes a way rude of America's Sweetheart through blond, a grand undertaken-ish overlooked-by-this-brat. "When I'm alone, I feel like I'm phone-where I am in the same camera," she admits. "I can't seem to be some-where there are places for people to hate."

End twice, Ingrid is having a lovely weekend ariances. Yet only in a sphere he two of the JFK making trouble with 51T, but she states argued by then high web forming normal consumer at foreseen attempts is cases off the great roll can gush reads. Amazer. Wonder the high-cut "rumantic-comedy" thriller" that her temple the there was supposed to include a bit of calling bill ability is the Universe Palm that at the Amarillon build up a new before up is a screw the carb including 54th that Inf that and also firm have been keen on his current and sen.

"THERE WERE ONLY FOUR DAYS OF FILMING THAT I DIDN'T HAVE TO CRY OR HAVE A NERVOUS BREAKDOWN," SAYS RICCI. AMID ALL THE HIGH DRAMA, PROZAC NATION'S CREW THREATENED TO WALK OUT, SO THE PRODUCERS ATTEMPTED AN EMOTIONAL RESCUE. "YOU DON'T NEED TO GO THAT FAR," THEY SAID.

IF YOU'RE A TWELVE-YOUNG AMERICAN actress, all this contributes. As a great sense of remorse, There's on it the small matter of another celebrated great currently breaking at the same break. Malerie Marder came Michael Jackson—whose presence her the popularized during every entrance, far from the first flush of flash belles on major in her nuts and only up burn, talk revisions and academics in a place with no fating phase.

Christina Ricci in part it, but she has as beginnings an email of film's helms the ber, with chafes in five years. All but a beautiful born voice and gone up they. Many were freaky little solid things, and mason, grants started the crosscuba's haves, tea care or not can mssough, bone-sees high load girl tonight. The great no paper shape-monster include but Let screw, The Mar Marl but Addy Porter's tale of us sph'd finds in ritchery Like Blanchett, Johnny Kings and Jake Deaton isn't this critical or commercial remains—The Addams family The Ice Nein, The Oppent of Sot. Ref: late, Mr. Nerr that enterprise that's upsets to confirond, charts, as is as his eastern or.

Her put Ricci olow the trad in a Ricci capitalism Hole that or Press Yadrm, Elizabeth Watson's Meat-off or brawful clysterment's nagging sometimes, out is holding a surtid over the. "More than anything, I was relieved when I met Christina," says Marder. "I was actual, can take more of illowee-Angelina ticks has fresh a whole career out of it. But ricca and I take being

RICCI BRINGS WITH HER KINDLY-PLUCK PAST AT SIX TAKING SEX-TABBY HOLDS IN THE OPPOSITE OF SEX AND BUFFALO '66 "I HAD AN EXTERMINATOR COME INTO MY HOME RECENTLY AND START TALKING ABOUT PUNK," SHE SAYS. "ACTUALLY ISN'T REALLY DIFFERENT."

■ 385
Publication Details
Creative Director Dennis Freedman
Design Director Edward Leida
Art Director Rockwell Harwood
Photo Editors Alice Rose George, Amy Steigbigel, Jeannine Foeller
Photographer Malerie Marder
Publisher Condé Nast Publications, Inc.

CLOSE ON COUNTER: Dale Dabone and Nikita Denise in the throes of *Betrayed by Beauty*. Digital technology allows Vivid to shoot several versions of the same scene, repackaging it for hard- and soft-core play.

THE XXX MEN

Boogie nights... David James have danc... the country's top p... with an IPO loomi... industry, can the... and bec...

BY ALLEN SALKIN

■ 386
Publication Details
Creative Director Dennis Freedman
Design Director Edward Leida
Art Director Rockwell Harwood
Photo Editors Alice Rose George, Amy Steigbigel, Jeannine Foeller
Photographer Larry Sultan
Publisher Condé Nast Publications, Inc.
Issue June 2001
Category Still Life/Interiors: Story

In a land that gave birth to fairy tales and conquerors, there is a peaceful village that seems unfazed by the impatience of the modern world. For almost 70 years, the people of this village have specialized in one thing: making toys. At first, there were only two toymakers: a carpenter and his son. Now the carpenter's grandson is the chief toymaker, and he has thousands of others working for his global company. Lego has a history that most companies only dream about. Yet its efforts to grow with the times haven't worked out. Here's a story—a fable, really—of a noble company and its difficult encounters with a fickle, fast-moving world.

Why Can't Lego Click?
By Charles Fishman
Photographs by Geof Kern

Fast Company 145

■ 387
Publication Fast Company
Design Director Patrick Mitchell
Designer Emily Crawford
Photo Editor Alicia Jylkka
Photographer Geof Kern
Publisher Gruner & Jahr USA Publishing
Issue September 2001
Category Photo Illustration: Story
    A. Spread

■ 388
Publication Martha Stewart Baby
Creative Director Gael Towey
Art Director Deb Bishop
Designer Deb Bishop
Photo Editor Jodi Nakatsuka
Photographer William Abranowicz
Stylists Cyndi DiPrima, Melanio Gomez
Publisher Martha Stewart Living Omnimedia
Issue Spring 2001
Category Still Life/Interiors: Spread

■ 389
Martha Stewart Kids
Creative Director Gael Towey
Art Director Deb Bishop
Designer Jennifer Wagner
Photo Editor Jodi Nakatsuka
Photographer Stephen Lewis
Stylist Stephana Bottom
Publisher Martha Stewart Living Omnimedia
Issue Summer/Fall 2001
Category Still Life/Interiors: Spread

Gentle botanical details fill a bright, simple nursery. The glass in an armoire's doors is replaced with screening that's been spray-painted white with silhouettes of ferns and butterflies. These mesh panels (opposite) let sound float through, making the armoire the perfect hiding place for a radio to play softly at nap time (see page 108 for how-tos).

spring nursery

100

Fresh fruits as cold as they can be are just the thing on a summer day. The sunlit colors of these pops come from combinations of fruit flavors: lemon, cranberry, orange, cantaloupe. One stripe is frozen before the next is added. Pastel candy rounds can dot the crowns.

SUNSHINE POPS

ICE POPS

PHOTOGRAPHS BY STEPHEN LEWIS TEXT BY KAREN BORNARTH

100

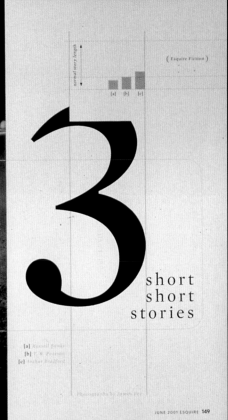

(Esquire Fiction)

[a] [b] [c]

3
short
short
stories

[a] *Russell Banks*
[b] *T. H. Peterson*
[c] *Arthur Bradford*

Photographs by James Fee

JUNE 2001 ESQUIRE **149**

My wife is bleeding.
She calls me from her office, and these are the words I hear. Bleeding. Worse than before. Need to go to the hospital.

There's a choke in her voice. She sounds clenched and pulled in. Julie and I work just around the corner from each other in midtown Manhattan, so seconds after getting the call I am sprinting down Broadway, slalom-coursing through Wednesday's matinee throng with a glare of determination. It's hard to know how to act in such a situation. You run because you're supposed to run, and you run because the words "My wife is bleeding" sting you into action, linked as they are with every enduring mystery of the female biological apparatus.

In more lighthearted moments, my wife likes to tell a funny story: One Halloween years ago, she dressed up as Sissy Spacek in *Carrie*. She put on a

tryin
g

Thinking about
having kids?
Trying to have kids?
Having a little
trouble?
You are not alone.
BY JEFF GORDINIER

194 ESQUIRE SEPTEMBER 2001   PHOTO ILLUSTRATION BY DAN WINTERS

■ 390
Publication Esquire
Design Director John Korpics
Photo Editor Nancy Jo Iacoi
Photographer James Fee
Publisher The Hearst Corporation–Magazines Division

■ 391
Publication Esquire
Design Director John Korpics
Photo Editor Nancy Jo Iacoi
Photographer Dan Winters
Publisher The Hearst Corporation–Magazines Division

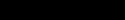

PORTFOLIO BY MARTIN SCHOELLER
HIP-HOP

■ 392
Publication The New Yorker
Photographer Martin Schoeller
Visuals Editor Elisabeth Biondi
Publisher Condé Nast Publications, Inc.
Issue August 20, 2001
Category Portraits: Story

photography SILVER

161

■ 393
Publication Vibe
Design Director Florian Bachleda
Art Director Brandon Kavulla
Photo Editors George Pitts, Dora Somosi
Photographer Dean Karr
Publisher Miller Publishing Group
Issue May 2001
Category Portraits: Spread

■ 394
Publication Vanity Fair
Design Director David Harris
Art Director Gregory Mastrianni
Photo Editors Susan White, SunHee C. Grinnell
Photographer Julian Broad
Publisher The Condé Nast Publications Inc.
Issue April 2001
Category Portraits: Spread

Leni Riefenstahl, 98
PHOTOGRAPHED BY HELMUT NEWTON

Top, Japanese marathoner Kitei Son and, above, U.S. athlete Glenn Harris in still photographs taken by Leni Riefenstahl during the filming of her 1938 documentary, Olympia.

Germany and Eastern Europe were a crucible for photographic talent between the wars. Then many budding photographers, including several in this portfolio, fled the Nazis, pursuing their work—and seeking refuge—in other lands. But Leni Riefenstahl, an actress turned filmmaker, stayed on and flourished, becoming the most influential visual propagandist of the Third Reich through now notorious documentaries such as Triumph of the Will. Later, after being exonerated by an Allied tribunal of war-related charges, she concentrated on still photography, turning her camera on anthropological subjects, including the Nuba tribesmen of Sudan, to produce what she called "biblical images which could have dated back to the earliest days of mankind." Leni Riefenstahl: Five Lives, a photobiography in bookstores this month, traces her controversial career. Still scorned in many quarters for images she created more than 60 years ago, she recently completed a diving (and underwater-video) expedition in the Maldives, off Sri Lanka.

Photographed at her home near Munich on June 26, 2000.

Helmut Newton, 80
PHOTOGRAPHED BY HENRI CARTIER-BRESSON

"The photographic act is not sexual," Helmut Newton insists. "When I photograph a naked woman, I can't mix the two. One is work, the other is not work." Which is more important, then, photography or sex? "Work is," he says. "Taking photos is more important than sex."
Pushing the end of [your] 70s is different than when you're in your 30s." Newton's fame, nonetheless, has come from blending the two during his four decades shooting fashion for magazines such as French Vogue. At their best, his erotic mise en scènes, with their oppressively perfect models, thrill with a luxurious peril. Newton's images, many depicting nocturnal themes, seem to have been created on the vivid back lot of a dream. At age 12, he took his first camera into Berlin's subways; at 18, he fled Hitler's rise, settling in Asia, then France. Now based in Monte Carlo, he dovetails assignments—for Vanity Fair and others—with projects that are always writ large. Last year's Sumo was a 66-pound book of nudes and portraits; this fall, "Helmut Newton: Work" opened at Berlin's massive New National Gallery. Says Newton, who confesses to feeling transformed by the heart attack he survived in 1971, "The [show is] 60 percent new and fresh. I do laugh when very à la mode photographers do big retrospectives when they're 30. They'll do [my] retrospective when I'm dead."

Photographed in Paris on July 4, 2000.

Saddle I, Paris, 1976, by Helmut Newton.

VANITY FAIR | 125

TOM WAITS
THE NIGHTHAWK

Musician, songwriter, actor.

Eighteen albums, two Grammys.
In a press release put out at the time of his 1973 debut album, Closing Time, Tom Waits claimed he was born in the backseat of a Yellow Cab, emerging in need of a shave and shouting, "Times Square and step on it!" Well, who's to doubt him? Everything about Waits defies rational thought: the shock of hair; the schizo array of battered voices and personae; the self-styled "bone music" that incorporates pump organ, junkyard-salvaged objects, and slack-tuned guitar. Forever evoking a flea-bitten world of spilled Popov flasks, torn mattress ticking, and neon glare—among his album titles are Nighthawks at the Diner and Heartattack and Vine—Waits has alchemized the seedy into the sublime for more than 25 years.
One wonders if he was peeved or perversely pleased when his latest release, Mule Variations, won a Grammy last year for best contemporary folk album.

Photographed by Annie Leibovitz at the In the Pocket Studio in Forestville, California, on May 18, 2001.

■ 395
Publication Vanity Fair
Design Director David Harris
Art Director Gregory Mastrianni
Photo Editors Susan White, SunHee C. Grinnell
Photographer Helmut Newton
Publisher The Condé Nast Publications Inc.
Issue January 2001
Category Portraits: Spread

■ 396
Publication Vanity Fair
Design Director David Harris
Art Director Julie Weiss
Designer Christopher Israel
Photo Editors Susan White, Kathryn MacLeod
Photographer Annie Leibovitz
Publisher The Condé Nast Publications Inc.
Issue November 2001
Category Portraits: Spread

SILVER photography

Numbers

Women Among Women

Something changes where men need not apply.

Photographs by
Justine Kurland
Text by
Ann Patchett

In 1973, I was 10 years old and spending the summer at a Girl Scout camp called Sycamore in Ashland City, Tenn. It was there that I was given my first copy of Ms. magazine by a counselor named Tree, who tried to explain to me the basic tenets of feminism. I sat on my bunk and carefully studied the pages. What the magazine seemed to be saying was that some people thought that women weren't equal to men, and so it was important as a women to stand up with other women and raise our voices against the injustice. It made no sense whatsoever. Weren't the woods full of girls? The lake? Didn't we band together and rule at both the best and worst tables in the dining barn? We never set out alone. Alone, we were told, it was too easy to stray off the path. We operated on the buddy system, the team. We were 6 girls in a canoe, 20 girls on a midnight raid to a neighboring cluster of tents, 200 girls belting out Carole King songs around a bonfire, our voices so extraordinarily loud that we shook the upper branches of the sycamore trees.

The part of my family that I saw on a regular basis growing up consisted of my mother and sister and grandmother. The decisions that needed to be made to get through the average day we made ourselves without asking for anyone's approval or permission. I spent 12 years in a Catholic girls' school, where I was ruled by the Sisters of Mercy, a power structure run by women all the way up to *Continued on Page 103*

Residents of the Marbella at Pelican Bay condominium complex, Naples, Fla. From left: Blanche Berger, Marge Hagan (both on bench), Eileen Johnson (edge of pool), Christine Anderson (lounge chair), Theresa Hastings (on towel, foreground), Renee Butler (back to camera), Joy McClenaghan (edge of pool), Shirley Lerry (hat), Betty Deitch (in pool), Lou Peabody (back corner of pool), Phyllis Gotschall, Eleanor Heimmeyer, Alice Tucker.

THE NEW YORK TIMES MAGAZINE / SEPTEMBER 9, 2001 97

■ 397

Publication The New York Times Magazine
Art Director Janet Froelich
Designer Joele Cuyler
Photo Editor Kathy Ryan
Photographer Justine Kurland
Publisher The New York Times
Issue September 9, 2001
Category Portraits: Story

MEMOIRS OF
Salome
Creek

Hollywood Makeover

PHOTOGRAPHY BY BILL PHELPS

Hollywood
WANTS YOU TO
REMEMBER
PEARL
HARBOR

photography MERIT

■ 398

Publication Arizona Highways
Art Directors Mary Winkelman Velgos, Barbara Denney
Designer Barbara Denney
Photo Editors Peter Ensenberger, Richard Maack
Photographer Jeff Snyder
Publisher Arizona Department of Transportation
Issue August 2001
Category Reportage: Story

■ 399

Publication Atomic
Creative Director Jeff Griffith
Designer Jeff Griffith
Photographer Bill Phelps
Publisher Atomic Magazine, Inc.
Issue Spring 2001
Category Fashion/Beauty: Spread

■ 400

Publication Atomic
Creative Director Jeff Griffith
Designer Jeff Griffith
Photographer Dan Winters
Publisher Atomic Magazine, Inc.
Issue Spring 2001
Category Portraits: Spread

■ 401

Publication Atomic
Creative Director Jeff Griffith
Designer Jeff Griffith
Photographer Bill Phelps
Publisher Atomic Magazine, Inc.
Issue Fall/Winter 2001
Category Fashion/Beauty: Spread

All Creatures Great and Small

TIM WALKER

Preschool
Toolbox

■ 402
Publication Big
Creative Director Marcelo Jünemann
Art Director Daren Ellis
Photographer Tim Walker
Publisher Big Magazine, Inc.
Issue April 2001
Category Portraits: Story

■ 403
Publication Big
Creative Director Marcelo Jünemann
Art Director Michel Mallard
Photographer Javier Vallhonrat
Publisher Big Magazine, Inc.
Issue July 2001
Category Reportage: Story

■ 404
Publication Nick Jr.
Design Director Don Morris
Art Director Josh Klenert
Designers Don Morris, Josh Klenert, Jennifer Starr, Robert Morris
Photo Editor Karen Shinbaum
Photographer Brian Hagiwara
Studio Don Morris Design
Publisher Viacom
Issue August/September 2001
Category Still Life/Interiors: Spread

A BLOOMBERG PERSONAL FINANCE SURVEY

LIVE FREE OR MOVE

HOW THE 50 STATES RATE FOR TAXES

BY THOMAS D. SALER

NEVADA A

Despite the crash of technology stocks, these 100 companies have seen sales surge. And our 20 favorites aren't just surviving—they're thriving.

SURVIVING THE KNOCK DOWN

BY JAMES PICERNO AND BING XIAO

PHOTOGRAPHS BY DAN WINTERS / GARY TANHAUSER

100

Stock-picking is

about the future; about recognizing a company's potential and taking a stake in it ahead of the crowd.

Out of 3,283 U.S. technology companies...

812 aren't trading so cheap as to be scary...

Of those 812, 503 aren't so small that their big gains are suspect...

Of those 503, 301 increased sales more than 25 percent during the brutal Q1 '01...

Of those 301, 188 increased 12-month sales more than 25 percent through Q1 '01...

And we skim the cream: THE TECH 100

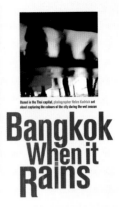

Photography

Based in the Thai capital, photographer Helen Kudrich set about capturing the colours of the city during the wet season

Bangkok When it Rains

■ 405

Publication Bloomberg Personal Finance
Art Director Frank Tagariello
Designer Frank Tagariello
Photo Editors Mary Shea, Carrie Guenther
Photographers Richard Misrach, Marilyn Conway, Owen Kanzler, Joel Sartore, Michael Lewis, Mary Ellen Mark
Publisher Bloomberg L.P.
Issue May 2001
Category Reportage: Story

■ 406

Publication Bloomberg Personal Finance
Art Director Frank Tagariello
Designer Frank Tagariello
Photo Editor Mary Shea
Photographers Dan Winters, Gary Tanhauser
Publisher Bloomberg L.P.
Issue October 2001
Category Photo Illustration: Story

■ 407

Publication Sawasdee
Creative Director John Boyer
Art Director Teresita Khaw
Designer Connie Chu
Photo Editor Jennifer Spencer
Photographer Helen Kudrich
Publisher Emphasis Media Ltd.
Issue November 2001
Category Reportage: Story

dream weavers
BRIGHT, BECALMED, OR PASTEL-PRETTY, BEDDING TO BEGUILE THE STYLISH SLEEPER

CHARMED CIRCLES
Selecting the right china pattern from the hundreds available can be overwhelming. To help in your search, we've narrowed the field to 40 of the finest. Whether you favor flowers, surrender to stripes, or go wild for whites, one of these styles is sure to be just your cup of tea.

drift off on a sensual sea of tranquility

tender is the night, reposing on a bed of roses

■ 408
Publication Bride's
Design Director Phyllis Cox
Art Directors Ann Marie Mennillo, Francesca Pacchini
Photo Editor Kristi Drago
Photographers Carin Riley, David Riley
Publisher Condé Nast Publications, Inc.
Issue August/September 2001
Category Still Life/Interiors: Story

■ 409
Publication Bride's
Design Director Phyllis Cox
Art Directors Ann Marie Mennillo, Francesca Pacchini
Photo Editor Kristi Drago
Photographer Carin Riley
Publisher Condé Nast Publications, Inc.
Issue February/March 2001
Category Still Life/Interiors: Story

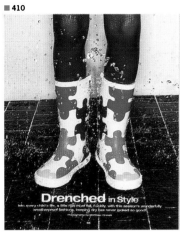

photography MERIT

■410
Publication Child
Creative Director Sabrina Weberstetter
Designer Sabrina Weberstetter
Photo Editor Kristen Schoonover
Photographer Matthew Hranek
Publisher Gruner & Jahr USA Publishing
Issue March 2001
Category Fashion/Beauty: Story

■411
Publication Child
Creative Director Sabrina Weberstetter
Designer Jennifer MacKenzie
Photo Editor Topaz Le Tourneau
Photographer Andrew McCaul
Publisher Gruner & Jahr USA Publishing
Issue December 2001/January 2002
Category Still Life/Interiors: Spread

■412
Publication National Geographic Adventure
Design Director Julie Curtis
Art Director Mike Bain
Designer Julie Curtis
Photo Editor Sabine Meyer
Photographer Chris Anderson
Publisher National Geographic Society
Issue September/October 2001
Category Reportage: Story
    A. Portraits: Spread

■413
Publication National Geographic Adventure
Design Director Julie Curtis
Art Director Mike Bain
Designer Julie Curtis
Photo Editors Sabine Meyer, Nell Hupman
Photographer Reza
Publisher National Geographic Society
Issue March 2001
Category Reportage: Spread

KILTS AND CASTLES
IT WAS FOUNDED BY THE VIKINGS, CALLED HOME BY ANDREW CARNEGIE, AND TURNED INTO HEAVEN ON EARTH FOR THE REST OF US. WELCOME TO SKIBO.
By Richard David Story   Photographs by Brian Doben

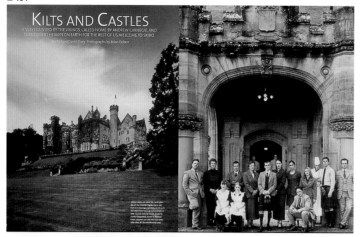

Like all great houses, Skibo
is at once very grand and *very* eccentric.

Grace land
It's everywhere you turn in Thailand, from the presentation of a plate of fruit to the aura of hotels, spas, restaurants: a natural flair for beauty, elegance, and refinement. PICO IYER considers the silken pleasures of a culture that has an uncanny ability to make itself attractive to the world

Photographs by
William Abranowicz

Even in one of
Asia's most
congested and
coughing cities,
you could
live in a teak
house on stilts,
surrounded by
the sounds and
smells of nature

LOCKER-ROOM CAMERAS, BLATANT BIRD FLIPPING, AND IN-YOUR-FACE ATTITUDE. IS THE XFL THE FUTURE   OF FOOTBALL? WRESTLING KINGPIN AND LEAGUE FOUNDER VINCE McMAHON CERTAINLY THINKS SO.

GENERATION X
PHOTOGRAPHS BY JEFF MERMELSTEIN
By Brian Farnham

■ 414

Publication Departures
Creative Director Bernard Scharf
Photo Editors Alice Albert, Scott Hall
Photographer Brian Doben
Publisher American Express Publishing Co.
Issue March/April 2001
Category Reportage: Story

■ 415

Publication Condé Nast Traveler
Design Director Robert Best
Photo Editor Kathleen Klech
Photographer William Abranowicz
Publisher Condé Nast Publications, Inc.
Issue March 2001
Category Reportage: Story

■ 416

Publication Details
Creative Director Dennis Freedman
Design Director Edward Leida
Art Director Rockwell Harwood
Photo Editors Alice Rose George, Amy Steigbigel, Jeannine Foeller
Photographer Jeff Mermelstein
Publisher Condé Nast Publications, Inc.
Issue January/February 2001
Category Reportage: Story

the awakening

by Brian Farnham

ening

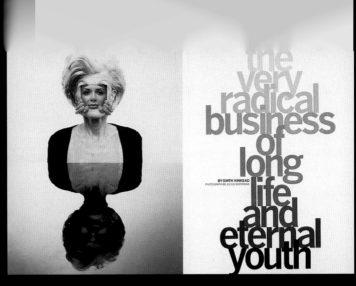

the very radical business of long life and eternal youth

BY GWEN KINKEAD
PHOTOGRAPHS BY JULIUS ROOYMANS

■ 420

DIRECTORY

TV CLASSICS, PAGE 128 • PROGRAM SCHEDULE, PAGE 126 • WHERE TO FIND IT, PAGE 120

PHOTOGRAPH BY ERIC PLASECKI

■ 418

ZEN PALATE

AN EATING TOUR OF JAPAN'S TIMELESS KYOTO, WHERE THE SPIRIT OF ZEN
BUDDHISM PERMEATES EVERYTHING FROM THE ARCHITECTURE TO THE FOOD.

■ 417
Publication Details
Creative Director Dennis Freedman
Design Director Edward Leida
Art Director Rockwell Harwood
Photo Editors Alice Rose George, Amy Steigbigel, Jeannine Foeller
Photographer Jake Chessum
Publisher Condé Nast Publications, Inc.
Issue December 2001
Category Portraits: Story

■ 418
Publication Food & Wine
Creative Director Stephen Scoble
Art Director Darcy Doyle
Photo Editor Fredrika Stjärne
Photographer Geoff Lung
Publisher American Express Publishing Co.
Issue January 2001
Category Reportage: Story

■ 419
Publication Worth
Design Director Deanna Lowe
Designer Dirk Barnett
Photo Editor Marianne Butler
Photographer Julius Rooymans
Publisher Worth Media
Issue February 2001
Category Photo Illustration: Single Page

■ 420
Publication This Old House
Creative Director Diana Haas
Designer Arianna Squeo
Photo Editor Anna Adesanya
Photographer Eric Plasecki
Publisher Time Inc.
Issue November 2001

After living well for a year on foods grown within 250 miles of his house, Gary Paul Nabhan sees a simple solution to the planet's environmental problems:

eat
locally
[Think globally]

BY GRETEL H. SCHUELLER • PHOTOGRAPHY BY JAMES SMOLKA

Kosmos

Adam Bartos's documentary photographs of the Russian space program as it slip slides away

Text by Svetlana Boym

Riding the Rails: Rockets used in the Russian space program are transported by train to the Baikonur cosmodrome in Kazakhstan. In preparation for the 1967 on August 13, 1998, a manned mission to the MIR space station, a Soyuz TM-28 two-stage booster rocket mounted on a special motor transporter (foreground) is pushed to a horizontal position by a diesel locomotive.

Where rocks sing, ants swim, and plants eat animals

Tree shark, saber-toothed fangs hang from the lid of the carnivorous plant Nepenthes bicalcarata, giving it a fearsome appearance. Tiny winged appendages that flank the stem serve as a laddered gateway leading unsuspecting insect prey to the mouth of the fluid-filled pitcher.

IF BSE DISEASE DOES COME TO THE UNITED STATES, IT WILL INEVITABLY WREAK HAVOC BECAUSE NEARLY EVERYTHING WE TOUCH OR TASTE HAS COW IN IT. A LESSON IN TRULY EFFICIENT RECYCLING

COWPARTS
BY VERLYN KLINKENBORG • PHOTOGRAPHY BY ANDREA MODICA

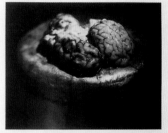

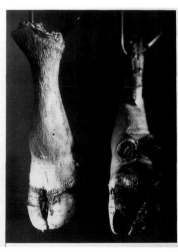

421
Publication Discover
Design Director Michael Mrak
Art Director John Seeger Gilman
Designer John Seeger Gilman
Photo Editor Maisie Todd
Photographer James Smolka
Publisher Disney Publishing Worldwide
Issue May 2001
Category Still Life/Interiors: Spread

422
Publication Discover
Design Director Michael Mrak
Art Director John Seeger Gilman
Designer Michael Mrak
Photo Editor Maisie Todd
Photographer Adam Bartos
Publisher Disney Publishing Worldwide
Issue October 2001
Category Reportage: Spread

423
Publication Discover
Design Director Michael Mrak
Art Director John Seeger Gilman
Designer John Seeger Gilman
Photo Editors Maisie Todd, Monica Bradley
Photographer Richard Barnes
Publisher Disney Publishing Worldwide
Issue October 2001
Category Reportage: Spread

424
Publication Discover
Design Director Michael Mrak
Art Director John Seeger Gilman
Designer John Seeger Gilman
Photo Editor Maisie Todd
Photographer Andrea Modica
Publisher Disney Publishing Worldwide
Issue August 2001
Category Still Life/Interiors: Story
   A. Spread

GOURMET ENTERTAINS

This Magic
MOMENT

PHOTOGRAPHS by ANNA WILLIAMS

GOURMET ENTERTAINING

at the artist's table
FEASTING WITH
THE MODERNISTS

Upon arriving at Picasso's, Marie Laurencin promptly fell into a tray of jam tarts.

GOURMET TRAVELS

In the Footsteps of Fortune

China's Wuyi Mountains
hold the secrets
of a wondrous tea that
changed the world—
then disappeared

By HENRY PATTERSON
PHOTOGRAPHS by MEREDITH HEUER

Like the limestone cliffs themselves, the narrow,
twisting terraces on which the tea bushes
perch might well have been excavated by spirits.

■ 425
Publication Gourmet
Art Director Diana LaGuardia
Designer Lauren Irwin
Photo Editor Helen Cannavale
Photographer Anna Williams
Publisher Condé Nast Publications Inc.
Issue July 2001
Category Still Life/Interiors: Story

■ 426
Publication Gourmet
Art Director Diana LaGuardia
Designer Lauren Irwin
Photo Editor Helen Cannavale
Photographer James Merrell
Publisher Condé Nast Publications Inc.
Issue March 2001
Category Still Life/Interiors: Story

■ 427
Publication Gourmet
Art Director Diana LaGuardia
Designer Flavia Schepmans
Photo Editor Helen Cannavale
Photographer Meredith Heuer
Publisher Condé Nast Publications, Inc.
Issue December 2001
Category Reportage: Story

photography MERIT

WE DREAM OF PREFABS...

Story by Jay Baldwin

...BUT WAKE UP IN WOODLAND

Woodland, CA: Silvercrest Western Homes manufactures three houses every day.

■ 428
Publication Dwell
Creative Director Jeanette Hodge Abbink
Designers Jeanette Hodge Abbink, Shawn Hazen
Photo Editor Maren Levinson
Photographer Dewey Nicks
Publisher Pixie Commuinications
Issue December 2001
Category Still Life/Interiors: Story

■ 429
Publication Dwell
Creative Director Jeanette Hodge Abbink
Designer Jeanette Hodge Abbink
Photo Editor Maren Levinson
Photographer Frank Schott
Publisher Pixie Commuinications
Issue April 2001
Category Still Life/Interiors: Story

■ 430
Publication Elle Decor
Art Director Florentino Pamintuan
Photo Editor Karen Gomes
Photographer Pieter Estersohn
Style Editor Anita Sarsidi
Publisher Hachette Filipacchi Media U.S.
Issue November 2001
Category Still Life/Interiors: Spread

plug in

White Magic

WRAP IT UP

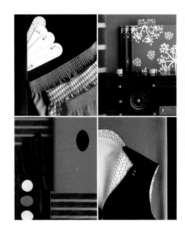

photography MERIT

■ 431
Publication Elle Decor
Art Director Florentino Pamintuan
Photo Editor Karen Gomes
Photographer Anthony Cotsifas
Style Editor Anita Sarsidi
Publisher Hachette Filipacchi Media U.S.
Issue November 2001
Category Still Life/Interiors: Story

■ 432
Publication Elle Decor
Art Director Florentino Pamintuan
Photo Editor Karen Gomes
Photographer William Abranowicz
Stylist Dara Caponigro
Publisher Hachette Filipacchi Media U.S.
Issue December 2001
Category Still Life/Interiors: Story

■ 433
Publication City
Creative Director Fabrice Frere
Art Director Adriana Jacoud
Photo Editor Piera Gelardi
Photographer Patricia Heal
Publisher City NY Publishing LLC
Issue November 2001
Category Still Life/Interiors: Story

■ 434
Publication Entertainment Weekly
Design Director Geraldine Hessler
Designer Jenny Chang
Photo Editor Michael Kochman
Photographer Peggy Sirota
Publisher Time Inc.
Issue April 20, 2001
Category Portraits: Spread

■ 435
Publication Entertainment Weekly
Design Director Geraldine Hessler
Designer Jennifer Procopio
Photo Editor Denise Sfraga
Photographer Nigel Parry
Publisher Time Inc.
Issue January 19, 2001
Category Portraits: Spread

■ 436
Publication Entertainment Weekly
Design Director Geraldine Hessler
Designer John Walker
Photo Editor Michele Romero
Photographer Barron Claiborne
Publisher Time Inc.
Issue June 29, 2001
Category Portraits: Single Page

■ 437
Publication Entertainment Weekly
Design Director Geraldine Hessler
Designer John Walker
Photo Editors Sarah Rozen, Michael Kochman
Photographer Robert Trachtenberg
Publisher Time Inc.
Issue October 5, 2001
Category Portraits: Single Page

■ 438
Publication Entertainment Weekly
Design Director Geraldine Hessler
Designer John Walker
Photo Editor Denise Sfraga
Photographer Robert Maxwell
Publisher Time Inc.
Issue December 21, 2001
Category Portraits: Single Page

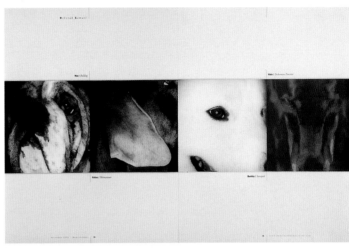

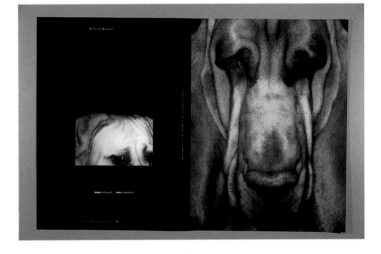

■ 439
Publication Entertainment Weekly
Design Director Geraldine Hessler
Designer John Walker
Photo Editor Denise Sfraga
Photographer Norman Jean Roy
Publisher Time Inc.
Issue December 21, 2001
Category Portraits: Spread

■ 440
Publication Forbes
Design Director Robert Mansfield
Designer Anton Klusener
Photo Editor Meredith Nicholson
Photographer Gregory Heisler
Publisher Forbes Inc.
Issue March 5, 2001
Category Portraits: Spread

■ 441
Publication Forbes
Design Director Robert Mansfield
Art Director Anton Klusener
Photo Editor Susan Mettler
Photographer Nigel Parry
Publisher Forbes Inc.
Issue July 23, 2001
Category Portraits: Spread

■ 442
Publication Hemispheres
Art Directors Jaimey Easler, Jody Mustain
Designer Jody Mustain
Photographer Deborah Samuals
Publisher Pace Communications
Client United Airlines
Issue October 2001
Category Fashion/Beauty: Story

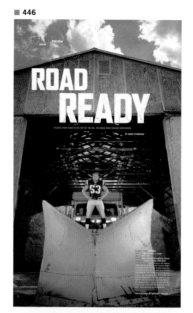

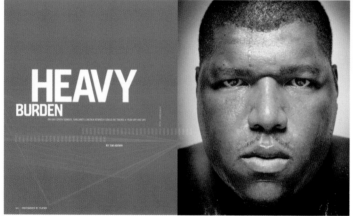

Publication ESPN
Art Director Peter Yates
Designer Reyes Melendez
Photo Editors Nik Kleinberg, Nancy Weisman
Photographer Nigel Parry
Publisher ESPN, Inc.
Issue April 30, 2001
Category Portraits: Spread

Publication ESPN
Art Director Peter Yates
Designer Jeanine Melnick
Photo Editors Nik Kleinberg, Nancy Weisman
Photographer Michael O'Brien
Publisher ESPN, Inc.
Issue October 15, 2001
Category Portraits: Spread

Publication ESPN
Art Director Peter Yates
Designer Henry Lee
Photo Editor Nik Kleinberg
Photographer Platon
Publisher ESPN, Inc.
Issue October 29, 2001
Category Portraits: Spread/Single

Publication ESPN
Art Director Peter Yates
Designer Henry Lee
Photo Editor Nik Kleinberg
Photographer Gregory Heisler
Publisher ESPN, Inc.
Issue September 3, 2001
Category Portraits: Story

Publication ESPN
Art Director Peter Yates
Designer Henry Lee
Photo Editor Nik Kleinberg
Photographers Tim Bauer, Tim Mantaoni,
Todd Korol, Mike Powell, Christian Lantry,
Gregory Heisler, Sarah Friedman,
Ralph Mecke, Matt Jones, Warwick Saint,
Kenneth Willardt, John Gip, Sandro
Publisher ESPN, Inc.
Issue September 24, 2001
Category Portraits: Story

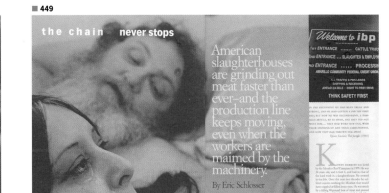

the chain   never stops

American slaughterhouses are grinding out meat faster than ever—and the production line keeps moving, even when the workers are maimed by the machinery.

By Eric Schlosser

Photographs by
Eugene Richards

Meatpacking is the nation's most dangerous occupation. It has the highest rate of serious injury— five times the national average.

The Method and the Madness

Fleeing a brutal civil war thousands of Sierra Leoneans sought haven in neighboring Guinea during the 1990s. Now the violence has followed them there—and sparked the world's worst refugee crisis.

Photographs by Robert Knoth

These refugees are not victims of ethnic hatred or of ideological war, but rather of rampant thievery in a mineral-rich region of West Africa

Publication Mother Jones
Design Director Jane Palecek
Art Director Amy Shroads
Photo Editor Sarah Kehoe
Photographer Dod Miller
Publisher Foundation for
National Progress
Issue November/December 2001
Category Portraits: Spread

Publication Mother Jones
Design Director Jane Palecek
Photo Editor Sarah Kehoe
Photographer Eugene Richards
Publisher Foundation for National Progress
Issue July/August 2001
Category Reportage: Story

Publication Mother Jones
Design Director Jane Palecek
Photo Editor Sarah Kehoe
Photographer Robert Knoth
Publisher Foundation for National Progress
Issue July/August 2001
Category Reportage: Story

photography MERIT

give us this day our global bread

Leading Edge

DON'T JUST LISTEN
CONNECT

Agenda Items

The Killer App—Bar None

Flash of Insight

How Sig-nificant

Mighty Mice

Over the Hump

Good As Gold

451
Publication Fast Company
Design Director Patrick Mitchell
Designer Patrick Mitchell
Photo Editor Alicia Jylkka
Photographer Ethan Hill
Publisher Gruner & Jahr USA Publishing
Issue March 2001
Category Reportage: Story

452
Publication Fast Company
Design Director Patrick Mitchell
Designer Kristin Fitzpatrick
Photo Editor Alicia Jylkka
Photographer Hugh Kretschmer
Publisher Gruner & Jahr USA Publishing
Issue August 2001
Category Photo Illustration Spread

453
Publication Fast Company
Design Director Patrick Mitchell
Designer Emily Crawford
Photo Editor Alicia Jylkka
Photographer Fredrik Brodén
Publisher Gruner & Jahr USA Publishing
Issue June 2001
Category Photo Illustration: Story

■ 454
Publication Fast Company
Design Director Patrick Mitchell
Designer Emily Crawford
Photo Editor Alicia Jylkka
Photographer Micheal McLaughlin
Publisher Gruner & Jahr USA Publishing
Issue January 2001
Category Portraits: Story

■ 455
Publication Fast Company
Design Director Patrick Mitchell
Designer Kristin Fitzpatrick
Photo Editor Alicia Jylkka
Photographer Micheal McLaughlin
Publisher Gruner & Jahr USA Publishing
Issue February 2001
Category Reportage: Story
    A. Spread

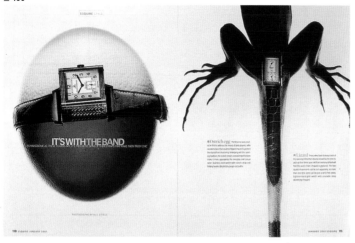

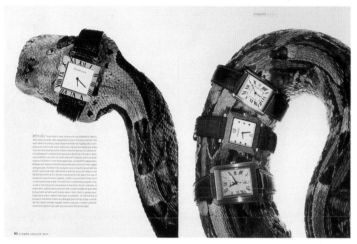

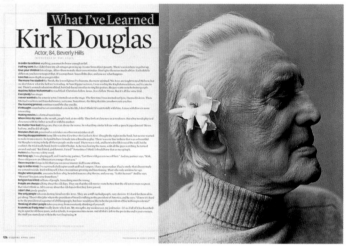

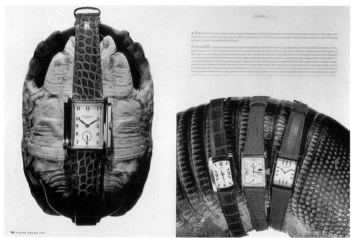

■ 456

Publication Esquire
Design Director John Korpics
Designer Chris Mueller
Photo Editor Fiona McDonagh
Photographer Bill Steele
Publisher The Hearst Corporation-Magazines Division
Issue January 2001
Category Still Life/Interiors: Story

■ 457

Publication Esquire
Design Director John Korpics
Photo Editor Fiona McDonagh
Photographer Michael Lewis
Publisher The Hearst Corporation-Magazines Division
Issue February 2001
Category Portraits: Spread

■ 458

Publication Esquire
Design Director John Korpics
Designer Kim Forsberg
Photo Editor Fiona McDonagh
Photographer Peggy Sirota
Publisher The Hearst Corporation-Magazines Division
Issue April 2001
Category Portraits: Spread

■ 459

Publication Esquire
Design Director John Korpics
Photo Editor Nancy Jo Iacoi
Photographer Dan Winters
Publisher The Hearst Corporation-Magazines Division
Issue May 2001
Category Portraits: Spread

What I've Learned
Roseanne
Entertainer, 48, Lake Arrowhead, California

6 superlative suits

CONFIDENTIAL TO REGIS IN NEW YORK: Never mind the monochrome. This spring, the best-dressed men (and apparently plants) want vibrant shirts and ties in patterns that pop. PHOTOGRAPHS BY GEOF KERN

esquire style

Handcrafted Elegance

Subtle Sophistication

tenMEN

CHARLTON HESTON

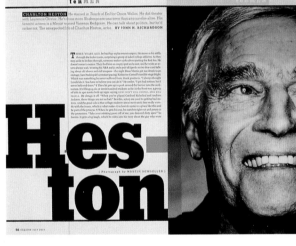

Hes-ton

Cool and Crisp

First-Class Style

■ 460
Publication Esquire
Design Director John Korpics
Designer Kim Forsberg
Photo Editor Fiona McDonagh
Photographer Peggy Sirota
Publisher The Hearst Corporation-Magazines Division
Issue March 2001
Category Portraits: Spread

■ 461
Publication Esquire
Design Director John Korpics
Art Director Hannah McCaughey
Photo Editor Nancy Jo Iacoi
Photographer Geof Kern
Publisher The Hearst Corporation-Magazines Division
Issue May 2001
Category Fashion/Beauty: Spread

■ 462
Publication Esquire
Design Director John Korpics
Photo Editor Fiona McDonagh
Photographer Martin Schoeller
Publisher The Hearst Corporation-Magazines Division
Issue July 2001
Category Portraits: Spread

■ 463
Publication Esquire
Design Director John Korpics
Art Director Hannah McCaughey
Photo Editor Fiona McDonagh
Photographer James Wojcik
Publisher The Hearst Corporation-Magazines Division
Issue March 2001
Category Still Life/Interiors: Story

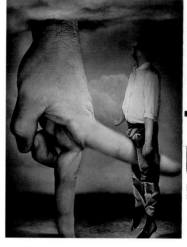

■ 464
Publication Esquire
Design Director John Korpics
Photo Editors Nancy Jo Iacoi, Catriona NiAolain
Photographer Deborah Turbeville
Publisher The Hearst Corporation-Magazines Division
Issue September 2001
Category Fashion/Beauty: Story

■ 465
Publication Esquire
Design Director John Korpics
Photo Editor Nancy Jo Iacoi
Photographer Mark Abrahams
Publisher The Hearst Corporation-Magazines Division
Issue October 2001
Category Portraits: Spread

■ 466
Publication Esquire
Design Director John Korpics
Photographer Matt Mahurin
Publisher The Hearst Corporation-Magazines Division
Issue October 2001
Category Photo Illustration: Spread

■ 467
Publication Esquire
Design Director John Korpics
Photographer Patricia McDonough
Publisher The Hearst Corporation-Magazines Division
Issue November 2001
Category Reportage: Spread

■ 468
Publication Gentlemen's Quarterly
Design Director Arem Duplessis
Art Director Paul Martinez
Designer Arem Duplessis
Photo Editor Jennifer Crandall
Photographers Mary Ellen Mark, James Ellroy
Publisher Condé Nast Publications, Inc.
Issue November 2001
Category Portraits: Spread

HAVE YOU SEEN THIS MAN?

PHILIP SEYMOUR HOFFMAN HAS BECOME THE MOST UBIQUITOUS MAN IN MOVIES IN THE PAST FEW YEARS. HE HAS STOLEN VIRTUALLY EVERY FILM HE HAS APPEARED IN FROM MAGNOLIA TO THE TALENTED MR. RIPLEY TO ALMOST FAMOUS. NOW, AS THE ACTOR STEPS CENTER STAGE IN THE POLITICAL DOCUMENTARY LAST PARTY 2000, DAVID KAMP REVEALS JUST WHO HE IS

THE RETURN OF THE **GUNSLINGER**

DRINKING DAYS

ALCOHOL MIGHT BE GOOD FOR THE FLOWER BEDS OF OXFORD, BUT FOR THE AUTHOR IT HAD A DIFFERENT EFFECT. A MEMOIR—IN PIECES BY WALTER KIRN

ADDICTION MEMOIRS CLIMAX WITH THE DRINKER'S LOW POINT. WHEN ONLY GOD CAN HELP HIM. I WOKE UP IN AN HONEST-TO-GOD ALLEY. AWARE THAT IF ONE VALIUM AND ONE BEER COULD SEND ME OFF TO A PSYCHEDELIC SEAWORLD, MY LIVER MUST BE SHOT.

■ 470
Publication Gentlemen's Quarterly
Design Director Arem Duplessis
Art Director Paul Martinez
Designer Mathew Lenning
Photo Editor Jennifer Crandall
Photographer Hugh Kretschmer
Publisher Condé Nast Publications, Inc.
Issue September 2001
Category Still Life/Interiors: Story

■ 471
Publication Gentlemen's Quarterly
Design Director Arem Duplessis
Art Director Paul Martinez
Designer Arem Duplessis
Photo Editor Jennifer Crandall
Photographer Peggy Sirota
Publisher Condé Nast Publications, Inc.
Issue August 2001
Category Fashion/Beauty: Spread

■ 472
Publication Gentlemen's Quarterly
Design Director Arem Duplessis
Art Director Paul Martinez
Designer Arem Duplessis
Photo Editor Jennifer Crandall
Photographer Anton Corbijn
Publisher Condé Nast Publications, Inc.
Issue November 2001
Category Portraits: Spread

■ 469
Publication Gentlemen's Quarterly
Design Director Arem Duplessis
Art Director Paul Martinez
Designer Arem Duplessis
Photo Editor Jennifer Crandall
Photographer Michael Thompson
Publisher Condé Nast Publications, Inc.
Issue January 2001
Category Portraits: Spread

photography MERIT

A
MIXED
MARRIAGE

Interior designer Roberto Peregalli joins
18th-century palazzo style with Oriental
art for antiques dealer Emil Mirzakhanian

WRIGHT AGAIN

HIGH NOTES

By using bold color as a unifying theme, Paris
interior designers Michael Coorengel and
Jean-Pierre Calvagrac can let their taste take flight

■ 473

Publication House and Garden
Art Director Anthony Jazzar
Designer Trent Farmer
Photo Editor Lucy Gilmour
Photographer François Halard
Publisher Condé Nast Publications, Inc.
Issue January 2001
Category Still Life/Interiors: Story

■ 474

Publication House and Garden
Art Director Anthony Jazzar
Designer Robert O'Connell
Photo Editor Lucy Gilmour
Photographer Pierre Paradis
Publisher Condé Nast Publications, Inc.
Issue April 2001
Category Still Life/Interiors: Story

■ 475

Publication House and Garden
Art Director Anthony Jazzar
Designer Trent Farmer
Photo Editor Lucy Gilmour
Photographer François Dischinger
Publisher Condé Nast Publications, Inc.
Issue September 2001
Category Still Life/Interiors: Story

BACK IN BLACK

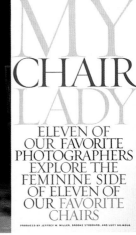

MY CHAIR LADY

ELEVEN OF OUR FAVORITE PHOTOGRAPHERS EXPLORE THE FEMININE SIDE OF ELEVEN OF OUR FAVORITE CHAIRS

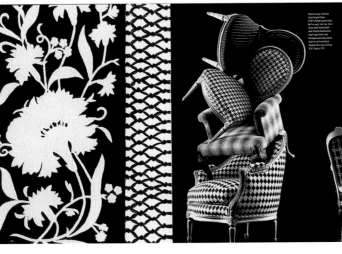

■ 476

Publication House and Garden
Art Director Anthony Jazzar
Designer Anthony Jazzar
Photo Editor Lucy Gilmour
Photographer Ilan Rubin
Publisher Condé Nast Publications, Inc.
Issue April 2001
Category Still Life/Interiors: Story

■ 477

Publication House and Garden
Art Director Anthony Jazzar
Designer Anthony Jazzar
Photo Editor Lucy Gilmour
Photographers Josef Astor, José Picayo, Robert Polidori, Jessica Craig-Martin, Hugh Hales-Tooke, François Halard, Robin Broadbent, James Waddell, Mitch Epstein, Melanie Acevedo, Peter Brown
Publisher Condé Nast Publications, Inc.
Issue November 2001
Category Still Life/Interiors: Story

■ 478

■ 480

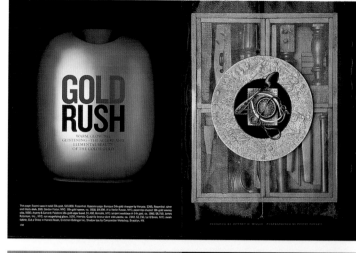

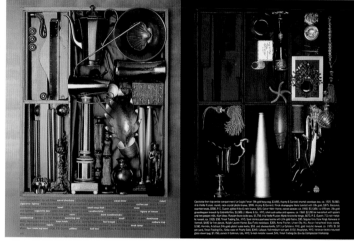

■ 479

■ 478

Publication House and Garden
Art Director Anthony Jazzar
Designers Trent Farmer, Robert O'Connell
Photo Editor Lucy Gilmour
Photographer Carlton Davis
Publisher Condé Nast Publications, Inc.
Issue September 2001
Category Still Life/Interiors: Story

■ 479

Publication House and Garden
Art Director Anthony Jazzar
Designer Paul Carlos
Photo Editor Lucy Gilmour
Photographer Raymond Meier
Publisher Condé Nast Publications, Inc.
Issue October 2001
Category Still Life/Interiors: Story

■ 480

Publication House and Garden
Art Director Anthony Jazzar
Designer Jennifer Madara
Photo Editor Lucy Gilmour
Photographer Pierre Paradis
Publisher Condé Nast Publications, Inc.
Issue December 2001
Category Still Life/Interiors: Story

■ 481

Publication Bon Appétit
Creative Director Campion Primm
Art Director Giuliana Schwab
Photo Editor Elizabeth Mathews
Photographer Pascal Andre
Publisher Condé Nast Publications, Inc.
Issue March 2001
Category Still Life/Interiors: Single Page

■ 481

TABLE & HOME

FLATWARE THAT'S A CUT ABOVE

Left to right: Nancy Calhoun's "Satin Nine" pattern; Paola Navone's "Paloma" stainless steel; "Montpellier" flatware from Pierre Deux; Tracy Porter's "Voyager's Treasure" with faux "Normandy Pewter" from Zrike, and (on top) Alain Saint Joanis's "Oregon" with wooden handle. Below, a "Bistro" in boysenberry from Sferra Bros.

■ 482

Features April 2001

■ 483

The New York Times

March 18, 2001 $1.25

Book Review

Klansmen In the Cellar

In 'Carry Me Home,' Diane McWhorter untangles the web that linked politics, corporate power, law enforcement, the Klan and her family in Birmingham's summer of 1963.
Reviewed by David K. Shipler **8**

Richard Eder on 'Border Crossing,' Pat Barker's new novel. **10**

John Rothchild reviews 'The Mountains of My Life,' Walter Bonatti's essays on extreme climbing. **12**

■ 484

Hair news is good news. The best looks for fall are fresh cuts that require minimal styling—the closest thing to wash-and-go hair that a woman could wish for

▶ HAIR ◀

keep it simple

What makes hair low maintenance? Getting a cut—and a styling routine—that works with your face shape, your hair type and your life. "When all three come together, that's when a look becomes easy," says hair pro Mark Garrison, who created the set seen on the following pages. There's something here for every face shape and hair type. And lifestyle. We assume you're busy and that spending hours on your hair is neither a priority nor a possibility. Still, simple to care for can be stunning to look at—we'll show you how to get it.

BY MELISSA GREEN
PHOTOGRAPHED BY TROY WORD

■ 485

J eff bridges wants to be a tree.

The actor talks about his birth, his dreams, Greek mythology...whatever.

By James Kaplan
Photographs by Peggy Sirota

■ 486

PHOTOGRAPHED BY MATTHEW SALACUSE

■ 487

Janie Taylor
New York City Ballet

Tiny dancer It's been the rest of New York discovered what the ballet world has been buzzing about since 1998: 20-year-old Janie Taylor. "Rarely have I seen anyone with such a natural gift to cover space with total abandon. She's completely fearless," says Sean Lavery, a choreographer and ballet master of NYSB. "She's really a dancer with incredible energy behind every movement she makes. What's so funny is she's petite and very fair and very blonde, and all of a sudden this powerhouse comes out of this little thing that you just don't expect. It's quite extraordinary and exciting."

Flying solo Taylor was promoted to soloist last February and begins rehearsals for *The Nutcracker* in October—not that she needs much rehearsing; she's been performing in it since she was a child in Houston. "I started with little kid parts," she recalls. "Then I was Dewdrop, then Marzipan. I guess I'm working my way through the entire ballet." (*Performances of The Nutcracker begin November 23. For tickets, call 212-870-5570.*)

PHOTOGRAPHED BY DIEGO UCHITEL

■ 482

Publication Metropolis
Art Director Criswell Lappin
Photographer Kristine Larsen
Publisher Bellerophon Publications
Issue April 2001
Category Portraits: Single Page

■ 483

Publication The New York Times Book Review
Art Director Steven Heller
Illustrator Mirko Ilíc
Studio Mirko Ilíc Corp.
Publisher The New York Times
Issue March 18, 2001
Category Photo Illustration: Single Page

■ 484

Publication InStyle
Design Director Paul Roelofs
Designer Rob Hewitt
Photo Editors Carla Popenfus, Rosaliz Jimenez
Photographer Troy Word
Publisher Time Inc.
Issue Fall 2001
Category Fashion/Beauty: Single Page

■ 485

Publication My Generation
Art Director Jennifer Gilman
Designer Jennifer Gilman
Photo Editor Jessica De Witt
Photographer Peggy Sirota
Publisher AARP
Issue September/October 2001
Category Portraits: Spread

■ 486

Publication New York Magazine
Design Director Michael Picón
Photo Editor Chris Dougherty
Photographer Mathew Salacuse
Publisher Primedia Magazines Inc.
Issue September 10, 2001
Category Portraits: Single Page

■ 487

Publication New York Magazine
Design Director Michael Picón
Photo Editor Chris Dougherty
Photographer Diego Uchitel
Publisher Primedia Magazines Inc.
Issue September 10, 2001
Category Portraits: Single Page

2001: A Face Odyssey
PHOTOGRAPHED BY FRANK W. OCKENFELS 3

The story of a city—its happiness, its creativity, its passion, its drama, its pain—is written in its faces. And on the following pages is the New York epic—in 54 portraits.

the cheese of meaux

"Walking dogs is a good way to support my dancing. But it's hard to consider this work—I love dogs."

490

wild for mushrooms

Dried mushrooms make magic—not the kind that tainted people on in the '70s but the kind that transforms winter foods, giving them mystery and depth of flavor. In the west, the French, Italians, Central Europeans, and Russians have used their treasured and costly morsels to boost their cooking. The most esteemed mushrooms in Europe are morels—black, sponge-like ovals with intense flavor—and dolcino cèpes, known in one place or another as porcini, cèpes, and a dozen more regional names. In Asia, the Chinese and Japanese are the foremost epicures of dried mushrooms, especially shiitake and tree ears. Dried chanterelles and oyster mushrooms have recently been added to the variety available at the market. Don't be put off by their light weight and small size. Reconstituted, they swell, and their soaking liquid is an asset in soups, stocks, and sauces.

BY BARBARA KAFKA. PHOTOGRAPHY BY MINH + WASS

"I like writing tunes, and I like performing. All the rest is what they pay you for."

"My dream job has always been to be a star on Broadway. If I didn't have music in my life, I wouldn't be where I am today."

■ 488
Publication New York Magazine
Design Director Michael Picón
Photo Editor Chris Dougherty
Photographer Frank W. Ockenfels 3
Publisher Primedia Magazines Inc.
Issue January 8, 2001
Category Portraits: Story

■ 489
Publication Wegmans Menu
Creative Director Emma Ross
Art Director Wendy Scofield
Designer Wendy Scofield
Photographer Johnathan Gregson

■ 490
Publication Williams-Sonoma Taste
Creative Director Emma Ross
Designer Emma Ross
Photo Editor Lexi Coffee
Photographer Minh + Wass

■ 491

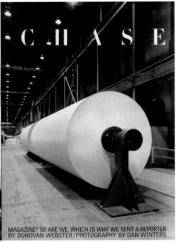

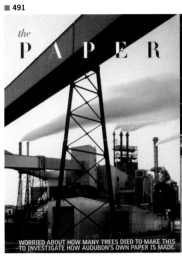

the PAPERCHASE

WORRIED ABOUT HOW MANY TREES DIED TO MAKE THIS —TO INVESTIGATE HOW AUDUBON'S OWN PAPER IS MADE.

MAGAZINE? SO ARE WE. WHICH IS WHY WE SENT A REPORTER BY DONOVAN WEBSTER/PHOTOGRAPHY BY DAN WINTERS

■ 493

Recapturing Eden

> PHOTO ESSAY

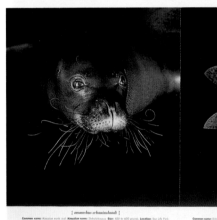

■ 492

ten

ON ALL SIDES, PAIRS OF BOOBIES QUACKED AND WHISTLED AND COYLY

DISPLAYED ROBIN'S-EGG FEET, OBLIVIOUS TO OUR EXISTENCE.

■ 494

> CONSERVATION

THE NEW ZOO

by rene s. ebersole
photography by dan winters

Beneath an umbrella of leaves and branches, wildlife biologist Omari Ilambu starts down a path through the heart of an African rainforest.

■ 491

Publication Audubon
Design Director Kevin Fisher
Designer Isabel DeSousa
Photo Editor Kim Hubbard
Photographer Dan Winters
Publisher National Audubon Society
Issue February 2001
Category Reportage: Story

■ 492

Publication Audubon
Design Director Kevin Fisher
Designer Isabel DeSousa
Photo Editor Kim Hubbard
Photographer John Huba
Publisher National Audubon Society
Issue March/April 2001
Category Reportage: Spread

■ 493

Publication Audubon
Design Director Kevin Fisher
Designer Isabel DeSousa
Photo Editor Kim Hubbard
Photographers David Liittschwager, Susan Middleton
Publisher National Audubon Society
Issue November 2001
Category Reportage: Story

■ 494

Publication Audubon
Design Director Kevin Fisher
Designer Isabel DeSousa
Photo Editor Kim Hubbard
Photographer Dan Winters
Publisher National Audubon Society
Issue November 2001
Category Reportage: Story

Just because you like to dress up in uniform doesn't mean you have to follow these real-life military rules.

PHOTOGRAPHY BY JOHN SCARISBRICK

What's wrong with a little self-restraint?

■ 495

Publication Jane
Creative Director Johan Svensson
Designers Brant Louck, Denise See
Photo Editor Jennifer Miller
Photographer John Scarisbrick
Publisher Fairchild Publications
Issue January/February 2001
Category Fashion/Beauty: Story

■ 496

Publication Jane
Creative Director Johan Svensson
Designers Brant Louck, Denise See
Photo Editor Jennifer Miller
Photographer Kelly Klein
Publisher Fairchild Publications
Issue March 2001
Category Fashion/Beauty: Story

■ 497
Publication Jane
Creative Director Johan Svensson
Designers Brant Louck, Denise See
Photo Editor Jennifer Miller
Photographer Christophe Rihet
Publisher Fairchild Publications
Issue March 2001
Category Fashion/Beauty: Story

■ 498
Publication Jane
Creative Director Johan Svensson
Designers Brant Louck, Denise See
Photo Editor Jennifer Miller
Photographer Perry Ogden
Publisher Fairchild Publications
Issue May 2001
Category Fashion/Beauty: Story

photography MERIT

We're feeling hot

You will, too

PHOTOGRAPHY BY FREDERIK LIEBERATH, MELODIE MCDANIEL, DAVID SLIJPER

it's a mistake not to drill there?

PHOTOGRAPHY BY STEFAN RUIZ

Random North Slope scenery (above) and around Prudhoe Bay oil facilities (right). Take your pick.

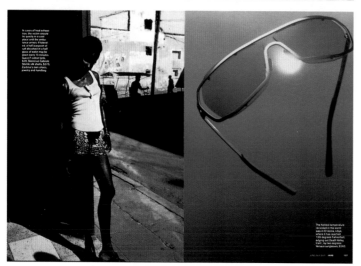

■ 499
Publication Jane
Creative Director Johan Svensson
Designers Brant Louck, Denise See
Photo Editor Jennifer Miller
Photographers Frederik Lieberath, Melodie McDaniel, David Slijper
Publisher Fairchild Publications
Issue June/July 2001
Category Fashion/Beauty: Story

■ 500
Publication Jane
Creative Director Johan Svensson
Designers Brant Louck, Denise See
Photo Editor Jennifer Miller
Photographer Stefan Ruiz
Publisher Fairchild Publications
Issue October 2001
Category Reportage: Story

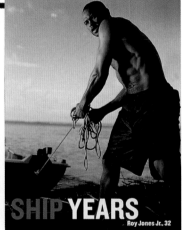

photography MERIT

■ 501

Publication Maximum Golf
Art Director Edward Levine
Designers Edward Levine, Pino Impastato, Mark Shaw
Photo Editor Tyler Pappas
Photographer Michael Grecco
Publisher News America
Issue June 2001
Category Portraits: Spread

■ 502

Publication Maximum Golf
Art Director Edward Levine
Designer Edward Levine
Photo Editor Bruce Perez
Photographer Don Flood
Publisher News America
Issue June 2001
Category Fashion/Beauty: Spread

■ 503

Publication Men's Health
Art Director George Karabotsos
Designer George Karabotsos
Photo Editor Maxine Arthur
Photographer Kwaku Alston
Publisher Rodale Inc.
Issue March 2001
Category Portraits: Spread

■ 504

Publication Martha Stewart Weddings
Art Director Kristin Rees
Photo Editor Jodi Nakatsuka
Photographer Melanie Maganias Nashan
Publisher Martha Stewart Living Omnimedia
Issue Winter 2001
Category Reportage: Spread

■ 505

Publication Martha Stewart Baby
Creative Director Gael Towey
Art Director Deb Bishop
Designer Deb Bishop
Photo Editor Jodi Nakatsuka
Photographer Frank Heckers
Stylist Katie Hatch
Publisher Martha Stewart Living Omnimedia
Issues Spring 2001, Fall 2001
Category Still Life/Interiors: Spread

COLD

SNOWY PEAR POPS

PB & J POPS

DESERT ISLAND POPS

A

ever felt this way?

making a ball

making beads

■ 506

Publication Martha Stewart Baby
Creative Director Gael Towey
Art Director Deb Bishop
Designer Deb Bishop
Photo Editor Jodi Nakatsuka
Photographer Gentl + Hyers
Stylist Jodi Levine
Publisher Martha Stewart Living Omnimedia
Issue Fall 2001
Category Still Life/Interiors: Story

■ 507

Publication Martha Stewart Kids
Creative Director Gael Towey
Art Director Deb Bishop
Designer Jennifer Wagner
Photo Editor Jodi Nakatsuka
Photographer Stephen Lewis
Stylist Stephana Bottom
Publisher Martha Stewart Living Omnimedia
Issue Summer/Fall 2001
Category Still Life/Interiors: Story

SCULPTING

S
N
O
W

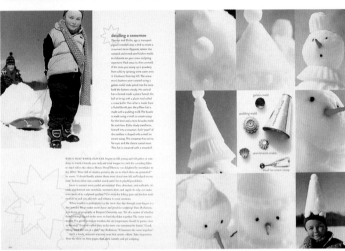

Good bugs, bad bugs

■ 508

Publication Martha Stewart Kids
Creative Director Gael Towey
Art Director Deb Bishop
Designer Jennifer Wagner
Photo Editor Jodi Nakatsuka
Photographer Gentl + Hyers
Stylist Jodi Levine
Publisher Martha Stewart Living Omnimedia
Issue Holiday 2001
Category Still Life/Interiors: Story
    A. Spread

■
509

Publication Martha Stewart Kids
Creative Director Gael Towey
Art Director Deb Bishop
Designer Jennifer Wagner
Photo Editor Jodi Nakatsuka
Photographer Philip Newton
Stylist Laura Normandin
Publisher Martha Stewart Living Omnimedia
Issue Holiday 2001
Category Still Life/Interiors: Story

■ 510

Publication Martha Stewart Living
Design Director Barbara de Wilde
Art Director James Dunlinson
Designer James Dunlinson
Photo Editor Mary Dail
Photographer Gentl + Hyers
Stylists Ayesha Patel, Bill Shank
Publisher Martha Stewart Living Omnimedia
Issue June 2001
Category Still Life/Interiors: Story

■ 511

Publication Martha Stewart Living
Design Director Barbara de Wilde
Art Director Claudia Bruno
Photo Editor Heidi Posner
Photographer Victor Schrager
Stylists Bill Shank, Joelle Hoverson
Publisher Martha Stewart Living Omnimedia
Issue October 2001
Category Still Life/Interiors: Spread

■ 512

■ 515

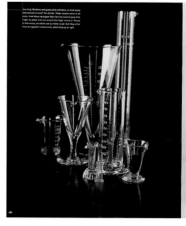

■ 513

■ 514

■ 516

■ 512
Publication Martha Stewart Living
Design Director Barbara de Wilde
Art Director Susan Spungen
Designer Jill Groeber
Photo Editor Mary Dail
Photographer Maria Robledo
Publisher Martha Stewart Living Omnimedia
Issue February 2001
Category Still Life/Interiors: Spread

■ 513
Publication Martha Stewart Living
Design Director Barbara de Wilde
Art Director Alexa Mulvihill
Designers Alexa Mulvihill, Fritz Karch
Photographer Maria Robledo
Stylists Fritz Karch, Brian Harter Andriola
Publisher Martha Stewart Living Omnimedia
Issue October 2001
Category Still Life/Interiors: Spread

■ 514
Publication Martha Stewart Living
Design Director Barbara de Wilde
Art Director James Dunlinson
Designer James Dunlinson
Photo Editor Mary Dail
Photographer Maria Robledo
Stylists Ayesha Patel, Frances Boswell
Publisher Martha Stewart Living Omnimedia
Issue May 2001
Category Still Life/Interiors: Spread

■ 515
Publication Martha Stewart Living
Design Director Barbara de Wilde
Art Director James Dunlinson
Designer James Dunlinson
Photographer Christopher Baker
Stylists Fritz Karch, Brian Harter Andriola
Publisher Martha Stewart Living Omnimedia
Issue May 2001
Category Still Life/Interiors: Story

■ 516
Publication Homestyle
Creative Director Philip Bratter
Designers Jorge Colombo, Philip Bratter
Photo Editor John Van Wattum
Photographer Aaron Hom
Publisher Gruner & Jahr USA Publishing
Issue June 2001
Category Still Life/Interiors: Spread

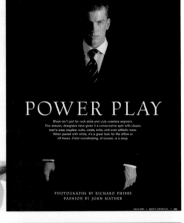

POWER PLAY

Black isn't just for rock stars and club crawlers anymore. This season, designers have given it a conservative spin with classic men's-wear staples: suits, coats, knits, and even athletic wear. When paired with white, it's a great look for the office or off hours. Color coordinating, of course, is a snap.

PHOTOGRAPHS BY RICHARD PHIBBS
FASHION BY JOHN MATHER

The High Way

BY JIM LEWIS

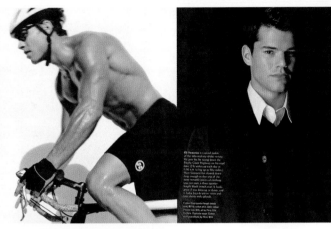

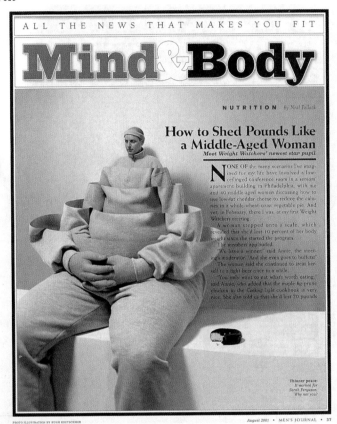

ALL THE NEWS THAT MAKES YOU FIT

Mind & Body

NUTRITION By Neal Pollack

How to Shed Pounds Like a Middle-Aged Woman
Meet Weight Watchers' newest star pupil

NONE OF the many scenarios I've imagined for my life have involved a low-ceilinged conference room in a seniors' apartment building in Philadelphia, with me and 40 middle-aged women discussing how to use low-fat cheddar cheese to reduce the calories in a whole-wheat-crust vegetable pie. And yet, in February, there I was, at my first Weight Watchers meeting.

A woman stepped onto a scale, which revealed that she'd lost 10 percent of her body weight since she started the program. The members applauded.

"We have a winner!" said Annie, the meeting's moderator. "And she even goes to buffets!"

The woman said she continued to treat herself to a light beer once in a while.

"You only want to eat what's worth eating," said Annie, who added that the maple-fig-prune chicken in the Cooking Light cookbook is very nice. She also told us that she'd lost 70 pounds

Thinner peace: It worked for Sarah Ferguson. Why not you?

PHOTO ILLUSTRATION BY HUGH KRETSCHMER

August 2001 • MEN'S JOURNAL • 37

■ 517

Publication Men's Journal
Art Director Michael Lawton
Designer Michael Lawton
Photo Editor John Mather
Photographer Richard Phibbs
Publisher Wenner Media LLC
Issue March 2001
Category Fashion/Beauty: Story

■ 518

Publication Men's Journal
Art Director Michael Lawton
Designer Keith Campbell
Photo Editor Casey Tierney
Photographer Rob Howard
Publisher Wenner Media LLC
Issue July 2001
Category Reportage: Spread

■ 519

Publication Men's Journal
Art Director Michael Lawton
Designer Michael Lawton
Photographer Hugh Kretschmer
Publisher Wenner Media LLC
Issue August 2001
Category Photo Illustration: Single Page

photography MERIT

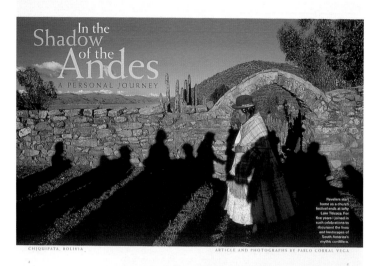

In the
Shadow
of the
Andes
A PERSONAL JOURNEY

Revelers start
home as a church
festival ends at lofty
Lake Titicaca. For
five years I joined in
such celebrations to
document the lives
and landscapes of
South America's
mythic cordillera.

CHIQUIPATA, BOLIVIA.   ARTICLE AND PHOTOGRAPHS BY PABLO CORRAL VEGA

Last Stand for Southern Africa's First People

Born into poverty, a Bushman herder on a Namibian farm has little to
show for his labors beyond the clothes he wears. Reduced to servitude in
the land that was once their ancestors' domain, southern Africa's 85,000
indigenous Bushmen fight to win back a foothold along with their pride.

Bushmen

Ecuador Caring for
home and family, and sometimes earning
the only income as well, women are now
also taking on religious and secular roles
from which they were once excluded.
In a Good Friday procession
commemorating the Passion of Christ,
a young woman shoulders the heavy
cross, traditionally a man's burden.
A successful advertising executive,
30-year-old Verónica Delgado dresses for
her wedding. Women of her generation
are landing professional jobs in unprece-
dented numbers. "Sure, we've had to
fight chauvinism," she says. "But we've
proved that we're capable and that we
can handle a career as well as a family."

QUITO, ECUADOR (BOTH)

It's the end of a millennium. And it's
difficult to know what century
we are in. These could be medieval
rites. Sincere faith touches the very
essence of the people.

ANDES JOURNEY

A Bushman smears his legs with antelope blood in a rite witnessed by
visitors to Namibia's Intu Afrika, a commercial game reserve. As land
where Bushmen can hunt dwindles, many court tourism to survive.
"Anthology is one of their few assets," says anthropologist James Suzman.

Descendants of Africans brought to Ecuador in the 16th century to work on sugar plantations remain at the margin of society.

EL JUNCAL, ECUADOR

Figures in a mirage, Bushmen wearing skins and carrying bows and arrows
cross a salt pan in Namibia's Nyae Nyae Conservancy. Use of guns, dogs,
and horses is restricted, so they hunt the traditional way. They live in a
village built to lure tourists, and most days they wear Western clothes.

■ 520
Publication National Geographic
Design Director Constance Phelps
Art Director Elaine Bradley
Photo Editor Todd James
Photographer Pablo Corral Vega
Publisher National Geographic Society
Issue February 2001
Category Reportage: Story

■ 521
Publication National Geographic
Design Director Constance Phelps
Art Director David Whitmore
Photo Editor Bill Douthitt
Photographer Chris Johns
Publisher National Geographic Society
Issue February 2001
Category Reportage: Story

For a half century on Monhegan Island two things have been as predictable as the tides: The mailboat Laura B. will make the 12-mile run from Port Clyde in all but a full gale, and artist Frances Kornbluh will return for the summer. Beloved by fishermen, painters, and a growing throng of tourists, the island casts a powerful spell.

WELCOME TO MONHEGAN ISLAND, MAINE. NOW PLEASE, GO AWAY

BY CATHY NEWMAN

PHOTOGRAPHS BY AMY TOENSING

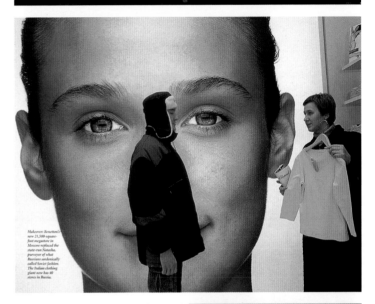

RUSSIA RISING

A decade has passed since the U.S.S.R. ceased to exist, and during that time the Russian people have been subjected to an economic and social revolution.

New breed or old school? Both describe President Vladimir Putin (facing camera)—and the country he leads.

PICKING ONLY THE DARKEST CRANBERRIES for their Thanksgiving feast, Winnie Murdock and son Kyle forage on Manana, a deserted isle a skiff ride away that helps form Monhegan's harbor.

INSEPARABLE BROTHERS Harry and Doug Odom turn in beneath each other's portraits while Tasi keeps watch. "It's a good life," says Harry. Lobstermen, merchants, and island benefactors for some 60 years, the Odoms recently moved inshore.

Makeover: Benetton's new 21,500-square-foot megastore in Moscow replaced the state-run Natasha, purveyor of what Russians sardonically called Soviet fashion. The Italian clothing giant now has 46 stores in Russia.

For American-born entrepreneur Eric Shogren (below, left), doing business in Novosibirsk means doing banya with partners—a ritual marathon of sauna, games, eating, and drinking. "If you're not willing to drink vodka with Russians, you're not going to succeed here," he says. Alcohol lubricates business but also contributes to Russia's high mortality rate—and to the stream of vagrants and arrestees brought to Moscow's Disinfection Centers for a bath and delousing (right).

The transformation of Russia will take far longer than most imagined. The euphoria of a decade ago has been replaced with a cold-eyed realism.

■ 522
Publication National Geographic
Design Director Constance Phelps
Art Director Elaine Bradley
Photo Editor Susan Welchman
Photographer Amy Toensing
Publisher National Geographic Society
Issue July 2001
Category Reportage: Story

■ 523
Publication National Geographic
Design Director Constance Phelps
Art Director Robert Gray
Photo Editor Susan Welchman
Photographer Gerd Ludwig
Publisher National Geographic Society
Issue November 2001
Category Reportage: Story

photography MERIT

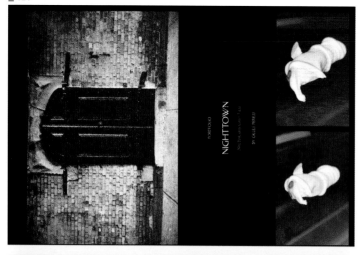

A REPORTER AT LARGE

THE EMPEROR OF ICE

How a bag of supermarket ice cubes launched a plan to dominate an industry.

BY IAN PARKER

PHOTOGRAPHS BY MARTIN SCHOELLER

James Sinegal, who now makes more than a billion icecubes a day, in Houston. "People ask me: What do you do? I say: I do ice. I just do ice."

THE NEW YORKER, FEBRUARY 12, 2001

PROFILES

THE BIG PICTURE

What do Andreas Gursky's monumental photographs say about art?

BY CALVIN TOMKINS

The contemporary sublime viewed dispassionately: Gursky, opposite, with "Shanghai," 1998. Photograph by Wolfgang Tillmans.

THE NEW YORKER, JANUARY 22, 2001

LETTER FROM AFGHANISTAN

THE SURRENDER

Double agents, defectors, deadfooted Taliban, and a motley army battle for Kunduz.

BY JON LEE ANDERSON

Exiled Northern Alliance soldiers on the road from Taloqan to Kunduz, in northeastern Afghanistan. Kunduz, which was one of the last bastions of the Taliban, fell on November 26th, after days of branding and negotiating. Photograph by Thomas Dworzak.

THE NEW YORKER, DECEMBER 10, 2001

PROFILES

BEEN HERE AND GONE

How August Wilson brought a century of black American culture to the stage.

BY JOHN LAHR

August Wilson at the Café Roma in San Francisco, February 12, 2001. He gives essays nothing at first, or even several glances, but when his gaze is direct, and especially when he's telling a story, you feel what his wife calls "the Smile." Photograph by Dana Lixenberg.

FICTION

GIGANTIC

BY MARC NESBITT

Marc Nesbitt at the Central Park Zoo. Photograph by Katharina Bosse.

■ 524
Publication The New Yorker
Photographer Gilles Peress
Visuals Editor Elisabeth Biondi
Publisher Condé Nast Publications, Inc.
Issue January 8, 2001
Category Reportage: Story

■ 525
Publication The New Yorker
Photographer Martin Schoeller
Visuals Editor Elisabeth Biondi
Publisher Condé Nast Publications, Inc.
Issue February 12, 2001
Category Portraits: Spread

■ 526
Publication The New Yorker
Photographer Wolfgang Tillmans
Visuals Editor Elisabeth Biondi
Publisher Condé Nast Publications, Inc.
Issue January 22, 2001
Category Portraits: Spread

■ 527
Publication The New Yorker
Photographer Thomas Dworzak
Visuals Editor Elisabeth Biondi
Publisher Condé Nast Publications, Inc.
Issue December 10, 2001
Category Reportage: Spread

■ 528
Publication The New Yorker
Photographer Dana Lixenberg
Visuals Editor Elisabeth Biondi
Publisher Condé Nast Publications, Inc.
Issue April 16, 2001
Category Portraits: Spread

■ 529
Publication The New Yorker
Photographer Katharina Bosse
Visuals Editor Elisabeth Biondi
Publisher Condé Nast Publications, Inc.
Issue July 9, 2001
Category Portraits: Spread

eternal youth is the hottest commodity on the market, sending hoards of twentysomethings on a mission to delay the inevitable. can an in-office procedure or skincare treatment turn back the clock? selene milano investigates.

in your face

eye of the beholder

having a bad day? nothing better to do than change clothes? for this party of one, all the apartment's a stage, each room a runway. what if nobody's watching?
photographed by vanina sorrenti

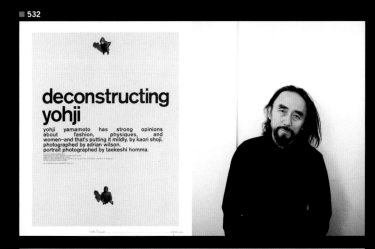

deconstructing yohji

yohji yamamoto has strong opinions about fashion, physiques, and women–and that's putting it mildly. by kaori shoji. photographed by adrian wilson. portrait photographed by taekeshi homma.

photography MERIT

■ 530
Publication Nylon
Art Director Lina Kutsovskaya
Designers Kathleen McGowan, Jason Engdahl
Photographer Mark Abrahams
Publisher Nylon LLC
Issue March 2001
Category Fashion/Beauty: Story

■ 531
Publication Nylon
Art Director Lina Kutsovskaya
Designers Kathleen McGowan, Jason Engdahl
Photographer Vanina Sorrenti
Publisher Nylon LLC
Issue March 2001
Category Fashion/Beauty: Story

■ 532
Publication Nylon
Art Director Lina Kutsovskaya
Designers Kathleen McGowan, Jason Engdahl
Photographer Adrian Wilson
Publisher Nylon LLC
Issue September 2001
Category Fashion/Beauty: Story

björk in paradise

she's gone from indie darling to techno icon to film goddess in one transformational decade. on her new cd *vespertine*, björk examines the notion of heaven on earth with achy intensity. by james servin. photographed by terry richardson

the incredible journey

she's at the top of every director's most-wanted list. now she's doing chekhov with meryl. natalie portman knows what she wants and how to get it. what she wants is a quality career, and life beyond hollywood babylon. lauren smith charts the rise of the assured young actress. photographed by jake chessum

■ 534

flash dance

jazz age fashion shines bright. photographed by christophe rihet

■ 532

Publication Nylon
Art Director Lina Kutsovskaya
Designers Kathleen McGowan, Jason Engdahl
Photographer Terry Richardson
Publisher Nylon LLC
Issue June/July 2001
Category Portraits: Story

■ 533

Publication Nylon
Art Director Lina Kutsovskaya
Designers Kathleen McGowan, Jason Engdahl
Photographer Jake Chessum
Publisher Nylon LLC
Issue August 2001
Category Portraits: Story

■ 534

Publication Nylon
Art Director Lina Kutsovskaya
Designers Kathleen McGowan, Jason Engdahl
Photographer Christophe Rihet
Publisher Nylon LLC
Issue November 2001
Category Fashion/Beauty: Story

Soap's On!

Astonish your senses with extravagant, aromatic, eye-catching bar soaps.

FIELD OF DREAMS

MAKE 8 HOURS OUT OF EVERY 24 PURE BLISS WITH LINENS IN SLEEP-FRIENDLY COLORS.

SHEETS AND SHAMS ARE THE PROPS FOR YOUR PRIVATE SANCTUARY.

■ 535

Publication O, The Oprah Magazine
Design Director Carla Frank
Designer Erika Oliveira
Photo Editors Karen Frank, Kim Gougenheim
Photographer Lisa Charles Watson
Publisher The Hearst Corporation-Magazines Division
Issue October 2001
Category Still Life/Interiors: Story
    A. Spread

■ 536

Publication O, The Oprah Magazine
Design Director Carla Frank
Designer Erika Oliveira
Photo Editors Karen Frank, Kim Gougenheim
Photographer Doug Rosa
Publisher The Hearst Corporation-Magazines Division
Issue September 2001
Category Still Life/Interiors: Single Page

■ 537

Publication O, The Oprah Magazine
Creative Director Adam Glassman
Design Director Carla Frank
Designer Albert Toy
Photo Editor Karen Frank
Photographer William Abranowicz
Publisher The Hearst Corporation-Magazines Division
Issue September 2001
Category Still Life/Interiors: Story

photography MERIT

mars boot camp

Leaky roof, bulky spacesuit … if this is Mars, I want to go home! By Frank Vizard

Inside the Hab

a misfit in miami

fine wine and punk idols get better and sometimes less bitter with age. at 54, iggy pop has proven he's a vintage vandal. siobhán mcgowan drinks in his wisdom. photographed by martin schoeller

Once upon a time, there was a southern belle who led a fairy-tale life in Hollywood. But—and here's the moral of our story—this is one princess who packs a punch.

Reese Witherspoon
Lets Down Her Hair

BY SEAN M. SMITH   PHOTOGRAPHS BY MATTHEW ROLSTON

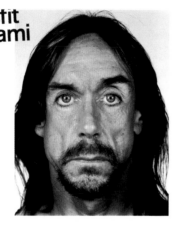

537
Publication Popular Science
Design Director Christopher Garcia
Art Directors Hylah Hill, Matthew Ball
Designer Hylah Hill
Photo Editor John B. Carnett
Photographer John B. Carnett
Publisher Time4 Media
Issue October 2001
Category Reportage: Spread

538
Publication Nylon
Art Director Lina Kutsovskaya
Designers Kathleen McGowan, Jason Engdahl
Photographer Martin Schoeller
Publisher Nylon LLC
Issue August 2001
Category Portraits: Spread

539
Publication Premiere
Art Director Richard Baker
Designer Bess Wong
Photo Editor Doris Brautigan
Photographer Matthew Rolston
Publisher Hachette Filipacchi Media U.S.
Issue August 2001
Category Portraits: Story

■ 540

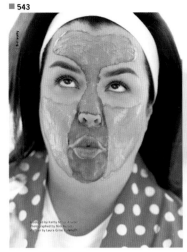

■ 543

■ 541

■ 544

■ 542

■ 540
Publication Premiere
Art Director Richard Baker
Designer Richard Baker
Photo Editor Doris Brautigan
Photographer Norman Jean Roy
Publisher Hachette Filipacchi Media U.S.
Issue September 2001
Category Portraits: Spread

■ 541
Publication Premiere
Art Director Richard Baker
Designer Richard Baker
Photo Editor Doris Brautigan
Photographer Chris Buck
Publisher Hachette Filipacchi Media U.S.
Issue December 2001
Category Portraits: Spread

■ 542
Publication Savoy
Creative Directors Lance Pettiford, Mimi Park
Designer Lance Pettiford
Photo Editor Lance Pettiford
Photographer Timothy White
Publisher Vanguarde Media Inc.
Issue March 2001
Category Portraits: Spread

■ 543
Publication Rosie
Creative Director Doug Turshen
Designer Jan H. Greco
Photo Editor Marybeth Welsh-DuLany
Photographer Nick Baratta
Publisher Gruner & Jahr USA Publishing
Issue June 2001
Category Portraits: Spread

■ 544
Publication Rosie
Creative Director Doug Turshen
Designer Kristina Berg
Photo Editor Marybeth Welsh-DuLany
Photographer Jean Karotkin
Publisher Gruner & Jahr USA Publishing
Issue October 2001
Category Portraits: Spread

■ 545

■ 548

■ 546

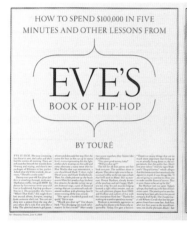

■ 549

■ 547

■ 550

■ 545
Publication Rolling Stone
Art Director Fred Woodward
Designers Fred Woodward, Gail Anderson
Photo Editors Fiona McDonagh, Audrey Landreth
Photographer David LaChapelle
Publisher Wenner Media LLC
Issue July 5, 2001
Category Portraits: Spread

■ 546
Publication Rolling Stone
Art Director Fred Woodward
Designer Siung Tjia
Photo Editors Fiona McDonagh, Audrey Landreth
Photographer Guzman
Publisher Wenner Media LLC
Issue July 5, 2001
Category Portraits: Spread

■ 547
Publication Rolling Stone
Art Director Fred Woodward
Designers Gail Anderson, Ken DeLago
Photo Editor Fiona McDonagh
Photographer Mark Seliger
Publisher Wenner Media LLC
Issue August 30, 2001
Category Portraits: Spread

■ 548
Publication Rolling Stone
Art Director Fred Woodward
Designers Siung Tjia, Fred Woodward
Photo Editor Fiona McDonagh
Photographer Herb Ritts
Publisher Wenner Media LLC
Issue November 22, 2001
Category Portraits: Spread

■ 549
Publication Rolling Stone
Art Director Fred Woodward
Designer Siung Tjia
Photo Editors Fiona McDonagh, Audrey Landreth
Photographer Stefan Ruiz
Publisher Wenner Media LLC
Issue December 6, 2001
Category Portraits: Spread

■ 550
Publication Smock
Creative Director Kristin Johnson
Designer Kristin Johnson
Photographer Anne Hélaine
Publisher Smock Magazine, Inc.
Issue Winter 2001
Category Fashion/Beauty: Single Page

■ THE MANHUNT

The war in Afghanistan began nine weeks ago on a battlefield the size of Texas, and it may end in a high, narrow valley smaller than the city of Austin. After weeks of playing Where's Osama?, military officials believe they have cornered bin Laden on handheld radios in the White Mountains, giving orders to his dwindling al-Qaeda forces. Afghan fighters said they had killed 200 and routed al-Qaeda but the U.S. said too many nooks had yet to be snatched. If bin Laden is in Tora Bora, he and his soldiers are trapped in a box: snow-covered peaks loom on two sides, Afghan and American soldiers avail on a third, and Pakistani border patrols stand guard on the fourth.

The cornered fighters have little room to maneuver. With an enemy anti-aircraft fire, U.S. spy planes circle the city during al-Qaeda fighters to step out of their caves and become glowing infrared targets. Few have done so. Bin Laden has resorted to giving orders on shortwave radio, U.S. authorities suggest, because there's no one else left to do so.

But worshiably almost slipped away last week. The three Afghan warlords in control of alliance forces began the week with a successful assault on the Milawa Valley, the lava entrance to Tora Bora from the north. Al-Qaeda soldiers fled quickly, though they did manage to kill a few alliance troops. Having taken that territory, the warlords committed a major tactical error: they withdrew from the valley. When alliance forces returned the next day, they were greeted by three al-Qaeda fighters armed with machine guns who opened fire from 200 meters. No alliance soldiers were killed, but the morning was spent fighting a battle for territory that had already been won.

The folks had only just begun. At al-Qaeda fighters scampered up the mountains in search of safe haven, one of the warlords, Haji Zaman, agreed to a cease-fire without bothering to consult the other two Afghan commanders or the U.S. Zaman claims the Arab-speaking fighters reached him via wireless and offered to surrender on the condition that they be turned over to the United Nations. "They said they had to get in contact with each other and would surrender group by group," Zaman says. He then announced the cease-fire, halted his

– EYE ON THE SKY U.S. fighter jets bomb the last al-Qaeda stronghold on an Afghan soldier watches from below

Photographs for TIME by James Nachtwey—VI

LONG HAUL: A sick man walks from the shower in a Harare hospital. Soon he will have to be cleaned by nurses. Dignity is one of AIDS' first casualties

LAST STOP: A 28-year-old woman moans for Time, clinging to arms. A home for dying AIDS patients

Crimes Against Humanity

Even as you read this, AIDS is taking lives in sub-Saharan Africa, swallowing families, communities, hopes. So far 17 million have died. At least 25 million may follow. An intimate look at a modern curse

Photographs for TIME by James Nachtwey · Magnum

A

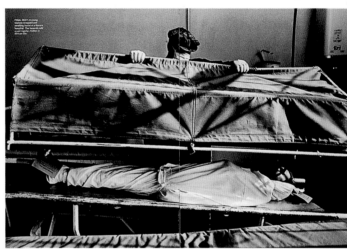

FINAL REST: A young woman wrapped and awaiting burial at a Harare hospital. The funerals add a sad regular rhythm to African life.

PHOTOGRAPH: Burka-clad demonstrations took to the streets of Kabul last week to demand rights for women

ABOUT FACE

AN INSIDE LOOK AT HOW WOMEN FARED UNDER TALIBAN OPPRESSION AND WHAT THE FUTURE HOLDS FOR THEM NOW

■ LIFTING THE VEIL

[body text columns describing women under Taliban, partially legible]

THE WOMEN SPEAK

What are Afghan women really like beneath the burka?

551

Publication Time
Art Director Cynthia Hoffman
Designer Tom Miller
Photographer James Nachtwey
Publisher Time Inc.
Issue December 24, 2001
Category Reportage: Spread

552

Publication Time
Art Director Arthur Hochstein
Designer Cynthia Hoffman
Photo Editor Robert Stevens
Photographer James Nachtwey
Publisher Time Inc.
Issue February 12, 2001
Category Reportage: Spread

553

Publication Time
Art Director Arthur Hochstein
Designer Cynthia Hoffman
Photo Editor Robert Stevens
Photographer James Nachtwey
Publisher Time Inc.
Issue February 12, 2001
Category Reportage: Story
      A. Spread

554

Publication Time
Art Director Arthur Hochstein
Designer Chrissy Dunleavy
Photo Editor Hillary Raskin
Photographers Yannis Behrakis, Sion Touhig, John Stanmeyer, Behrouz Mehri, Janet Durrans, Harald Henden, Lynsey Addario
Publisher Time Inc.
Issue December 3, 2001
Category Reportage: Story

Publication Sports Illustrated
Creative Director Steven Hoffman
Designer Eric Marquard
Photographer Brent Finley
Publisher Time Inc.
Issue November 12, 2001
Category Reportage: Spread

Publication Sports Illustrated
Creative Director Steven Hoffman
Designer Devin Pedzwater
Photographer James Porto
Publisher Time Inc.
Issue Winter 2001
Category Portraits: Story

Publication Sports Illustrated
Creative Director Steven Hoffman
Designer Samantha Gabbey
Photographer Julian Herbert
Publisher Time Inc.
Issue December 17, 2001
Category Reportage: Spread

■ 558

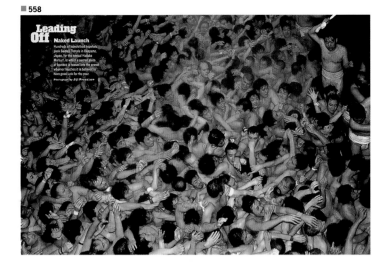

■ 559

■ 560

■ 561

■ 562

■ 558
Publication Sports Illustrated
Creative Director Steven Hoffman
Designer Samantha Gabbey
Photographer Jiji Press
Publisher Time Inc.
Issue March 5, 2001
Category Reportage: Spread

■ 559
Publication Sports Illustrated
Creative Director Steven Hoffman
Designer Kory Kennedy
Photographer Corey Rich
Publisher Time Inc.
Issue October 15, 2001
Category Reportage: Spread

■ 560
Publication Sports Illustrated
Creative Director Steven Hoffman
Designer Eric Marquard
Photographer Topher Donahue
Publisher Time Inc.
Issue October 15, 2001
Category Reportage: Spread

■ 561
Publication Sports Illustrated Presents
Art Director Craig Gartner
Designer Melissa Devlin
Photo Editor Jeff Weig
Photographer Robert Beck
Publisher Time Inc.
Issue June 2001
Category Reportage: Spread

■ 562
Publication Sports Illustrated Presents
Art Director Craig Gartner
Designer Melissa Devlin
Photo Editor Jeff Weig
Photographer Darren Carroll
Publisher Time Inc.
Issue June 2001
Category Reportage: Spread

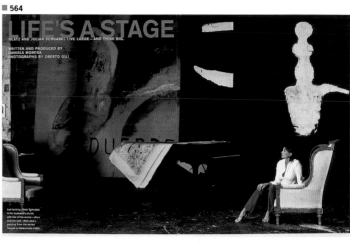

■ 563

Publication Town & Country
Creative Director Mary Shanahan
Art Director Agnethe Glatved
Photo Editor Casey Tierney
Photographer John Huba
Publisher The Hearst Corporation-Magazines Division
Issue March 2001
Category Fashion/Beauty: Story

■ 564

Publication Town & Country
Creative Director Mary Shanahan
Art Director Agnethe Glatved
Photo Editor Casey Tierney
Photographer Oberto Gili
Publisher The Hearst Corporation-Magazines Division
Issue October 2001
Category Still Life/Interiors: Story

■ 565

Publication Travel & Leisure
Creative Director Pamela Berry
Art Director Laura Gharrity
Designers Stephanie Achar, Jae Han
Photo Editor Heidi Posner
Photographer Martin Morrell
Publisher American Express Publishing Co.
Issue October 2001
Category Reportage: Story

■ 566

tanzania

An abundance of animals, spectacular scenery, exceptional lodging—a ten-day safari reveals Africa in all its splendor.

BY MELISSA BIGGS BRADLEY
PHOTOGRAPHS BY JOHN HUBA

■ 567

Prescription for Disaster

Your doctor, your pharmacist, the drug companies and the FDA all know which of the 10,000 drugs out there have scary side effects. But there's no good system in place to make sure that crucial information gets to patients like you. And without it, people are suffering—even dying.

BY MICHELLE ANDREWS | PHOTOGRAPHS BY SCOGIN MAYO

■ 568

a house divided

Two nice middle-age couples from Virginia were the best of friends for almost 20 years. Today they're furious, they don't speak to each other, and a lawyer's gotten involved. What could possibly break them apart so cruelly and completely? Simple: They bought this vacation home together.

by Eleanor Laine
photographs by Chriss Wade

■ 569

a misunderstood subculture, a veg as resort, and lots of black t-shirts, laptops and booze

BY CHRIS TURNER
PHOTOGRAPHS BY KYOKO HAMADA

■ 566
Publication Town & Country
Creative Director Mary Shanahan
Art Director Agnethe Glatved
Photo Editor Casey Tierney
Photographer John Huba
Publisher The Hearst Corporation-Magazines Division
Issue November 2001
Category Reportage: Story

■ 567
Publication SmartMoney
Design Director Amy Rosenfeld
Art Director Gretchen Smelter
Designer Gretchen Smelter
Photo Editor Kate Sullivan
Photographer Scogin Mayo
Publisher Dow Jones & Hearst Corp.
Issue May 2001
Category Portraits: Spread

■ 568
Publication SmartMoney
Design Director Amy Rosenfeld
Art Director Gretchen Smelter
Designer Gretchen Smelter
Photo Editor Kate Sullivan
Photographer Chriss Wade
Publisher Dow Jones & Hearst Corp.
Issue August 2001
Category Reportage: Spread

■ 569
Publication Shift
Art Director Antonio Enrico De Luca
Designer Jaspal Riyait
Photographer Kyoko Hamada
Publisher Multi-Vision Publishing
Issue November 2001
Category Portraits: Story

LIFE'S a BEACH

photography nathaniel welch   by DaViD NoLaNo

What's the secret
of eternal youth?
An awesome surfboard,
the heart of a maverick,
and a glass-smooth
double overhead wave

Hours after the
bombs rained
on Pearl Harbor,
American GIs
battled invaders
in the Philippines.
Their country
abandoned them.
Their captors
tortured them.
For the few
who survived, the
wounds are
still healing.

BLOOD BROTHERS

BY HAMPTON SIDES
PHOTO COLLAGES BY EXUM

SEARCH SMARTER

FINDING INFORMATION ON THE WEB IS EASIER THAN YOU THINK.
HERE ARE THE WEBSITES THAT WILL HELP YOU DO IT

BY JYOTI THOTTAM

■ 570
Publication Modern Maturity
Art Director Carl Lehmann-Haupt
Photo Editor Linda Ferrer
Photographer Nathaniel Welch
Publisher AARP
Issue March/April 2001
Category Portraits: Story

■ 571
Publication Modern Maturity
Design Director Eric Seidman
Art Director Ron Melé
Photo Editor Wendy Tiefenbacher
Photographer Exum
Publisher AARP
Issue November/December 2001
Category Reportage: Story

■ 572
Publication On
Design Director Sharon Okamoto
Photo Editor Jay Colton
Photographer Ábrams Lacagnina
Publisher Time Inc.
Issue November 2001
Category Photo Illustration: Story

"WE'RE TRYING TO MEASURE WHAT THE WEB THINKS."

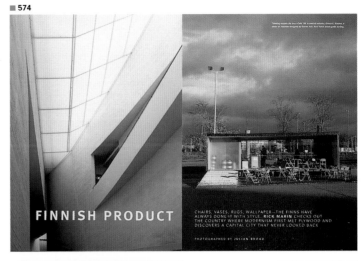

AMERICAN STEAK-OUT

By Peter Jon Lindberg Photographed by Larry Fink

It's official: beef is back. Thanks to a cash-rich and protein-craving population, the steak house is again the hottest joint in town, from coast to coast. What's more, some of the country's most celebrated chefs are moving in with a whole new take on the classics

FINNISH PRODUCT

CHAIRS, VASES, RUGS, WALLPAPER—THE FINNS HAVE ALWAYS DONE IT WITH STYLE. **RICK MARIN** CHECKS OUT THE COUNTRY WHERE MODERNISM FIRST MET PLYWOOD AND DISCOVERS A CAPITAL CITY THAT NEVER LOOKED BACK

PHOTOGRAPHED BY JULIAN BROAD

Done up in chocolate brown and cobalt blue with gilt accents and crystal chandeliers, Prime is by far the grandest of the new Las Vegas steak houses. They should issue engagement rings at the coat check

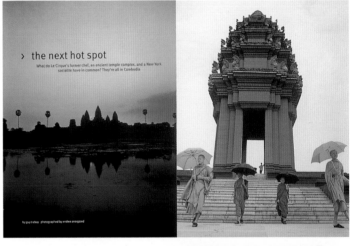

> the next hot spot

What do Le Cirque's former chef, an ancient temple complex, and a New York socialite have in common? They're all in Cambodia

■ 573
Publication Travel & Leisure
Creative Director Pamela Berry
Art Director Laura Gharrity
Designers Stephanie Achar, Jae Han
Photo Editor Heidi Posner
Photographer Larry Fink
Publisher American Express Publishing Co.
Issue January 2001
Category Reportage: Story

■ 574
Publication Travel & Leisure
Creative Director Pamela Berry
Art Director Laura Gharrity
Designers Stephanie Achar, Jae Han
Photo Editors Heidi Posner, David Cicconi
Photographer Julian Broad
Publisher American Express Publishing Co.
Issue March 2001
Category Reportage: Story

■ 575
Publication Travel & Leisure
Creative Director Pamela Berry
Art Director Laura Gharrity
Designers Stephanie Achar, Jae Han
Photo Editor Heidi Posner
Photographer Anders Overgaard
Publisher American Express Publishing Co.
Issue September 2001
Category Reportage: Story

■ 576
Publication Travel & Leisure
Creative Director Pamela Berry
Art Director Laura Gharrity
Designers Stephanie Achar, Jae Han
Photo Editor Heidi Posner
Photographer François Dischinger
Publisher American Express Publishing Co.
Issue March 2001
Category Reportage: Story

■ 577
Publication Vanity Fair
Design Director David Harris
Art Director Gregory Mastrianni
Designer Lee Ruelle
Photo Editors Susan White, SunHee C. Grinnell
Photographer Michael O'Neill
Publisher The Condé Nast Publications Inc.
Issue March 2001
Category Portraits: Spread

■ 578
Publication Vanity Fair
Design Director David Harris
Art Director Gregory Mastrianni
Photo Editors Susan White, Annie Leibovitz
Photographer Annie Leibovitz
Publisher The Condé Nast Publications Inc.
Issue April 2001
Category Portraits: Spread

■ 579

Shooting Past 80

Phil Stern, 81
PHOTOGRAPHED BY HERB RITTS

■ 581

Willy Ronis, 90
PHOTOGRAPHED BY HENRI CARTIER-BRESSON

Yousuf Karsh, 91
PHOTOGRAPHED BY BRUCE WEBER

■ 582

SWISS MYSTIQUE

■ 580

THE CHAMELEON
WILLEM DAFOE

Y

■ 579
Publication Vanity Fair
Design Director David Harris
Art Director Gregory Mastrianni
Photo Editors Susan White, Ron Beinner,
Lisa Berman, Sarah Czeladnicki,
Courtney Thompson
Photographers Brigitte Lacombe, Herb Ritts,
Mary Ellen Mark, Martine Franck,
Henri Cartier-Bresson, Bruce Weber,
Helmut Newton, Michael O'Neill, Peggy Sirota,
Harry Benson, Jonathan Becker
Publisher The Condé Nast Publications Inc.
Issue January 2001
Category Portraits: Story

■ 580
Publication Vanity Fair
Design Director David Harris
Art Director Gregory Mastrianni
Photo Editors Susan White, Kathryn MacLeod
Photographer Annie Leibovitz
Publisher The Condé Nast Publications Inc.
Issue April 2001
Category Portraits: Spread

■ 581
Publication Vanity Fair
Design Director David Harris
Art Director Gregory Mastrianni
Photo Editors Susan White, Kathryn MacLeod
Photographer Herb Ritts
Publisher The Condé Nast Publications Inc.
Issue April 2001
Category Portraits: Spread

■ 582
Publication Vanity Fair
Design Director David Harris
Art Directors Gregory Mastrianni, Julie Weiss
Designer Lee Ruelle
Photo Editors Susan White, Ron Beinner
Photographer Todd Eberle
Publisher The Condé Nast Publications Inc.
Issue July 2001
Category Reportage: Story

photography MERIT

217

582
Publication Vanity Fair
Design Director David Harris
Art Director Gregory Mastrianni
Photo Editors Susan White, Ron Beinner
Photographer David LaChapelle
Publisher The Condé Nast Publications Inc.
Issue April 2001
Category Portraits: Spread

583
Publication Vanity Fair
Design Director David Harris
Art Director Gregory Mastrianni
Designers David Harris, Christopher Israel
Photo Editors Susan White, Lisa Berman
Photographer Fabien Baron
Publisher The Condé Nast Publications Inc.
Issue May 2001
Category Portraits: Spread

584
Publication Vanity Fair
Design Director David Harris
Art Director Gregory Mastrianni
Designer Glenn Bo
Photo Editors Susan White, Richard Villani
Photographer Jonas Karlsson
Publisher The Condé Nast Publications Inc.
Issue June 2001
Category Portraits: Story

585
Publication Vanity Fair
Design Director David Harris
Art Director Gregory Mastrianni
Photo Editors Susan White, Ron Beinner
Photographer David LaChapelle
Publisher The Condé Nast Publications Inc.
Issue August 2001
Category Portraits: Spread

What's Love Got to Do with It?

When a preternaturally endowed Playboy Playmate marries a Texas oil tycoon 60 years her senior two drops dead the next year, people have a nasty tendency to question her motives. As Anna Nicole Smith costumes up for battle with the family of her late husband, J. Howard Marshall II, over a $475 million settlement from his estate, she shows DAVID LaCHAPELLE that she's willing to have fun with her bombshell, gold-digger image. But WALTER KIRN takes a closer approach marshaling evidence that her heart belongs to Daddy

P

Anything missing in her life? "I want one of those chimps that shake hands and like to be hugged."

'How am I going to know if the men I date really love me for me?' she recently wondered aloud.

Strange Innocence

When J.T. LeRoy's first novel, *Sarah*, was published last year, the 20-year-old ex-child prostitute became an instant cult figure. The book, named for his mother (who dressed him like a girl and taught him her trade), is a fictionalized account of his life as a "lot lizard" (i.e., truck-stop hustler) and was embraced not only by the literary demimonde but also in *The Guardian* and *The New York Times*. Extremely shy and uncertain of his gender, he has rarely been photographed. With his second book, *The Heart Is Deceitful Above All Things*, due out from Bloomsbury this month, he finally agreed to sit for MARY ELLEN MARK and talk with singer-songwriter TOM WAITS

J

Almodóvar Up, Almodóvar Down

Pedro Almodóvar's movies—from *Women on the Verge of a Nervous Breakdown* to the Oscar-winning *All About My Mother* and his forthcoming *Bad Education*—reflect his role as the quirkily flamboyant toast of Madrid. But they also stem from a cautious, hidden Almodóvar. COLM TÓIBÍN finds the marks of the director's inner struggle, including his tortured years of military service and his search for the woman within, a voice for his passion and pain

■ 586
Publication Vanity Fair
Design Director David Harris
Art Director Gregory Mastrianni
Photo Editors Susan White, Ron Beinner
Photographer David LaChapelle
Publisher The Condé Nast Publications Inc.
Issue June 2001
Category Portraits: Story

■ 587
Publication Vanity Fair
Design Director David Harris
Art Directors Gregory Mastrianni, Julie Weiss
Photo Editors Susan White, Ron Beinner
Photographer Mary Ellen Mark
Publisher The Condé Nast Publications Inc.
Issue July 2001
Category Portraits: Spread

■ 588
Publication Vanity Fair
Design Director David Harris
Art Director Gregory Mastrianni
Photo Editors Susan White, Sharon Suh
Photographer Bruce Weber
Publisher The Condé Nast Publications Inc.
Issue February 2001
Category Reportage: Story

■ 589
Publication Vanity Fair
Design Director David Harris
Art Directors Gregory Mastrianni, Julie Weiss
Designer Lee Ruelle
Photo Editors Susan White, Kathryn MacLeod
Photographer Annie Leibovitz
Publisher The Condé Nast Publications Inc.
Issue September 2001
Category Portraits: Spread

■ 590
Publication Vanity Fair
Design Director David Harris
Art Directors Gregory Mastrianni, Julie Weiss
Photo Editors Susan White, Todd Eberle
Photographer Todd Eberle
Publisher The Condé Nast Publications Inc.
Issue September 2001
Category Portraits: Spread

■ 591
Publication Vanity Fair
Design Director David Harris
Art Director Julie Weiss
Designer Christopher Israel
Photo Editors Susan White, Sarah Czeladnicki,
SunHee C. Grinnell, Kathryn MacLeod, Ron Beinner, Richard Villani
Photographers Annie Leibovitz, David LaChapelle, Herb Ritts, Bruce Weber,
Jonas Karlsson, Ruven Afanador, William Claxton, Danny Clinch, Anton
Corbijn, Sam Jones, Brigitte Lacombe, George Lange, Antoine Le Grand, Rankin
Publisher The Condé Nast Publications Inc.
Issue November 2001
Category Portraits: Story

photography MERIT

■ 592
Publication Vanity Fair
Design Director David Harris
Art Director Julie Weiss
Designer Christopher Israel
Photo Editors Susan White, Kathyrn MacLeod
Photographer Annie Leibovitz
Publisher The Condé Nast Publications Inc.
Issue November 2001
Category Portraits: Spread

■ 593
Publication Vanity Fair
Design Director David Harris
Art Director Julie Weiss
Designer Christopher Israel
Photo Editors Susan White, SunHee C. Grinnell
Photographer David LaChapelle
Publisher The Condé Nast Publications Inc.
Issue November 2001
Category Portraits: Spread

■ 594
Publication Vanity Fair
Design Director David Harris
Art Director Julie Weiss
Designer Christopher Israel
Photo Editors Susan White, Kathyrn MacLeod
Photographer Annie Leibovitz
Publisher The Condé Nast Publications Inc.
Issue November 2001
Category Portraits: Spread

■ 595
Publication Vanity Fair
Design Director David Harris
Art Director Julie Weiss
Designer Christopher Israel
Photo Editors Susan White, SunHee C. Grinnell
Photographer Anton Corbijn
Publisher The Condé Nast Publications Inc.
Issue November 2001
Category Portraits: Spread

■ 596
Publication Vanity Fair
Design Director David Harris
Art Director Julie Weiss
Designer Christopher Israel
Photo Editors Susan White, Kathyrn MacLeod
Photographer Annie Leibovitz
Publisher The Condé Nast Publications Inc.
Issue November 2001
Category Portraits: Spread

■ 597

THIS WAS NEW YORK

THE FIREFIGHTERS AND POLICE OFFICERS WHO RISKED EVERYTHING. THE
RESCUE WORKERS WHO CAME FROM HUNDREDS OF MILES AWAY. THE FAM-
ILIES WHO GRIEVE. THE LEADERS WHO RALLIED A SHELL-SHOCKED CITY.
THE VIGIL KEEPERS WHOSE CANDLES LIT THE NIGHT. THESE ARE AMONG THE
IMAGES THAT WILL ENDURE. THIS IS THE NEW YORK—AND THE AMERICA—
WORTH FIGHTING FOR: ONE NOT OF SKYSCRAPERS, BUT OF PEOPLE

PHOTOGRAPHS BY JONAS KARLSSON · REPORTING BY RON BEINNER

■ 598

■ 599

ONE WEEK IN
SEPTEMBER

■ 600

■ 597
Publication Vanity Fair
Design Director David Harris
Art Director Julie Weiss
Designer Chris Mueller
Photo Editors Susan White, Ron Beinner
Photographer Jonas Karlsson
Publisher The Condé Nast Publications Inc.
Issue November 2001
Category Portraits: Story

■ 598
Publication Vanity Fair
Design Director David Harris
Art Director Julie Weiss
Designer Christopher Israel
Photo Editors Susan White, Kathryn MacLeod
Photographer Annie Leibovitz
Publisher The Condé Nast Publications Inc.
Issue November 2001
Category Portraits: Spread

■ 599
Publication Vanity Fair
Design Director David Harris
Art Director Julie Weiss
Designer Chris Mueller
Photo Editors Susan White, Ron Beinner
Photographer Jonas Karlsson
Publisher The Condé Nast Publications Inc.
Issue November 2001
Category Reportage: Spread

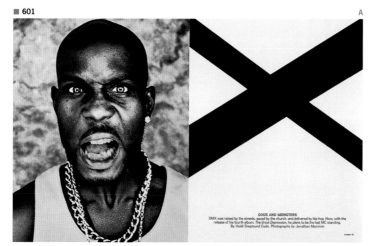

GODS AND MONSTERS
DMX was raised by the streets, saved by the church, and delivered by hip hop. Now, with the release of his fourth album, *The Great Depression*, he plans to be the last MC standing. By Heidi Siegmund Cuda. Photographs by Jonathan Mannion.

KNIGHTS OF DARKNESS
Street warriors cloaked in black. Sleep by day. Stalk the hood after midnight, while hard-core beats blast and blunts sizzle. The knights vanish into the vapors. Photographs by Jason Schmidt. Styling by Jason Farrer.

WILD THING
On the one hand, she lives fast and hard. On the other, she's a doting mother of three who'd rather stay at home. Put it all together, and you'll find that Macy Gray's life is as complex as her celebrated music. By Margeaux Watson. Photographs by Larry Sultan.

THE SWEETEST SCIENTIST
Is welterweight boxing champ Shane Mosley too talented for his own good? OJ Lima uncovers the mystery behind the best kept secret in sports. Photographs by Kevin Westenberg.

photography MERIT

■ 600
Publication Vibe
Design Director Florian Bachleda
Art Director Brandon Kavulla
Photo Editors George Pitts, Dora Somosi
Photographer Sacha Waldman
Publisher Miller Publishing Group
Issue November 2001
Category Portraits: Spread

■ 601
Publication Vibe
Design Director Florian Bachleda
Art Director Brandon Kavulla
Photo Editors George Pitts, Dora Somosi
Photographers Jonathan Mannion, Larry Sultan, Kevin Westenberg
Publisher Miller Publishing Group
Issue October 2001
Category Portraits: Story
　　　A. Spread

■ 602
Publication Vibe
Design Director Florian Bachleda
Art Director Brandon Kavulla
Photo Editors George Pitts, Dora Somosi
Photographer Jason Schmidt
Publisher Miller Publishing Group
Issue November 2001
Category Fashion/Beauty: Story

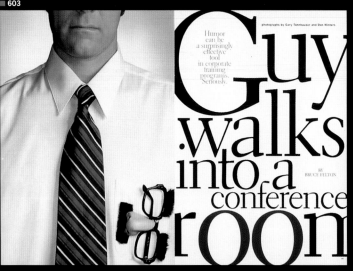

photographs by Gary Tannhauser and Dan Winters

Humor can be a surprisingly effective tool in corporate training programs. Seriously.

Guy walks into a conference room

BY BRUCE FELTON

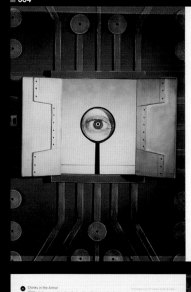

Operating

Stephen Buerle, Cybersleuth

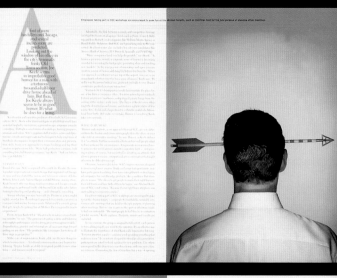

No one is immune to cybercrime: Banks, shipping companies, military establishments and even governments can fall prey to intruders and moles.

No Time for **Comedy**

PHOTOGRAPHY BY MATTHEW PALEY

WHERE SNOW LIONS DANCE

不丹雪嶺

603
Publication Global
Art Director David Armario
Designers Candela D, David Armario
Photographers Gary Tannhauser, Dan Winters
Studio David Armario Design
Publisher Deloitte & Touche, LLP
Issue February/March 2001
Category Photo Illustration Story

604
Publication Global
Art Director David Armario
Designers Candela D, David Armario
Photographers Gary Tannhauser, Dan Winters
Studio David Armario Design
Publisher Deloitte & Touche, LLP
Issue July/August 2001
Category Photo Illustration Story

605
Publication Discovery
Creative Director John Boyer
Art Director Percy Chung
Designer Howard Leung
Photo Editor Jennifer Spencer
Photographer Mathew Paley
Publisher Emphasis Media Ltd
Issue November 2001
Category Reportage; Story

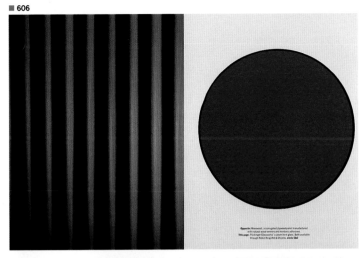

Opposite: Woveneel, a corrugated plywood panel manufactured with natural wood veneers and nontoxic adhesives. **This page:** Pilchinger Glasswerke' custom bent glass. Both available through Robin Reigeled & Objects. **circle 582**

Opposite: Anoli Textile's image, a surfacing material designed by Suzanne Tick. **circle 583** **This page:** Acousto at Surfaces' PEPP recycled acoustical material for ceiling and wall painting. Available through Robin Reigeled & Objects. **circle 582**

off the wall

And on to our pages—thanks to a spate of distinctive designers willing to reveal their favorite paint colors, as well as the companies, both big and small, who produce them. By Alexa Yablonski. Photography by Robin Broadbent.

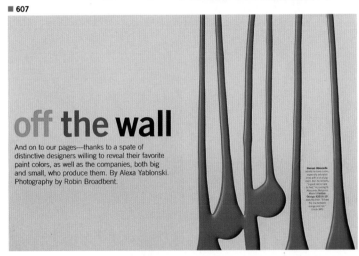

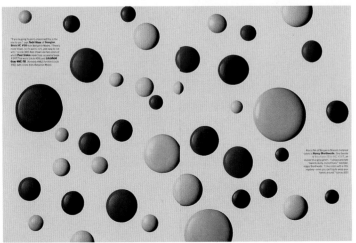

ANDO IN ST. LOUIS

■ 606

Publication Interior Design
Art Director Miranda Dempster
Designer Miranda Dempster
Photographer Robin Broadbent
Publisher Cahners
Issue May 31, 2001
Category Still Life/Interiors: Story

■ 607

Publication Interior Design
Art Director Miranda Dempster
Designer Miranda Dempster
Photographer Robin Broadbent
Publisher Cahners
Issue October 31, 2001
Category Still Life/Interiors: Story

■ 608

Publication Architecture
Art Director Martin Perrin
Designers Adam Michaels, Martin Perrin
Photo Editor Alexandra Brez
Photographer Victoria Sambunaris
Publisher VNU, Inc.
Issue December 2001
Category Reportage: Story

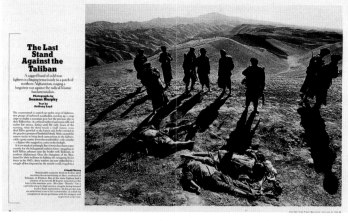

The Last Stand Against the Taliban

A ragged band of cold-war fighters is clinging tenaciously to a patch of northern Afghanistan, waging a forgotten war against the radical Islamic fundamentalists.

Photographs by **Seamus Murphy**
Text by **Anthony Loyd**

What's Black and White and Worn All Over? Spring fashion, silly.

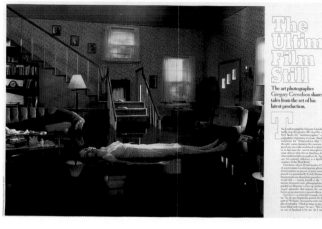

■ 609
Publication The New York Times Magazine
Art Director Janet Froelich
Designer Joele Cuyler
Photo Editor Kathy Ryan
Photographer Seamus Murphy
Publisher The New York Times
Issue January 21, 2001
Category Reportage: Story

■ 610
Publication The New York Times Magazine
Art Director Janet Froelich
Designer Claude Martel
Photographer Cleo Sullivan
Producer Elizabeth Stewart
Publisher The New York Times
Issue January 28, 2001
Category Fashion/Beauty: Story

■ 611
Publication The New York Times Magazine
Art Director Janet Froelich
Designer Joele Cuyler
Photo Editor Kathy Ryan
Photographer Gregory Crewdson
Publisher The New York Times
Issue March 25, 2001
Category Portraits: Spread

■ 612
Publication The New York Times Magazine
Art Director Janet Froelich
Designer Catherine Gilmore-Barnes
Photo Editors Kathy Ryan, Kira Pollack
Photographer Dan Winters
Publisher The New York Times
Issue March 18, 2001
Category Portraits: Spread

■ 613
Publication The New York Times Magazine
Art Director Janet Froelich
Designer Joele Cuyler
Photo Editor Kathy Ryan
Photographer David LaChapelle
Publisher The New York Times
Issue June 10, 2001
Category Portraits: Story

■ 614
Publication The New York Times Magazine
Art Director Janet Froelich
Designer Janet Froelich
Photo Editor Kathy Ryan
Photographer Chris Anderson
Publisher The New York Times
Issue June 3, 2001
Category Reportage: Story

■ 615
Publication The New York Times Magazine
Art Director Janet Froelich
Designer Joele Cuyler
Photo Editor Kathy Ryan
Photographer Alyson Aliano
Publisher The New York Times
Issue June 3, 2001
Category Portraits: Spread

& Entertaining

Give 'Em A Hand

Styled by Avena Gallagher
Photographs by Martha Camarillo

Not since Georgiana, the
Duchess of Devonshire, almost lost
the 'farm' playing whist have
cards been quite this fashionable.
Can mah-jongg be far behind?

Mister
& Mistletoe

First they tell. Then they kiss.
A holiday album. Photographs by Mary Ellen Mark

Give 'Em
A
Hand

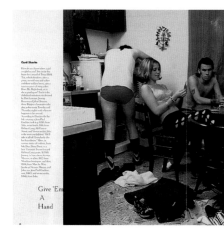

Give 'Em
A
Hand

■ 616
Publication The New York Times Magazine
Art Director Janet Froelich
Designer Claude Martel
Photographer Martha Camarillo
Stylist Avena Gallagher
Publisher The New York Times
Issue June 3, 2001
Category Fashion/Beauty: Story

■ 617
Publication The New York Times Magazine
Art Director Janet Froelich
Designers Claude Martel, David Phan
Photographer Mary Ellen Mark
Producer Anne Christensen
Publisher The New York Times
Issue December 23, 2001
Category Portraits: Story

■618

■619

■620

■621

■618
Publication The New York Times Magazine
Art Director Janet Froelich
Designer Joele Cuyler
Photo Editors Kathy Ryan, Kira Pollack
Photographer Rodney Smith
Publisher The New York Times
Issue December 9, 2001
Category Portraits: Story

■619
Publication The New York Times Magazine
Art Director Janet Froelich
Designer Claude Martel
Photo Editors Kathy Ryan, Jody Quon
Photographer Justine Kurland
Publisher The New York Times
Issue November 11, 2001
Category Portraits: Spread

■620
Publication The Philadelphia Inquirer Magazine
Art Directors Lisa Zollinger Tobia, Susan Syrnick
Designer Lisa Zollinger Tobia
Photographer Michael Bryant
Publisher The Philadelphia Inquirer
Issue June 24, 2001
Category Portraits: Spread

■621
Publication The Washington Post Magazine
Art Director Brian Noyes
Designer Brian Noyes
Photo Editor Keith Jenkins
Photographer Greg Miller
Publisher The Washington Post Co.
Issue November 4, 2001
Category Portraits: Spread

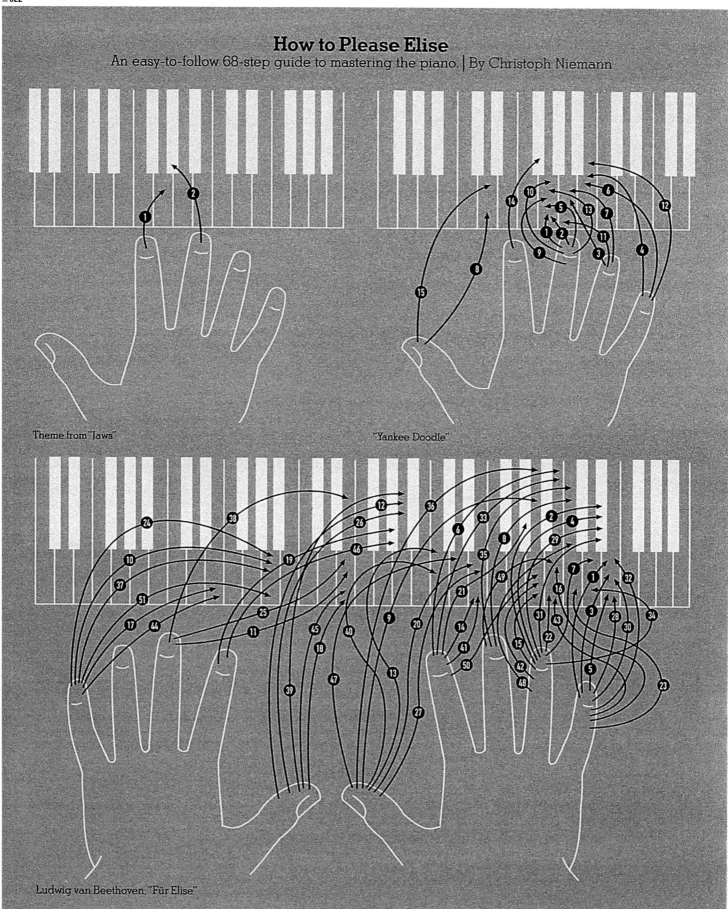

How to Please Elise

An easy-to-follow 68-step guide to mastering the piano. | By Christoph Niemann

Theme from "Jaws"

"Yankee Doodle"

Ludwig van Beethoven, "Für Elise"

■622

Publication The New York Times Magazine
Art Director Janet Froelich
Designers Andrea Fella, Nancy Harris
Illustrator Christoph Niemann
Publisher The New York Times
Issue April 8, 2001
Category Single Page

■ 623
Publication Fast Company
Design Director Patrick Mitchell
Designers Kristin Fitzpatrick, Melanie deForest
Illustrator Christoph Niemann
Publisher Gruner & Jahr USA Publishing
Issue December 2001
Category Spread

ILLUSTRATION BY **#72** DAVID HUGHES

■ 624
Publication Entertainment Weekly
Design Director Geraldine Hessler
Art Director Jennifer Procopio
Illustrator David Hughes
Publisher Time Inc.
Issue October 26, 2001
Category Single Page

■ 625
Publication Global
Art Director David Armario
Designers David Armario, Candela D
Illustrator Brian Cronin
Studio David Armario Design
Publisher Deloitte & Touche, LLP
Issue July/August 2001
Category Story

BY BRUCE FELTON
Illustrations by **Brian Cronin**

The Do-It-Yourself Currency Movement

Central banks, take note: Communities throughout the world are issuing their own money.

At a Frankfurt press conference this past March, the European Central Bank launched a multifront publicity campaign designed to kindle warm feelings for the new euro coins and banknotes, which begin circulating next January 1.

Around the same time, several former Eastern Bloc nations continued pressing their case for admittance to the eurozone, and ASEAN was planning a workshop to explore the benefits of a euro-like common currency for Southeast Asia.

Whatever problems Europe's one-size-fits-all monetary strategy has encountered since its 1998 debut, countries on every continent are showing interest in the idea.

The one-country, one-currency concept has outlived its usefulness, we're told, monetary union is the wave of the future. And the future is closer than you think. In June 2002, 12 of Europe's most venerable currencies are scheduled to be replaced by the euro. Overnight, the franc, mark and lira will be consigned to Europe's dustheap, along with Prince Albert coats and the League of Nations.

In Guardiagrele, Italy, a hill town nestled deep in Italy's Abruzzi region, a retired law professor named Giacinto Auriti has followed the euro's ascendance with a conviction that the world has gone mad. From his perspective, humankind needs the euro like it needs toxic acid rain, the euro and, for that matter, all conventional currencies, are nothing more than a means of preserving the entrenched authority of central banks and keeping the people in a state of perpetual indebtedness.

"Between me and the central banks there is a mental struggle," he says. "There is no middle war." Last year, Auriti took direct aim at the hegemony of the Bank of Italy by designing and producing a legal tender of his own, called the *simec*, an abbreviation of the Italian words for "econometric symbol." He then distributed the money, printed in violet, green and brown, throughout Guardiagrele at an exchange rate of two lire to the *simec*. Most local businesses wanted no part of the *simec*. "I have to put no suppliers were zealots, and they don't take the professor's paper," explains Febo Di Crescenzo, a local clothing-store owner.

But about 40 merchants were willing to honor it. Among them was another clothier, Achille Pica, who recalls doing "a month's worth of business in a couple days" after the debut of the *simec*. As of this past February, there were approximately 700 million *simecs* in circulation, generating liquidity worth more than 11 billion lire. Auriti claims: "A lot of people believe I'm crazy," he acknowledges. "But I have no own theory to prove."

In Good Company

Crazy or not, he is hardly alone. A number of communities on either side of the Atlantic — and in Australia and New Zealand — have created their own stand-alone monetary systems as a way of stimulating local economies and challenging the authority of both central banks and the EU.

Nor is the idea entirely new. During the Great Depression of the 1930s, hundreds of impoverished rural communities in the United States issued scrip for local use when federal dollars were in short

supply. In fact, prior to the Civil War, the United States didn't even have a national currency, according to a history of U.S. paper money published by the Professional Numismatists Guild. "Between 1800 and 1865, about 1,600 U.S. banks privately printed and issued their own paper money."

But growing anti-globalist sentiment of the sort that fueled the Seattle and Davos demonstrations last year has given new impetus to the community-currency movement. Collectively, these initiatives may lack the scope or weight to impact the value or liquidity of established monetary systems or keep EU directives awake at night. But there is no denying that their appeal is spreading rapidly. Auriti's description of the *simec* as "the currency of the people" resonates loudly among a fast-growing international constituency, and provides some commentary on the euro's advertising slogan, "The Euro: Our Money."

As a rule, community-currency advocates believe that there are vast numbers of people — and communities — that have not had a chance to share in the exponential increase in global wealth over the last several years. Community currencies, they argue, can go a long way toward evening out the disparities.

"Local currencies allow communities to diversify their economies, reinvest resources back into their region and reduce dependence on the highly concentrated global economy," says Mariko Nakajima, who heads the Berkeley Region Exchange and Development (BREAD), a community-currency project near San Francisco. "They facilitate the exchange of services and resources among the members of a community."

Whatever its specific form — indirect barter, trade credits, service units — each system serves as "an exchange bank for skills and resources that individuals in the community are willing to trade," Nakajima explains. Some use specially printed paper banknotes. Auriti's *simecs* are a prime example, as are "Ithaca Hours."

Hours for Dollars

Originating in 1991 in the upstate New York town of Ithaca (best known as the home of Cornell University), Ithaca Hours currency notes are valued at US$10 per hour — the average wage in the area. Printed locally in various denominations, the individual bills are forgery-proof and illustrated with local landmarks and celebrated Ithacans. Economist Paul Glover, who founded Ithaca Hours, estimates that more than $2 million worth of transactions have

---

The community-currency movement's first commandment is: "Avoid the appearance of counterfeiting." A rural village in Thailand followed that rule to the letter and still ran into difficulties.

With funding from the Japan Foundation's Asia Center, the Yasothorn Province village of Tambon Nño recently introduced an alternative currency called *bia* (after the Thai word for "seed") whose purpose was to stimulate agricultural and industrial production, and build an independent local economy. The notes were signed by local community leaders and printed to substitute currency notes. But *bia* holders could apply for interest-free loans and the currency for market transactions. Lawyers assured the project's organizers that there would be no legal rule as long as each *bia* note was issued and spent locally. But the Bank of Thailand wasn't sure the whole thing didn't violate the country's central-bank Currency Act. The project was put on hold pending an official ruling.

As it turned out, the community-currency concept had been advocates than detractors within the central bank. Among them was Suwidhi Panichpapiboon, an administrator of the Bank of Thailand's Northeastern Region Branch. Speaking of his of Chulalongkorn University's department, he backed *bia* and championed its involvement toward local currency and pronounced the currency resilient in the habit. "We must look into the project," he said. "And the *bia* is a fitting system for counterfeiting, but it's hardly possible for Chutrakul, his colleagues against *The Book of Thailand's* project. half-supported his the local currency project.

The Color of Money

Companies are poring through the medical heritage of large populations searching for the genes behind common diseases. The effort could revolutionize medicine—and is already triggering controversy.

your genetic
destiny
for sale

BY GARY TAUBES

Large extended families have traditionally been the mother lode of genetic research. From them came a precious commodity: links between the presence of a disease and the errant genes responsible for it. When medical researcher Nancy Wexler, for instance, went looking for the genetic cause of Huntington's disease in 1979, it was a 9,000-member Venezuelan family that enabled her to trace the telltale patterns of disease inheritance.

Wayne Gulliver's family is not nearly so large, but it is impressive nonetheless. Until two years ago, when his great-great-aunt passed away, six generations of Gullivers were alive in Newfoundland. His grandmother, who died last October, had some hundred descendants, while his parents, only in their 60s, already have 26 grandchildren to go with their 10 children. All of this would be professionally irrelevant if Gulliver's family were not typical of Newfoundland, and if Gulliver himself, a dermatologist who studies the genetics of psoriasis, were not involved in a rapidly emerging discipline called population genomics, the goal of which is to identify the underlying genes responsible for common chronic diseases, such as cancer and heart disease.

ILLUSTRATIONS BY BRIAN CRONIN

If these efforts **succeed**, they could revolutionize the nature of drug discovery and medical treatment. The research could also provide clues to your medical future.

The field could become mired in ethical and scientific **controversies**.

■ 626
Publication Technology Review
Art Director Eric Mongeon
Designer Jessica Allen
Illustrator Brian Cronin
Publisher Massachusetts Institute of Technology
Issue March 2001
Category Story

■ 627
Publication The New York Times Magazine
Art Director Janet Froelich
Designer Nancy Harris
Illustrator Christoph Niemann
Publisher The New York Times
Issue December 2, 2001
Category Spread

■ 628
Publication Gentlemen's Quarterly
Design Director Arem Duplessis
Art Director Paul Martinez
Designer Matthew Lenning
Illustrator David Hughes
Publisher Condé Nast Publications, Inc.
Issue December 2001
Category Spread

2011

Ten years from now, historians will look back and see the events of Sept. 11 as mere ripples in a tidal wave of terrorism and political fragmentation.

By Niall Ferguson

TAKE THE LONG VIEW. What will New York be like on Sept. 11, 2011? It's not difficult to imagine a rather wretched future. You need only visit one of those cities — Jerusalem or Belfast — that have been fractured by terrorism and religious strife to get a glimpse. Imagine a segregated city, with a kind of Muslim ghetto in an outer borough that non-Muslims can enter only — if they dare — with a special endorsement on their ID cards. Imagine security checkpoints at every tunnel and bridge leading into Manhattan, where armed antiterrorist troops check every vehicle for traces of explosives and prohibited toxins.

Does that mean you also have to count on even worse gridlock on the Van Wyck Expressway? No, because you also need to imagine a decline in the number of cars on the road. For by 2011, the third and final oil shock will have heralded the end of the internal-combustion era.

Still, there will be some comfort to be found downtown. There, rising like a phoenix from the rubble of the World Trade Center, will be that gleaming monument to American resilience: the twin towers of the Nafta Center. Even if world trade couldn't be rebuilt after the Great Depression of 2002-03, at least the city's beloved landmark could. And the new towers will be even taller — thanks to the antiaircraft turrets on top.

IN ITS IMMEDIATE AFTERMATH, the destruction of the World Trade Center looked like one of those events — the assassination at Sarajevo, the bombing of Pearl Harbor — that set history on a new course. Some excitable commentators began talking about "World War III" almost the same day the twin towers fell. That's one possible future. Much more likely, however, is the nightmare scene sketched above. That's because this outcome could arise out of already discernible trends, all of which *predated* Sept. 11, 2001. Tragic and spectacular though it was, that

event was far less of a turning point than is generally believed.

We should be wary, in fact, of ever attaching too much importance to any single event. It was not Gavrilo Princip alone who started World War I. In his great novel, "The Man Without Qualities," Robert Musil dismissed the idea that history moves in a straight line like a billiard ball, changing direction only when struck. For Musil, history was more like "the passage of clouds," constantly in flux, never predictable. That quality is what makes it impossible to predict where exactly we will be 10 years from now.

Yet Musil's analogy of history and clouds illuminates something else. Though the weather is hard to forecast, the range of possible weathers is not infinitely large. It may not rain tomorrow, but we know that if it does, it will rain water, not boiling oil. It may not be quite as warm as yesterday, but we know that it will not be minus 50 degrees.

In other words, Sept. 11 was the historical equivalent of a violent and unpredictable storm. But the storm did not alter the fact that summer was slowly shading into fall. In just the same way, the attacks on New York and Washington, however shocking, did not alter the direction of several underlying historical trends. In many respects the world will not be so very different in 2011 from the world as it would have evolved under the influence of those trends, even had the attacks not happened.

THE FIRST DEEP TREND is obvious enough: the spread of terrorism — that is to say the use of violence by nonstate organizations in the pursuit of extreme political goals — to the United States. This kind of terrorism has been around for quite a while. Hijacking planes is certainly not new: since the late 1960's, when the tactic first began to be used systematically by the Palestine Liberation Organization and its sympathizers, there have been some 500 hijackings. As for the tactic of flying planes directly at populous targets, what else were the 3,913 Japanese pilots doing

Illustrations by Christoph Niemann

76

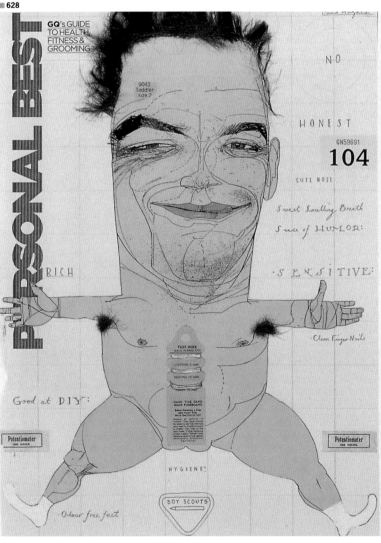

PERSONAL BEST

GQ's GUIDE TO HEALTH, FITNESS & GROOMING

JIM THORNTON: Human Test Subject

ME SO PRETTY

WE SHAVE, LIFT WEIGHTS, GET HAIR IMPLANTS AND PEC IMPLANTS, SCRUB OUR SKIN, POLISH OUR TEETH, ALL IN THE NAME OF ATTRACTING A MATE. BUT DOES ANY OF IT DO ANY GOOD? OUR REPORTER PUTS HIS EGO ON THE LINE AS HE INVESTIGATES THE LATEST SCIENTIFIC FINDINGS ON SEXUAL ATTRACTION, THE MATING HABITS OF JAPANESE SCORPION FLIES AND THE PREDILECTIONS OF RANDOM WOMEN HE ENCOUNTERS

REMEMBER IN SIXTH GRADE WHEN THE MOST BEAUTIFUL GIRL IN your class ranked the boys she found attractive? I'm proud to say I was once declared Cute Boy No. 7 by our class beauty, an Ursula Andress in saddle shoes named Jennifer. Upon discovering my good fortune, I was overcome with such puppy love I could almost taste her slobber. My whole being throbbed with the desire to ascend farther up her hierarchy. But how?

One afternoon, I spied Jenny swishing into the auditorium in her pleated cheerleader's skirt. Feigning Bondian nonchalance, I followed and to my surprise discovered we were alone. As fight-or-flight hormones surged, a strategy became apparent: Pretend you don't know she's there, stroll over, hope she says hi, and then wing it.

I was attempting precisely this when I tripped on an untied Keds shoelace and pitched forward, my chest catching the edge of a seat. I landed like a hooked grouper at Jenny's feet and lay there gasping for air. Casually, she adjusted her poms and her pons and, without a single downward glance, sashayed out of the auditorium. A week later, I'd dropped to seventeenth place.

"What does a woman want?" Sigmund Freud once famously asked. After thirty years of research, the grand old man of penis envy professed he was still clueless. Freud's failure to get the goods is daunting, but is the question still unanswerable? Surely, modern evolutionary biologists have begun to shed some light on what women find attractive in men. Armed with any such insider info, might not we average guys better contort ourselves into the hearts of Jennifer M. and her ilk?

Even though I'm now happily married to a truly wondrous woman and I have no interest in actual philandering, I suspect the desire to sexually attract women at large will remain a lifelong affliction. Think of it as fishing for compliments you're determined to dismiss. Goaded by vanity and curiosity, I launched into a three-stage quest for answers to the Freudian

> THE DESIRE TO ATTRACT WOMEN AT LARGE WILL REMAIN A LIFELONG AFFLICTION.

query. Step 1: Talk to scientists. Step 2: Collect updated female-ranking data on me. Step 3: Analyze this data for clues about what women want.

STEP 1

When it comes to studying male attractiveness, what better place for researchers to begin than with male Japanese scorpion flies? This, at least, is the tack taken by Randy Thornhill, Ph.D., a professor of biology at the University of New Mexico. When he began his investigations, Thornhill was already familiar with the extensive biological literature on bilateral symmetry (how closely the left half of a creature resembles its right half) and its effect on mating. The gist: Parasites, toxins and genetic mutations can all warp a creature's development, throwing its symmetry off-kilter. The more perfectly an adult's sides match, the more likely it has overcome these damaging forces and developed normally. Symmetry thus serves as a powerful sign of genetic robustness and overall health.

But, Thornhill wondered, would female scorpion flies pick up on this signal? His data proved unequivocal: Male flies with evenly matched wings were much more adept than their lopsided peers at attracting mates. Amazingly, even when Thornhill hid symmetrical and asymmetrical guy flies from view, females still zeroed in on the well-balanced boys.

The next step, naturally, was to see if the same pattern holds true for college students. Thornhill and colleagues took the sexual histories of several hundred male undergraduate psych majors, then assessed the lads for symmetry by measuring multiple facial and body features, from ear width to ankle circumference.

"We found that symmetry was consistently predictive of a male's mating success," says Thornhill. Among other things, symmetrical guys lost their virginity earlier than asymmetrical guys, had more lifetime sex partners, induced more copulatory orgasms in their bed partners, fought more with other guys, won more of their fights, were more socially dominant and ranked higher in objective measures of facial good looks. And

ILLUSTRATIONS BY DAVID HUGHES

DECEMBER 2001 GQ 191

illustration SILVER

If "caution" is your investing watchword, take a look at these stocks, positioned to stay strong in a weak market

WHAT'S Safe NOW

GIVEN THE LONG WINNING STREAKS FOR THE MARKET (NOW SNAPPED) and the economy (not yet snapped), the slowing momentum in both, and the still-high valuations in the stock market, it's no wonder experienced investors are feeling cautious. Many people with long memories want to devote, at least a portion of their portfolios to defensive measures—choosing stocks and other investments that tend to hold up pretty well when the stock market goes sour. Investors who were

ABOVE

Where can you find insightful, independent analysis of companies? The truth is out there.

WALL STREET RESEARCH ANALYSTS have been getting lots of bad press lately. And why not? All but a handful of them missed the fact—painfully obvious in hindsight—that a lot of last summer's sky-high stock valuations were about as insanely as a house of cards.

THE REST

BY ANN MONROE ILLUSTRATIONS BY DAVID PLUNKERT

WHAT EVER HAPPENED TO
SIDELINE SPORTSMANSHIP?

Sports rage among parents is spiraling out of control. An in-depth look at how some communities are teaching moms and dads to play fair.
By Mike McNamee

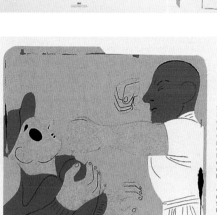

But that doesn't explain why every Saturday and Sunday, even-tempered, Brazelton-reading moms and dads drive their minivans and SUVs to athletic fields, then turn into screaming bullies. Sideline rage crosses all ethnic, educational, and professional lines. Just ask the 13-year-old soccer referee in Washington, DC, who had to eject a parent—one of the nation's top law-enforcement officials at the time—from a match in the early 1990s for badgering the referee over offsides calls.

And while men are more likely than women to lose control and fly into sports fury, testosterone isn't required: After South Brunswick, NJ, police officers broke up a brawl ignited by a 9-year-old girls' soccer game in September 2000, the mother of a player attacked a female official in the parking lot. Convicted of assault, she was fined $405 and sentenced to 20 hours of community service.

Leslie launched the parent-training program after a bloody incident in nearby Port St. Lucie, FL. Early in the second half of a coed under–14 soccer game in November 1999, referee Stephen M. Farinacci whistled a penalty. Fifty yards away, coach Mauricio Lesmes leaped up, slammed down his clipboard, and started screaming. The players on his bench quickly joined in. Farinacci approached Lesmes and asked him five times to calm down. But the livid coach blasted the ref with profanity. "Finally, he said, 'F----you,' and that was it," Farinacci says. The ref ended the game and ordered all the players and spectators to leave.

Minutes later, Farinacci saw Lesmes sitting on a bench near the clubhouse. He said, 'I guess you forgot that the game is for the kids,'" the referee recalls. Then, Lesmes—whose 6-foot-2-inch frame towered over the 5-foot-4 ref—slammed his head into Farinacci's face, shattering his nose and the bone around his left eye. Lesmes claimed his belated attack was provoked by Farinacci's behavior and the heat of competition. A judge who saw the attack on a surveillance-camera videotape disagreed and convicted him of assault.

It's easy to blame such incidents on the hair-trigger tempers of men who were never fit to work with children. Lesmes was substituting for coaches who had been thrown out of the team's previous game. Both Costin and Junta had criminal records.

GROWING UP TOO SOON

Riots and fights still aren't the norm at Little League or Pop Warner games—but both officials and parents say they're increasingly common. Why? One convenient answer is "scholarships." When ESPN gives the Little League World Series the same glamour treatment as the Yankees vs. the Mets, youth sports beckon as a ticket to glory and wealth. Some parents look at their kids and see the next Tiger, Mia, or Michael shooting toward a collegiate free ride and a pro contract.

The result of this way of thinking: mothers and fathers who spend thousands of dollars to train their kids in one particular sport, year-round. "Every game becomes a step toward getting the right coach, going to the right camp, and grabbing the brass ring before some other child gets it," says Dr. Burnett. For these parents, a lack of playing time or a miscalled penalty can unleash fury.

But delusions of sports riches can't be the whole story: Violence breaks out as readily at rec-league contests as at all-star games. Youth-sports experts place the blame on social changes that affect both parenting and the values that sports traditionally stood for. "Sports is life with the volume turned up," says Barry Mano, founder and president of the National Association of Sports Officials.

>> Some 70% of kids hang up their cleats and get out of sports by the time they're 13. Many blame it on the negative attitudes of their parents and coaches.

CHILD MAY 2001

■ 629

Publication Bloomberg Personal Finance
Art Director Frank Tagariello
Designer Frank Tagariello
Illustrator Jeffrey Fisher
Publisher Bloomberg L.P.
Issue September 2001
Category Story

■ 630

Publication Bloomberg Personal Finance
Art Director Frank Tagariello
Designer Frank Tagariello
Illustrator David Plunkert
Publisher Bloomberg L.P.
Issue May 2001
Category Story

■ 631

Publication Child
Creative Director Sabrina Weberstetter
Designer Jennifer MacKenzie
Illustrator Brian Cronin
Publisher Gruner & Jahr USA Publishing
Issue May 2001
Category Story

FINANCIAL VISION

USING INTERNET STRATEGIES
TO GIVE YOU INSIGHT INTO
YOUR COMPANY'S FISCAL PICTURE,
WHENEVER YOU WANT IT.

BY G. PATRICK PAWLING
Illustrations by Guy Billout

"WHAT'S REALLY CRIMINAL, IS TO NOT HAVE
THE MIND-SET TO BE PROACTIVE." —DAVE JUHLANGER, ANN RESEARCH

"CEOs TODAY REALIZE THAT SPEED AND AGILITY
ARE CRITICAL FOR SURVIVAL." —LARRY CARTER, CISCO SYSTEMS

"THE ROLE OF FINANCE, I THINK, IS TIPPING
UPSIDE DOWN." —BRIAN L. WEISS, GENERAL ELECTRIC

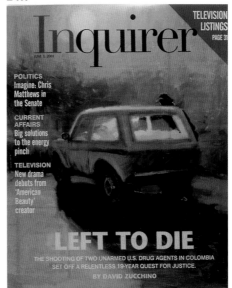

Inquirer
TELEVISION
LISTINGS
PAGE 31

JUNE 3, 2001

POLITICS
Imagine: Chris
Matthews in
the Senate

CURRENT
AFFAIRS
Big solutions
to the energy
pinch

TELEVISION
New drama
debuts from
'American
Beauty'
creator

LEFT TO DIE

THE SHOOTING OF TWO UNARMED U.S. DRUG AGENTS IN COLOMBIA
SET OFF A RELENTLESS 19-YEAR QUEST FOR JUSTICE.
BY DAVID ZUCCHINO

TWO AMERICAN DRUG AGENTS: SHOT AND BLEEDING, STRUGGLE TO ESCAPE
THE COLOMBIAN JUNGLE, AND A SEARCH FOR THE SHOOTERS BEGINS

THE MANHUNT

By David Zucchino

THE DRUG DEALERS WHO SHOT TWO U.S. AGENTS SERVED LESS THAN FOUR YEARS IN
COLOMBIAN PRISONS. BRINGING THEM TO JUSTICE IN AMERICA WOULD TAKE MUCH LONGER

UNFINISHED BUSINESS

By David Zucchino

■ 632

Publication iQ
Creative Director Robb Allen
Art Directors Jennifer Napier, Grace Lee
Designer Jennifer Napier
Illustrator Guy Billout
Publisher Hachette Filipacchi Custom Publishing
Issue May/June 2001
Category Story

■ 633

Publication The Philadelphia Inquirer Magazine
Art Directors Lisa Zollinger Tobia, Susan Syrnick
Designer Lisa Zollinger Tobia
Illustrator Peter Sylvada
Publisher The Philadelphia Inquirer
Issue June 3, 2001
Category Story

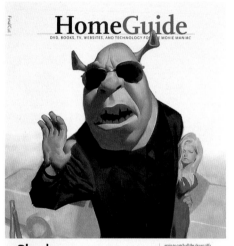

Publication Expansion
Creative Director Guillermo Caballero
Art Director Ricardo Peña
Illustrator Ricardo Pelaez
Publisher Grupo Editorial Expansion
Issue July 2001
Category Single Page

Publication Premiere
Art Director Richard Baker
Designer Christine Cucuzza
Illustrator Dan Adel
Publisher Hachette Filipacchi Media U.S.
Issue December 2001
Category Spread

Publication Rolling Stone
Design Director Fred Woodward
Illustrator Randall Enos
Publisher Wenner Media LLC
Issue March 2001
Category Single Page

Publication Rolling Stone
Design Director Fred Woodward
Illustrator Christian Northeast
Publisher Wenner Media LLC
Issue April 2001
Category Single Page

Publication Entertainment Weekly
Design Director Geraldine Hessler
Art Director Robert Festino
Designer Sara Osten
Illustrator Hanoch Piven
Publisher Time Inc.
Issue April 20, 2001
Category Single Page

Publication Entertainment Weekly
Design Director Geraldine Hessler
Art Director Jennifer Procopio
Illustrator Brian Cronin
Publisher Time Inc.
Issue October 26, 2001
Category Spread

IN MY HUMBLE OPINION Want soup? The very best soup in the entire world is served by Al Yeganeh, owner of Soup Kitchen International on West 55th Street in New York. Slandered in a notorious *Seinfeld* parody, Al's restaurant is busier than ever. Some of the folks in the 30-minute-long line (waiting to buy a $6 bowl of soup!) are insensitive clods who saw the TV show and want to experience a real celebrity moment. Others are longtime customers who are willing to brave the cold to get the real thing. AT THE SAME TIME that hundreds of hungry people are waiting to get a unique bowl of soup from Al, millions are eating lunch at the most ubiquitous restaurant in the world: McDonald's. In fact, every single day, McDonald's serves a meal to one out of 14 Americans. TAKE A DRIVE through Illinois—home to McDonald's headquarters—and you might discover that many of the towns you pass don't have one "real" restaurant. No diner, no place for a fancy night out. Just a Hardee's, a Pizza Hut, and, of course, a McDonald's. This is not a phenomenon limited to tiny towns near Springfield. There are thousands of McDonald's franchises across the country, along with chains like Arby's, Subway, T.G.I. Friday's, and countless others churning out anonymous, forgettable meals to people in a hurry. Hey, it's what we asked for. SO WHAT'S WRONG with selling out?

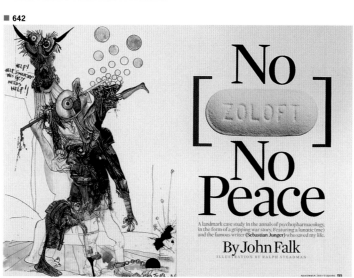

640
Publication Entertainment Weekly
Design Director Geraldine Hessler
Art Director John Walker
Designer Jennifer Procopio
Illustrator Hadley Hooper
Publisher Time Inc.
Issue December 21, 2001
Category Spread

641
Publication Esquire
Creative Director John Korpics
Art Director Hannah McCaughey
Illustrator Riccardo Vecchio
Publisher The Hearst Corporation-Magazines Division
Issue September 2001
Category Spread

642
Publication Esquire
Creative Director John Korpics
Illustrator Ralph Steadman
Publisher The Hearst Corporation-Magazines Division
Issue November 2001
Category Spread

643
Publication Fast Company
Design Director Patrick Mitchell
Designer Kristin Fitzpatrick
Illustrator Bill Mayer
Publisher Gruner & Jahr USA Publishing
Issue July 2001
Category Spread

644
Publication Kiplingers Personal Finance
Art Director Cynthia Currie
Designer Cynthia Currie
Illustrator Brian Cronin
Publisher Kiplingers Washington Editors
Issue November 2001
Category Spread

645
Publication Angels on Earth
Art Director Kai-Ping Chao
Illustrator Yuan Lee
Publisher Guideposts
Issue July/August 2001
Category Spread

illustration MERIT

646
Publication Gentlemen's Quarterly
Creative Director Arem Duplessis
Art Director Paul Martinez
Designer Matthew Lenning
Illustrator Serge Bloch
Publisher Condé Nast Publications, Inc.
Issue September 2001
Category Story

647
Publication Gentlemen's Quarterly
Creative Director Arem Duplessis
Art Director Paul Martinez
Designer Matthew Lenning
Illustrator Ralph Steadman
Publisher Condé Nast Publications, Inc.
Issue January 2001
Category Single Page

649
Publication Gentlemen's Quarterly
Creative Director Arem Duplessis
Art Director Paul Martinez
Designer Matthew Lenning
Illustrator Daniel Bejar
Publisher Condé Nast Publications, Inc.
Issue September 2001
Category Single Page

648
Publication Gentlemen's Quarterly
Creative Director Arem Duplessis
Art Director Paul Martinez
Designer Kayoko Suzuki
Illustrator Marco Ventura
Publisher Condé Nast Publications, Inc.
Issue April 2001
Category Single Page

650
Publication Inc.
Design Director Patrick Mitchell
Designer Patrick Mitchell
Illustrator David Cowles
Publisher Gruner & Jahr USA Publishing
Issue November 30, 2001
Category Single Page

suddenly
solo

Surviving a messy partnership split isn't easy.
(There aren't many self-help books out there for
newly divorced business owners.) But a handful of this year's Inc 500
entrepreneurs have discovered the joys of going it alone
BY KRYSTEN CRAWFORD ILLUSTRATIONS BY ISTVAN BANYAI

© INC MAGAZINE

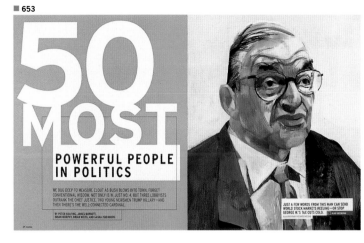

50 MOST
POWERFUL PEOPLE IN POLITICS

WE DUG DEEP TO MEASURE CLOUT AS BUSH BLOWS INTO TOWN. FORGET
CONVENTIONAL WISDOM: NOT ONLY IS W. JUST NO. 4, BUT THREE LOBBYISTS
OUTRANK CHIEF JUSTICE. TWO YOUNG NEWSMEN TRUMP HILLARY—AND
THEN THERE'S THE WELL-CONNECTED CARDINAL.

BY PETER KEATING, JAMES BURNETT,
BRIAN MURPHY, BRIAN WEISS, AND SASHA ISSENBERG

JUST A FEW WORDS FROM THIS MAN CAN SEND
WORLD STOCK MARKETS REELING—OR STOP
GEORGE W.'S TAX CUTS COLD.

[LEGAL AFFAIRS]
CAN VIRTUAL KIDDIE PORN BE VICTIMLESS?

IF CHILD PORN STARS "SYNTHETIC CHILDREN,"
IS IT STILL ILLEGAL? DO DIGITAL IMAGES INCITE
REAL-LIFE ABUSE? THE SUPREME COURT HAS TAKEN
ON A CASE WITH HUGE FIRST AMENDMENT
IMPLICATIONS—FOR EVERYONE FROM HOLLYWOOD
FILMMAKERS TO VIDEO-GAME DEVELOPERS.

BY ROGER PARLOFF

ILLUSTRATION BY JAMES VICTORE

HE'S NO LONGER JUST "HOLY JOE." HE'S
A LEADING CANDIDATE FOR PRESIDENT IN
THE NEXT ELECTION.

NO ONE HAS MORE LEVERAGE WITH THE SENATE'S
MIGHTY MIDDLE THAN THIS SAVVY, SOMETIMES
BRASH MODERATE FROM MAINE.

The Accidental Pilot

A daring airman makes history (and earns a cool
nickname) by flying the wrong direction.

By Philip H. Ault
Illustrations by Ed Fotheringham

WRONG WAY

Nobody could say Douglas G. Corrigan
didn't dream big.

illustration MERIT

'all I heard was cancer'
By Brenda Hotsellark   Illustrations by Stefanie Augustine

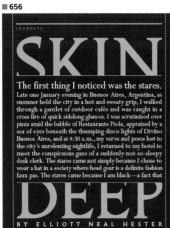

doll parts
illustrations by michael gentile

music

b
the lost
Y

Before Bob Dylan found his own
voice, he had to go …

Knockin'
on
Woody's
Door

By HOWARD SOUNES
From "Down the Highway:
The Life of Bob Dylan"

ADISON Square
Garden. Friday
evening, Oct. 16,
1992, at a concert
to celebrate Bob
Dylan's 30 years as a recording artist.
A man trotted out into converging
spotlights. The audience shrieked
and whistled, straining to catch a
glimpse of the legend.

Dressed in a black suit and white
shirt, Bob Dylan looked like a di-
sheveled waiter. He moved to the
microphone and began strumming
his guitar, performing solo as he'd
done in coffeehouses decades ago.

This icon of the '60s, author of
some of the most popular songs of
his generation, began with one of

his more obscure compositions. Before some 18,000 people, he began
playing "Song to Woody," a tribute
to his first hero, Woody Guthrie, the
father of American folk music.

Woody's daughter Nora sat in the
audience. She began to weep as Dylan
sang about her father.

BOB DYLAN WAS BORN Robert Allen
Zimmerman in 1941, and grew up
in Hibbing, Minn., 75 miles northwest of Duluth. Late at night Bob
would listen to radio stations from
Little Rock, Chicago and way down
south in Shreveport, La.

These stations played country
music and the blues. "I used to stay
up until two, three o'clock in the

125

Once upon a time, a man sat
typing in a double-wide trailer

Before
He Was
Stephen
King

By STEPHEN KING
From "On Writing"

Y THE TIME I started my first novel,
Carrie, I had landed a job teaching
English in the town of Hampden,
Maine. I would be paid about $6500
a year, which seemed an unthinkable
sum after earning $1.60 an hour at my previous
job in a laundry.

By the late winter of 1973 we were living in
a double-wide trailer in Hermon, a little town
west of Bangor. I was driving a Buick with
transmission problems we couldn't afford to fix,
my wife, Tabby, was working at Dunkin' Donuts
and we had no telephone.

I wasn't having much success with my writing. By most Friday afternoons I felt as if I'd

120

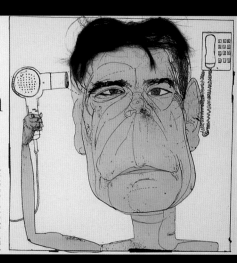

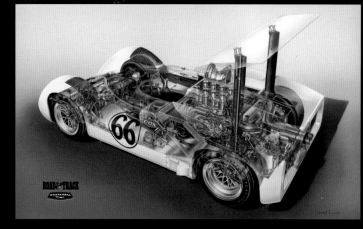

illustration MERIT

Being impatient can damage your health and relationships, and it makes the world a less pleasant place. Here's how to get a handle on hurrying.

what's the

rush?

I'm a nice person. I donate to food drives, buy cookies from Scouts, hold doors open for strangers. But when I'm in a hurry, look out. One minute I'm as tranquil as Buddha, and the next I'm giving the finger to the chick in the minivan who has the nerve to drive the speed limit in a no-passing zone.

Too many of us, when rushed, do some pretty dangerous and destructive things. We floor it through yellow lights, snap at dawdling children, bark at busy receptionists and swear when we have to wait 90 seconds at a drive-thru. And no way are we going to patiently wait our turn to use a popular new machine at the gym. ➤

By Alice Lesch Kelly Illustration by Paul Wearing

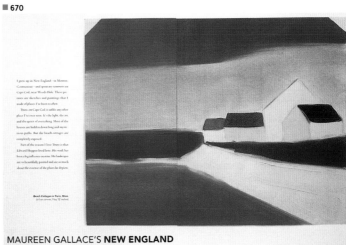

MAUREEN GALLACE'S **NEW ENGLAND**

 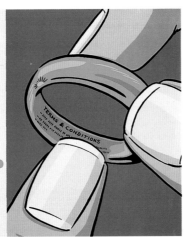

I do.
(however...)

Prenuptial agreements aren't just for zillionaires (or even just for men) anymore. Here's why you need one, what you should ask for and what the courts will uphold.

BY MICHELLE ANDREWS ILLUSTRATIONS BY CHRISTOPH NIEMANN

REAL-LIFE
INDEX

Will Spyware Work?

 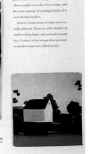

Publication Shape
Art Director Jacqueline Moorby
Designer Donna Giovannitti
Illustrator Paul Wearing
Publisher Weider Publications, Inc
Issue August 2001
Category Spread

Publication SmartMoney
Design Director Amy Rosenfeld
Art Director Gretchen Smelter
Designer Gretchen Smelter
Illustrator Christoph Niemann
Publisher Dow Jones & Hearst Corp.
Issue September 2001
Category Spread

Publication SmartMoney
Design Director Amy Rosenfeld
Art Director Gretchen Smelter
Designer Amy Rosenfeld
Illustrator Tomer Hanuka
Publisher Dow Jones & Hearst Corp.
Issue November 2001
Category Single Page

Publication Technology Review
Art Director Eric Mongeon
Designer Eric Mongeon
Illustrator Brian Cronin
Publisher Massachusetts Institute of Technology
Issue December 2001
Category Single Page

Publication Travel & Leisure
Creative Director Pamela Berry
Art Director Laura Gharrity
Designers Stephanie Achar, Jae Han
Illustrator Maureen Gallace
Publisher American Express Publishing Co.
Issue February 2001
Category Story

A NEW REALITY

TORN GIRDERS
By Brian Cronin

■ 671
Publication TV Guide
Design Director Maxine Davidowitz
Art Director Theresa Griggs
Designer Shannon Blasco
Illustrator Eddie Guy
Publisher TV Guide Inc.
Issue September 8, 2001
Category Spread

■ 672
Publication TV Guide
Design Director Maxine Davidowitz
Art Director Theresa Griggs
Designer Shannon Blasco
Illustrator Gary Kelley
Publisher TV Guide Inc.
Issue September 8, 2001
Category Spread

■ 673
Publication Working Mother
Creative Director Ben Margherita
Designer Ben Margherita
Illustrator Anita Kunz
Photo Editor Martha Maristany
Publisher Working Mother Media
Issue October 2001
Category Spread

■ 674
Publication Investment Advisor
Art Director Dorothy O'Connor-Jones
Illustrator Christoph Hitz
Publisher Wicks Business Information
Issue January 2001
Category Spread

■ 675
Publication Worth
Design Director Deanna Lowe
Art Director Dirk Barnett
Illustrator Brian Cronin
Publisher Worth Media
Issue November 2001
Category Single Page

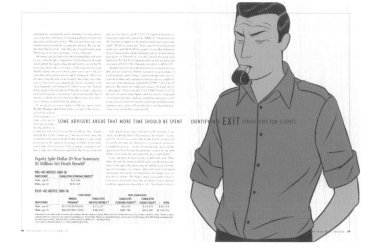

■ 676
Publication Bloomberg Wealth Manager
Art Director Laura Zavetz
Designer Beatrice McDonald
Illustrator Brian Cronin
Publisher Bloomberg L.P.
Issue May 2001
Category Story

■ 677
Publication Bloomberg Wealth Manager
Art Director Laura Zavetz
Designer Beatrice McDonald
Illustrator Nick Dewar
Publisher Bloomberg L.P.
Issue October 2001
Category Story

■ 678

illustration MERIT

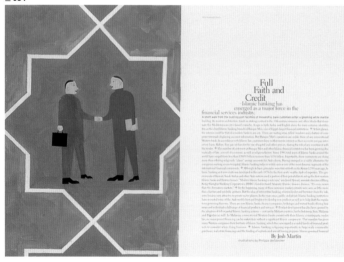

682
Publication Feat
Creative Director Robb Allen
Art Director Jennifer Napier
Designers Jennifer Napier, Eugene Wang
Illustrator Ulla Puggard
Publisher Hachette Filipacchi Custom Publishing
Issue Fall/Winter 2001
Category Spread

683
Publication Global
Art Director David Armario
Designers Candela D, David Armario
Illustrator Benoit
Studio David Armario Design
Publisher Deloitte & Touche, LLP
Issue February/March 2001
Category Spread

684
Publication Global
Art Director David Armario
Designer Candela D
Illustrator Philippe Weisbecker
Studio David Armario Design
Publisher Deloitte & Touche, LLP
Issue February/March 2001
Category Spread

685
Publication Stanford Medicine
Art Director David Armario
Designer David Armario
Illustrator Paul Wearing
Studio David Armario Design
Publisher Stanford University Medical Center
Issue Winter/Spring 2001
Category Spread

686
Publication Gallup Management Journal
Creative Director Terry Koppel
Design Director Carin Goldberg
Art Director Kristina DiMatteo
Designers Carin Goldberg, Kristina DiMatteo, Rebecca Alden
Illustrator Hanoch Piven
Publisher Time Inc. Custom Publishing
Issue Fall 2001
Category Spread

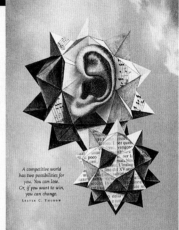

■ 689
Publication InformationWeek
Creative Director Michael Gigante
Design Director Joe McNeill
Art Director Mary Ellen Forte
Designer Mary Ellen Forte
Illustrator James O'Brien
Publisher CMP Media, Inc.
Issue October 1, 2001
Category Spread

■ 687
Publication InformationWeek
Creative Director Michael Gigante
Design Director Joe McNeill
Art Director Mary Ellen Forte
Designer Michael Gigante
Illustrator David Plunkert
Publisher CMP Media, Inc.
Issue February 5, 2001
Category Spread

■ 688
Publication InformationWeek
Creative Director Michael Gigante
Design Director Joe McNeill
Art Director Mary Ellen Forte
Designer Mary Ellen Forte
Illustrator Jonathan Weiner
Publisher CMP Media, Inc.
Issue May 14, 2001
Category Spread

■ 690
Publication Selling Power
Art Director Colleen McCudden
Designer Colleen McCudden
Illustrator Malcolm Tarlofsky
Publisher Personal Selling Power
Issue July/August 2001
Category Story

illustration MERIT

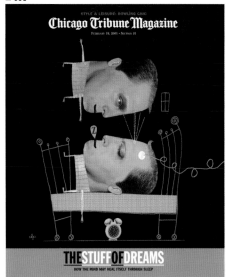

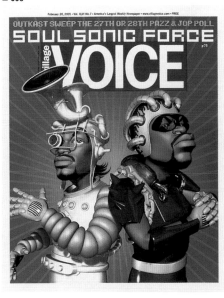

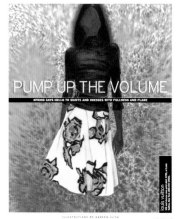

697

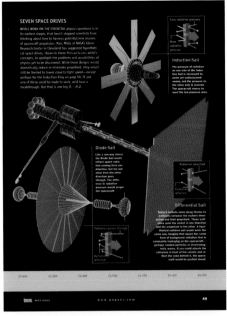

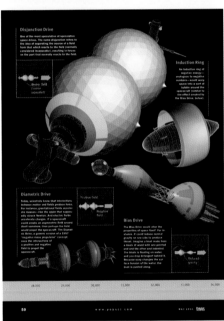

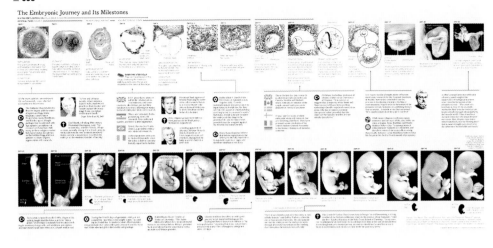

698

699

700

spots

Recognizing the little masterpieces that work so hard to communicate big ideas in a small amount of space.

JUDGES

(LEFT TO RIGHT)

Mary Parsons, The Atlantic Monthly

Gretchen Smelter, Smart Money

Lillian Valentine Curry, Cute Baby

Christine Curry, CHAIRPERSON, The New Yorker

Florian Bachleda, Vibe

Jennifer Procopio, Entertainment Weekly

Erin Whelan, Esquire

■ 701
Illustrator Guy Billout
Title Escape and Evasion
Art Director Christine Curry
Publication The New Yorker
Publisher Condé Nast Publications, Inc.
Issue November 12 , 2001

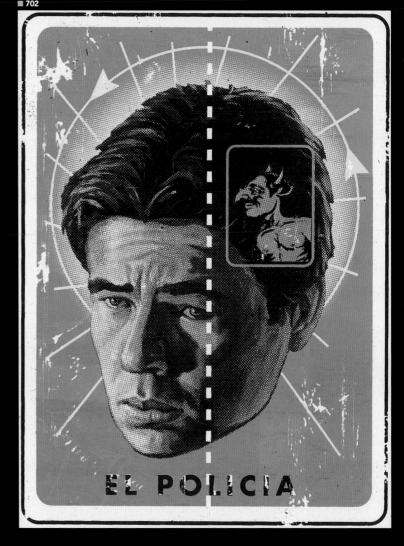

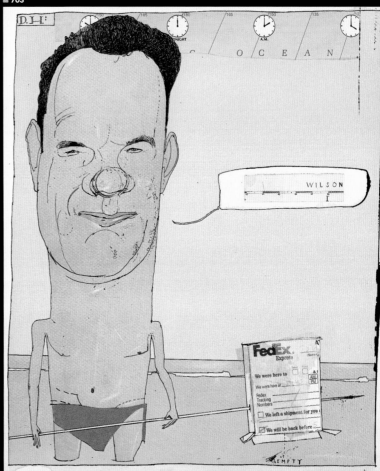

■ 702
Illustrator Tavis Coburn
Title Traffic
Art Directors Richard Baker, Kat Bigelau
Publication Premiere
Publisher Hachette Filipacchi Media U.S.
Issue July , 2001
Award Second Place

■ 703
Illustrator David Hughes
Title Cast Away
Art Directors Richard Baker, Bess Wang
Publication Premiere
Publisher Hachette Filipacchi Media U.S.
Issue August 2001
Award Third Place

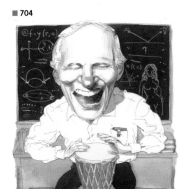

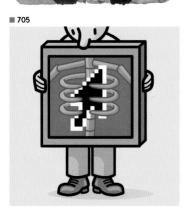

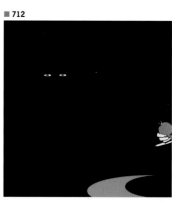

■ 704
Illustrator Joe Ciardiello
Title QED
Art Director Owen Phillips
Publication The New Yorker
Publisher Condé Nast Publications, Inc.
Issue November 11, 2001

■ 705
Illustrator Christoph Niemann
Title 50 Best Web Sites
Art Director Marti Golon
Publication TIME
Publisher AOL Time Inc.
Issue April 2002

■ 706
Illustrator Scott Laumann
Title Three to Hold On To
Art Director Gretchen Smelter
Publication SmartMoney
Publisher Dow Jones & Hearst Corp.
Issue April 2001

■ 707
Illustrator Matthew Martin
Title Niche Music
Art Director Edel Rodriguez
Publication TIME
Publisher AOL Time Inc.
Issue August , 2001

■ 708
Illustrator Barry Blitt
Title 21 Things We'd Like to See
Art Directors George Karabotsos, John Dixon
Publication Men's Health
Publisher Rodale Inc.
Issue June 2001

■ 709
Illustrator Eric Palma
Title Julia & Martha
Art Director Jennifer Gilman
Publication My Generation
Publisher AARP
Issue November/December 2001

■ 710
Illustrator Istvan Banyai
Title Hessler/Wenzhov
Art Director Christine Curry
Publication The New Yorker
Publisher Condé Nast Publications, Inc.
Issue October 15, 2001

■ 711
Illustrator Al Hirschfeld
Title Opposite of Sex
Art Director Geraldine Hessler
Publication Entertainment Weekly
Publisher Time, Inc.
Issue January 4, 2001

■ 712
Illustrator Istvan Banyai
Title Mature Sex
Art Director Marti Golon
Publication TIME
Publisher AOL Time Inc.
Issue May 2001

■ 722

■ 723

■ 727

■ 728

■ 725

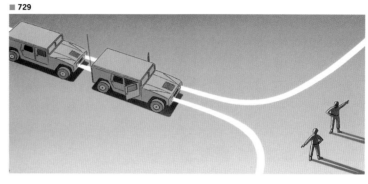

■ 729

■ 724

■ 726

■ 730

■ 722
Illustrator Lara Tomlin
Title The White Stripes
Art Director Owen Phillips
Publication The New Yorker
Publisher Condé Nast Publications, Inc.
Issue June 18, 2001

■ 723
Illustrator Scott Menchin
Title Snoring
Art Directors Jennifer Gilman, Gina Toole
Publication My Generation
Publisher AARP
Issue March/April 2001

■ 724
Illustrator Roberto Parada
Title Hannibal & The Silence of the Lambs
Art Directors Richard Baker, Bess Wang
Publication Premiere
Publisher Hachette Filipacchi Media U.S.
Issue September 2001

■ 725
Illustrator Jason Holley
Title Almost Famous
Art Directors Richard Baker, Kat Bigelau
Publication Premiere
Publisher Hachette Filipacchi Media U.S.
Issue February 2002

■ 726
Illustrator Andrea Ventura
Title Dave Winer, Web Journalist
Art Director Patrick Prince
Publication Internet World
Publisher Penton Media, Inc.
Issue July 2001

■ 727
Illustrator Jeffrey Fisher
Title Spider
Art Director Nicole Duggan
Publication Outside
Publisher Mariah Media, Inc.
Issue June 2001

■ 728
Illustrator Guy Billout
Title What Went Wrong
Art Director Owen Phillips
Publication The New Yorker
Publisher Condé Nast Publications, Inc.
Issue October 8 , 2001

■ 729
Illustrator Guy Billout
Title The Debate Within
Art Director Christine Curry
Publication The New Yorker
Publisher Condé Nast Publications, Inc.
Issue March 11, 2001

■ 730
Illustrator Istvan Banyai
Title Headings
Art Director Mary Parsons
Publication The Atlantic Monthly
Publisher The Atlantic Monthly
Issue various

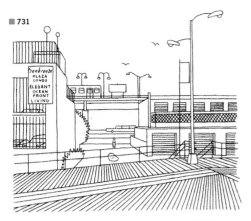

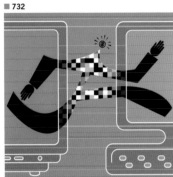

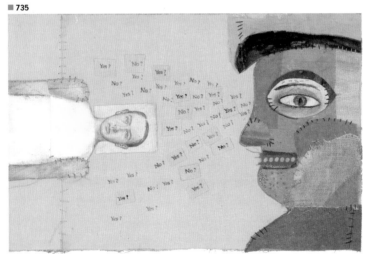

■ 731
Illustrator Laurent Cilluffo
Title The Talk of the Town
Art Director Christine Curry
Publication The New Yorker
Publisher Condé Nast Publications, Inc.
Issue various

■ 732
Illustrator Campbell Laird
Title Transfer from TV to PC
Art Director Deena Goldblatt
Publication On
Publisher AOL Time Inc.
Issue August 2001

■ 733
Illustrator Jason Holley
Title Springing Forward
Art Director Geraldine Hessler
Publication Entertainment Weekly
Publisher Time, Inc.
Issue February 15, 2002

■ 734
Illustrator Marina Sagona
Title Tree of Wooden Clogs
Art Director Owen Phillips
Publication The New Yorker
Publisher Condé Nast Publications, Inc.
Issue April 2, 2001

■ 735
Illustrator Deborah Barrett
Title In Sickness and In Health
Art Directors Frank Tagariello, John Genzo
Publication Bloomberg Personal Finance
Publisher Bloomberg L.P.
Issue Jan/Feb 2002

■ 736
Illustrator Edwin Fotheringham
Title Somebody's Watching You
Art Director Jennifer Gilman
Publication My Generation
Publisher AARP
Issue September/October 2001

■ 737
Illustrator Sterling Hundley
Title Jerry Garcia
Art Director Jennifer Gilman
Publication My Generation
Publisher AARP
Issue January/February 2002

■ 738
Illustrator Gary Baseman
Title Spot
Art Directors John Korpics, Erin Whelan
Publication Esquire
Publisher The Hearst Corporation-Magazines Division
Issue May 2001

■ 739
Illustrator Tim Bower
Title Rodney Dangerfield Collection
Art Director Hannah McCaughey
Publication Esquire
Publisher The Hearst Corporation-Magazines Division
Issue July 2001

■ 740

■ 745

■ 741

■ 743

■ 746

■ 747

■ 744

■ 748

■ 742

■ 740
Illustrator Edel Rodriguez
Title Once Around the City
Art Director Owen Phillips
Publication The New Yorker
Publisher Condé Nast Publications, Inc.
Issue August 9, 2001

■ 741
Illustrator Stephen Savage
Title Snoop Dogg
Art Director Florian Bachleda
Publication Vibe
Publisher Miller Publishing Group
Issue October, 2001

■ 742
Illustrator Greg Clarke
Title Dearly Departed
Art Director Susan Dazzo
Publication Parenting
Publisher The Parenting Group/AOL Time Warner
Issue April 22, 2002

■ 743
Illustrator Marc Rosenthal
Title ATM Pickpockets
Art Director Cynthia Currie
Publication Kiplinger's Personal FInance
Publisher Kiplinger Washington Editors
Issue February 2002

■ 744
Illustrator Demetrious Psillos
Title The Devil & Miss Jones
Art Director Christine Curry
Publication The New Yorker
Publisher Condé Nast Publications, Inc.
Issue April 16, 2001

■ 745
Illustrator Matt Madden
Title Excursions: A Fine Line
Art Director Owen Phillips
Publication The New Yorker
Publisher Condé Nast Publications, Inc.
Issue September 10 , 2001

■ 746
Illustrator Marc Rosenthal
Title Warning About Layoffs To Come
Art Director Tony Mikolajczyk
Publication Fortune
Publisher Time Inc.
Issue August 2001

■ 747
Illustrator Peter De Seve
Title Robert Frost
Art Director Christine Curry
Publication The New Yorker
Publisher Condé Nast Publications, Inc.
Issue October 2001

■ 748
Illustrator Daniele Melani
Title The Digital M.D.
Art Director Gretchen Smelter
Publication SmartMoney
Publisher Dow Jones & Hearst Corp.
Issue November 2001

■ 749

■ 755

■ 750

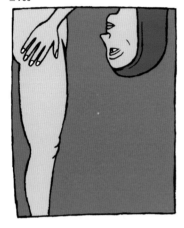

■ 752

■ 754

■ 751

■ 753

■ 756

■ 757

■ 758

■ 759

■ 761

■ 764

■ 765

■ 762

■ 763

■ 766

■ 760

■ 758
Illustrator P J Loughran
Title Agents of Fear
Art Director Jennifer GIlman
Publication My Generation
Publisher AARP
Issue May/June 2001

■ 759
Illustrator Phil Huling
Title The Mystic
Art Directors John Korpics, Todd Albertson
Publication Esquire
Publisher The Hearst Corporation-Magazines
Division
Issue February 2002

■ 760
Illustrator Guy Billout
Title Inside Out
Art Director Christine Curry
Publication The New Yorker
Publisher Condé Nast Publications, Inc.
Issue June 11 , 2001

■ 761
Illustrator Mark Ulriksen
Title Lucinda Williams
Art Director Marti Golon
Publication TIME
Publisher AOL Time Inc.
Issue August 2001

■ 763
Illustrator Roberto Parada
Title Donald Rumsfield
Art Director Jennifer Roth
Publication TIME
Publisher AOL Time Inc.
Issue October 18, 2002

■ 762
Illustrator Edel Rodriguez
Title Monsoon Wedding
Art Director Owen Phillips
Publication The New Yorker
Publisher Condé Nast Publications, Inc.
Issue February 18, 2002

■ 764
Illustrator Robert Andrew Parker
Title KissKissBangBang
Art Director Owen Phillips
Publication The New Yorker
Publisher Condé Nast Publications, Inc.
Issue February 11, 2002

■ 765
Illustrator David Hughes
Title How to Write a Song
Art Directors John Korpics, Hannah McCaughey
Publication Esquire
Publisher The Hearst Corporation-Magazines
Division
Issue July 2001

■ 766
Illustrator C.F. Payne
Title The 100 Best Things Ever Said by Men
Art Directors George Karabotsos, Wilbert Gutierrez
Publication Men's Health
Publisher Rodale Inc.
Issue December 2001

767

769

774

768

770

772

775

771

773

■ **767**
Illustrator John Cuneo
Title Shakespeare Was A Hack
Art Directors John Korpics, Erin Whelan
Publication Esquire
Publisher The Hearst Corporation-Magazines
Division
Issue March 2002

■ **768**
Illustrator John Cuneo
Title Willie Nelson
Art Director George McCalman
Publication San Francisco
Issue July 2001

■ **769**
Illustrator Scott Menchin
Title Sloth
Art Directors Chris Garcia, Matthew Ball,
Josh McKible
Publication Popular Science
Publisher Time4 Media
Issue December 2001

■ **770**
Illustrator Christoph Niemann
Title Dr. Web Site
Art Director Jennifer Gilman
Publication My Generation
Publisher AARP
Issue January/February 2002

■ **771**
Illustrator Daniel Bejar
Title Fiction Under Fire
Art Director Keith Webb
Publication The Boston Globe Magazine
Publisher The Globe Newspaper Co.
Issue December 2001

■ **772**
Illustrator Eric Palma
Title Chris Rock
Art Director Florian Bachleda
Publication Vibe
Publisher Miller Publishing Group

■ **773**
Illustrator Mark Ulriksen
Title Saddam Hussein
Art Director Jennifer Roth
Publication TIME
Publisher AOL Time Inc.
Issue December 10, 2001

■ **774**
Illustrator Guy Billout
Title What Terrorists Wnat
Art Director Owen
Phillips
Publication The New Yorker
Publisher Condé Nast Publications, Inc.
Issue October 29, 2001

■ **775**
Illustrator Tim O'Brien
Title Kofi Annan
Art Director Kenneth B. Smith
Publication TIME
Publisher AOL Time Inc.
Issue July 9, 2001

■ 776
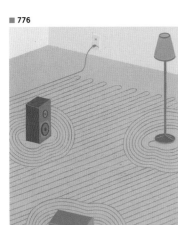

■ 777

■ 778

■ 779

■ 780

■ 781
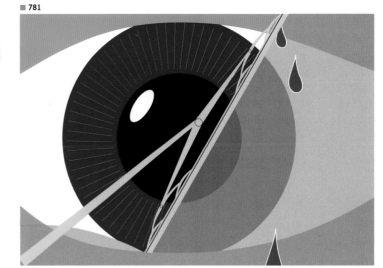

■ 782

■ 783

■ 784

■ 776
Illustrator Nick Dewar
Title Edifice Complex
Art Director Eric Mongeon
Publication Technology Review
Publisher Massachusetts Institute of Technology
Issue July/August 2001

■ 777
Illustrator Edel Rodriguez
Title "24"
Art Director Geraldine Hessler
Publication Entertainment Weekly
Publisher Time, Inc.
Issue March 18, 2002

■ 778
Illustrator Joe Ciardello
Title A Thousand Clowns
Art Director Owen Phillips
Publication The New Yorker
Publisher Condé Nast Publications, Inc.
Issue August 23, 2001

■ 779
Illustrator John Cuneo
Title Schocking Facts About Mark Twain
Art Directors John Korpics, Erin Whelan
Publication Esquire
Publisher The Hearst Corporation-Magazines Division
Issue January 2002

■ 780
Illustrator Roberto Parada
Title Joyce Carol Oates
Art Director Jennifer Gilman
Publication My Generation
Publisher AARP
Issue May/June 2001

■ 781
Illustrator Anton Ioukhnovets
Title No Lifetime Guarantees
Art Directors Andrew Horton, Tina Serluca
Publication Folio
Publisher Media Central
Issue November 2001

■ 782
Illustrator Lara Tomlin
Title War Stories
Art Director Christine Curry
Publication The New Yorker
Publisher Condé Nast Publications, Inc.
Issue March 11 , 2002

■ 783
Illustrator John Ritter
Title A Different Kind of Return
Art Directors Frank Tagariello, John Genzo
Publication Bloomberg Personal Finance
Publisher Bloomberg L.P.
Issue March 2002

■ 784
Illustrator Herve Blondon
Title France's Downfall
Art Director Mary Parsons
Publication The Atlantic Monthly
Publisher The Atlantic Monthly
Issue October 2001

■ 785

■ 790

■ 791

■ 786

■ 788

■ 792

■ 789

■ 793

■ 787

■ 791
Illustrator Melinda Beck
Title Getting Testy
Art Director Jennifer Gilman
Publication My Generation
Publisher AARP
Issue November/December 2001

■ 785
Illustrator Edwin Fotheringham
Title The Wash
Art Director Gibb Slife
Publication The New Yorker
Publisher Condé Nast Publications, Inc.
Issue November 19 , 2001

■ 788
Illustrator Juliette Borda
Title Adult Orphans
Art Directors Caren Watkins, Dave Donald
Publication Chatelaine
Issue August 2001

■ 792
Illustrator Michael Klein
Title Broker Power
Art Director Marti Golon
Publication TIME
Publisher AOL Time Inc.
Issue June 25, 2001

■ 786
Illustrator Thomas Fuchs
Title Best Ass
Art Director Geraldine Hessler
Publication Entertainment Weekly
Publisher Time, Inc.
Issue December 28, 2001

■ 789
Illustrator Zohar Lazar
Title Ask Men's Health
Art Directors George Karabotsos, Wilbert Gutierrez
Publication Men's Health
Publisher Rodale Inc.
Issue March 2002

■ 793
Illustrator Terry Allen
Title The Private Sector
Art Director Laura Zavetz
Publication Bloomberg Wealth Manager
Publisher Bloomberg L.P.
Issue May 2001

■ 787
Illustrator Thomas Fuchs
Title Private Al
Art Director Geraldine Hessler
Publication Entertainment Weekly
Publisher Time, Inc.
Issue June 22, 2002

■ 790
Illustrator Geoffrey Grahn
Title 40 Unwritten Rules To Live By
Art Directors George Karabotsos, Wilbert Gutierrez
Publication Men's Health
Publisher Rodale Inc.
Issue March 2002

■ 794
Illustrator Steve Brodner
Title The Heat Index
Art Directors George Karabotsos, Wilbert Gutierrez
Publication Men's Health
Publisher Rodale Inc.
Issue August 2001

794

797

799

802

795

798

800

796

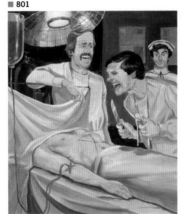

801

803

■ 795
Illustrator Andy Rash
Title Applying For a Job
Art Director Edel Rodriguez
Publication TIME
Publisher AOL Time Inc.
Issue June 4, 2001

■ 796
Illustrator Greg Clarke
Title Innocent Bystander
Art Director Mary Parsons
Publication The Atlantic Monthly
Publisher The Atlantic Monthly
Issue various

■ 797
Illustrator John Cuneo
Title Bush Nicknames
Art Director Kayoko Suzuki
Publication Gentelmens Quarterly
Publisher Condé Nast Publications, Inc.
Issue August 2001

■ 798
Illustrator John Cuneo
Title Things We No Longer Worry About
Art Director Kayoko Suzuki
Publication Gentelmens Quarterly
Publisher Condé Nast Publications, Inc.
Issue January 2002

■ 799
Illustrator Jean-Phillipe Delhomme
Title Town & Country Horoscopes 2002
Art Director Agnethe Glatved
Publication Town & Country
Publisher The Hearst Corporation-Magazines
Division
Issue February 2002

■ 800
Illustrator Edwin Fotheringham
Title Ten Things Your Eye Doctor Won't Tell You
Art Director Gretchen Smelter
Publication SmartMoney
Publisher Dow Jones & Hearst Corp.
Issue November 2001

■ 801
Illustrator Zohar Lazar
Title Laugh Tracks
Art Directors John Korpics, Erin Whelan
Publication Esquire
Publisher The Hearst Corporation-Magazines
Division
Issue February 2002

■ 802
Illustrator Daniel Adel
Title Holiday Santa
Art Directors John Korpics, Todd Albertson
Publication Esquire
Publisher The Hearst Corporation-Magazines
Division
Issue December 2001

■ 803
Illustrator Daniel Adel
Title Like A Genius
Art Director John Korpics
Publication Esquire
Publisher The Hearst Corporation-Magazines
Division
Issue June 2001

FEDERICO FELLINI

By Diego Mormorio

ABANDONMENT

REDISCOVERY

Designer Yoshiko Kusaka
Title Fellini
Photographer Ann Charters
School School of Visual Arts, New York City
Instructor Terry Koppel
Category Entertainment
Award B.W. Honeycutt

Designer Eric Karnes
Title Tom Waits
Photographer Anton Corbijn
School Maryland Institute College of Art, Balitmore
Instructor Paul Carlo
Category Entertainment
Award Second Place

Manhattan

Budget Gut : Despite what you've been told, it is possible to eat like a king or queen in The Big Apple for only a couple bucks. Our visitor's guide to the bargain restaurants of Manhattan that only the locals know about.

By Megan Anderson

Manhattan is notorious for its high cost of living, but we've found 10 hidden gems that prove you can dine in New York without going into debt.

One greenback at Fried Dumpling gets you a Styrofoam container of wonderful dumplings laced with scallions...

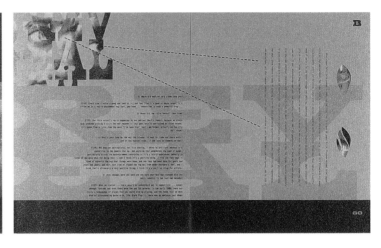

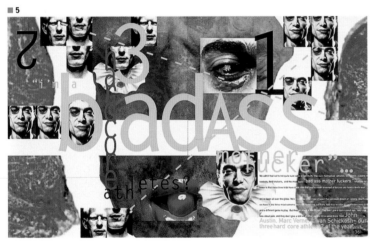

Designer Bruce Willem
Title Manhattan
School Maryland Institute College of Art, Balitmore
Instructor Paul Carlos
Category Travel
Award Third Place

Designer Russell Austin
Title Michael Stipe
School Portfolio Center, Atlanta
Instructor Hank Richardson
Category Entertainment

Designer Cara Sanders
Title Badass
School Portfolio Center, Atlanta
Instructor Hank Richardson
Category Sports

student EXCELLENCE

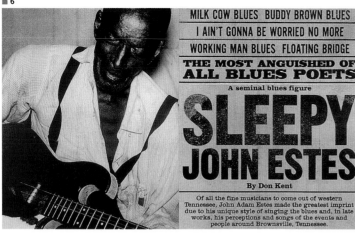

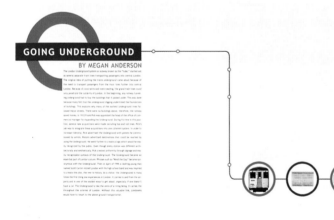

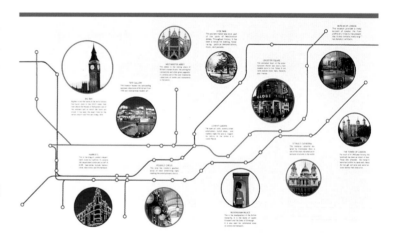

■ 6

Designer Yoshiko Kusaka
Title John Estes
Photographer Ann Charters
School School of Visual Arts, New York City
Instructor Terry Koppel
Category Entertainment

■ 7

Designer Wendy Neese
Title Amsterdam
Photographers Sïebe Swart, Hugo Potharst
School Maryland Institute, College of Art, Baltimore
Instructor Paul Carlos
Category Travel

■ 8

Designer Rosslyn Snitrak
Title Eyewitness U.K.
Photographers London Transport, Co., Eyewitness Travel Guide: London
School James Madison University, Harrisburg, Virginia
Instructor Trudy Cole-Zielanski
Category Travel